NATIONAL SECURITY SURVEILLANCE
IN SOUTHERN AFRICA

NATIONAL SECURITY SURVEILLANCE IN SOUTHERN AFRICA

An Anti-Capitalist Perspective

Jane Duncan

ZED

LONDON • NEW YORK • OXFORD • NEW DELHI • SYDNEY

Zed Books
Bloomsbury Publishing Plc
50 Bedford Square, London, WC1B 3DP, UK
1385 Broadway, New York, NY 10018, USA
29 Earlsfort Terrace, Dublin 2, Ireland

BLOOMSBURY and Zed Books are trademarks of Bloomsbury Publishing Plc

First published in Great Britain 2022

Cover design by Adriana Brioso
Cover image © filo/iStock

A catalogue record for this book is available from the British Library.

Library of Congress Cataloging-in-Publication Data
Names: Duncan, Jane, author.
Title: National security surveillance in southern Africa: an anti-capitalist perspective / Jane Duncan.
Description: New York: Zed, 2022. | Includes bibliographical references and index.
Identifiers: LCCN 2021052007 (print) | LCCN 2021052008 (ebook) | ISBN 9780755640225 (hardback) | ISBN 9780755640249 (pdf) | ISBN 9780755640232 (epub) | ISBN 9780755640256
Subjects: LCSH: Electronic surveillance–Africa, Southern. | Electronic surveillance–Political aspects–Africa, Southern. | National security–Africa, Southern.
Classification: LCC HM853 .D86 2022 (print) | LCC HM853 (ebook) | DDC 363.10630968–dc23/eng/20211021
LC record available at https://lccn.loc.gov/2021052007
LC ebook record available at https://lccn.loc.gov/2021052008

ISBN: HB: 978-0-7556-4022-5
        PB: 978-0-7556-4021-8
     ePDF: 978-0-7556-4024-9
   eBook: 978-0-7556-4023-2

Typeset by Deanta Global Publishing Services, Chennai, India

To find out more about our authors and books visit www.bloomsbury.com and sign up for our newsletters.

This book is dedicated to three people who have passed on from this world, but whose ideas and political contributions continue to live on. The first is Neville Alexander, who remains the single biggest intellectual and political influence on my life. The second is Aziz Choudry, who passed away tragically while I was completing this manuscript. His work on surveillance and anti-capitalism was ground breaking and helped shape my thinking in fundamental ways. The third is academic, colleague and comrade Pier Paolo Frassinelli, who passed away a month after I had submitted the manuscript. Capitalism remains the single biggest threat to mental health.
Another world is possible, and their efforts and sacrifices have brought it that much closer.

CONTENTS

PREFACE

When I was conducting the research for this book, one of my interviewees asked me, 'But how does someone with an art history background get to be interested in state spying?' After all, my degrees were in fine art and art history. My journey to this point has been long and circuitous, spanning over three decades.

My interest in national security surveillance extends beyond being purely academic, as I have been what researchers would probably call a 'participant-observer'. In fact, it is my experiential learning about how intelligence agencies use and abuse national security surveillance powers that eventually led to this book. This learning has taught me that intelligence infiltration and harassment of social movements, and the maintenance of our highly unequal and unjust social 'orders' more generally, are not a departure from what these agencies do. It *is* what they do. Yet, there is an alarming paucity of literature documenting and analysing this real history of state spying.

My interest in this issue developed when I was Executive Director of a South African–based non-governmental organization called the Freedom of Expression Institute (FXI). This was from 2001 to 2009, which was a time when the anti-globalization, anti-capitalist movement matured into a global fighting force. Shortly after activists shut down the World Trade Centre negotiations in Seattle in 1999, South Africa hosted two global summits. At the time, governments vied with one another to host these mega-events, as they brought prestige and tourism to the host countries. By then, paranoia had gripped intelligence and security agencies, as they feared that the burgeoning anti-globalization and anti-capitalist movement would shut down the events they hosted, too. During the run-up to the World Conference against Racism in Durban in 2001 and the World Summit on Sustainable Development in Johannesburg in 2002, South Africa's then-civilian intelligence agency, the National Intelligence Agency (NIA), infiltrated social movements and put activists under surveillance, leading to the police pre-emptively arresting some of them. We documented and analysed activists' experiences in an edited volume (N'dungu 2003). The September 11 attacks had just taken place, and the US was trying hard to conscript South Africa into its 'war on terror'. While claiming to remain non-aligned, the government nevertheless rushed pieces of legislation through to consolidate its surveillance capabilities and the fight against terrorism. I was involved in civil society and social movement efforts to push back against these wide-ranging powers.

In 2004, protests broke out in the Free State province, and we handled a case that was a post-apartheid first. The state charged protestors with sedition for participating in a protest that became violent. However, it was not the protestors who became violent, but the police. They shot and killed a seventeen-year-old youth, Tebogo Mkhonza – a killing the police have not been held accountable for. The accused police members would visit our FXI offices for legal assistance, followed by people in cars who self-identified as members of the NIA. These experiences told me that the spies were moving far beyond their stated aim of protecting national security and into the politically loaded area of maintaining domestic (in)stability.

From 2011 onwards, I was involved in an organization called the Right2Know Campaign, which became a target for infiltration and surveillance by the NIA's successor, the State Security Agency (SSA). The fact that this was the case was hardly surprising as the organization had mounted a very successful campaign, for a time, against a draft law (known as the Protection of Information Bill) that threatened to draw a shroud of secrecy over the government's intelligence, policing and military activities. The extent of the challenge, which galvanized thousands of people across the country, shook the spies to the core.

In 2015, I was teaching at the University of Johannesburg when student protests organized under the hashtag #feesmustfall broke out across the country. At the time, I became aware of how the spy agencies were moving far beyond what they claimed to be doing – namely countering violent protests – and using the protests to fight factional battles in the ruling African National Congress (ANC). In 2018, I was one of ten people appointed by President Cyril Ramaphosa to a High Level Review Panel to investigate abuses in the SSA. Most of the findings of this panel are public knowledge (Mufamadi et al. 2018), and the panel's report formed the basis of detailed testimony at the Commission of Enquiry into State Capture (otherwise known as the Zondo Commission, after its chair Raymond Zondo), which was still sitting at the time of writing. The panel found evidence of spies in the SSA having set up a parallel intelligence agency to maintain former president Jacob Zuma's dwindling grip on power. This parallel agency put under surveillance trade unions that broke politically with the ANC, and penetrated civil society organizations, environmental movements and the media with the purpose of neutralizing and impeding them as sources of counter-power. My serving on the panel was a life-changing experience, as it exposed me to the inner workings of an intelligence agency, and how the spies and their political masters could repurpose it with abuse in mind. It also sensitized me to the fact that such an agency can be uneven. As much as there are rogue spies intent on entrenching corrupt extractive capitalism, and as much as the agency may be system-maintaining in its overall objective, there are also spies of conscience willing to stand up and resist these abuses from within. Much of what we know about recent abuses of surveillance powers locally and globally come from such spies.

While teaching in academia, I encouraged research and journalism on surveillance and intelligence in South Africa. Many of my postgraduate students come from the southern African region, and so it seemed logical to extend this work to the region. As will be explained in the introduction, this book draws on some of that work as a source of inspiration. Post-apartheid South Africa has had ongoing problems with abusive state spying on national security grounds. However, we are still in a relatively privileged position compared to the rest of the region, where controls barely exist and where the political classes can abuse surveillance powers with abandon. As they acquire more digital surveillance capabilities, the problem is growing. In this book, I focus on the scale of the problem and on what to do about it, drawing on insights from journalists, academics and spies of conscience.

One last piece of the puzzle may help to explain my approach to this book, or at least its anti-capitalist orientation and its embedment in the theory of racial capitalism. I was a member of a now-defunct independent left organization called the Workers' Organization for Socialist Action (WOSA). Formed as a political alternative to the South African Communist Party, with its highly problematic history of alignment with Stalinist Russia and the ANC, WOSA brought together socialist organizations from around the country. Some of its founding members made great sacrifices in the struggle against racial capitalism, including spending time imprisoned on Robben Island by the apartheid regime. Although he would be deeply unhappy about my singling him out, one of WOSA's founder members, the lifelong socialist activist Neville Alexander, recognized the indivisibility of social struggles and consequently was instrumental in theorizing the concept of racial capitalism. Consequently, racial capitalism has always made sense as a lens through which to view contemporary society and its problems, and as a guide to action for how to change it, nationally and globally.

ACKNOWLEDGEMENTS

I would like to acknowledge and thank all the interviewees who agreed to participate in the research that informs this book. Some participated on conditions of anonymity, as having their views attributed to them could have exposed them to risks. I must emphasize that they cannot be held responsible for the ideological orientation of this book, which is mine and mine alone.

This book would not have been possible without the sabbatical I was granted by my university, the University of Johannesburg. If it is not a contradiction in terms to say so, the Department of Communication and Media and the School of Communication went out of their way to leave me alone during this period, to give me space to research, think and write, and I hope I put that space to good use. Many thanks, too, to my publishers, Zed Books, an imprint of Bloomsbury Books, for having steered me through my first international book publication, and for having organized peer reviews of the proposal and book. These reviews challenged me and enriched the final product. Many of my ideas for this book were incubated while writing commentary for the media on various intelligence and surveillance issues, including for the *Daily Maverick* online news site, *The Conversation*, a collaboration between the media and academic institutions to promote research-based media commentary, and About.Intel, an intelligence blog based in Berlin and run by the Stiftung Neue Verantwortung. I thank the editors of all these sites for providing me with the space to develop my thinking on these issues.

Given the state of the region, it could reasonably be assumed that research on national security surveillance in southern Africa is an impossible undertaking, as democratic space is in short supply in the region, and is shrinking all the time. However, I was helped by the fact that I am principal investigator on a research and journalism project on surveillance and intelligence in southern Africa. The project has involved forming a network of journalists and communication researchers on surveillance issues in southern Africa, funded by the philanthropic organization Luminate. Members of this network work with one another to produce research and journalism on the spread of communication surveillance technologies and practices in the region. I drew on the researchers and journalists on this project as sources of information, although Luminate did not fund the research for this book. It was not possible to focus on all southern African countries, so I confined myself to countries where the project had a presence. These were Namibia, Botswana, South Africa, Zimbabwe, Angola, Malawi, Mozambique, the Democratic Republic of the Congo (DRC) and Zambia. I also included Mauritius, as I already had contacts in the country from some years back. I would like to acknowledge the unstinting work of the project leader on this project, Dr Allen Munoriyarwa, who has far surpassed me as his supervisor and grown into being an important academic voice on digital rights in the region.

The research and journalism project was undertaken under the auspices of the Media Policy and Democracy Project (MPDP), which was launched in 2012. The MPDP is an inter-university collaborative research project between the Department of Communication Science at the University of South Africa (UNISA), and the Department of Communication and Media at the University of Johannesburg (UJ), where I am based. The MPDP aims to promote participatory media and communications policymaking in the public interest. Since its launch, the MPDP has collaborated with academics and researchers from various institutions across the world, but with a focus on Southern Africa. The project has three specific focus areas, namely, internet freedom, privacy online and communications surveillance; media diversity; and transformation and communications policy in the public interest. The findings inform advocacy and activism efforts, and campaigns on communications and media rights and democratic space more generally, and this book has been shaped by these collaborations, with their embodiment of 'theory in action' or praxis.

ABBREVIATIONS

ABIS	Automated Biometric Identification System
AI	Artificial Intelligence
ANC	African National Congress
AU	African Union
BDP	Botswana Democratic Party
BMA	Border Management Authority
BRICS	Brazil-Russia-India-China-South Africa
CAAT	Campaign Against Arms Trade
CALEA	Communications Assistance for Law Enforcement Act
CCM	Chama Cha Mapinduzi
CCTV	Closed-Circuit Television
CIA	Central Intelligence Agency
COMINT	Communications Intelligence
DIS	Directorate of Intelligence and Security
DRC	Democratic Republic of the Congo
ETSI	European Telecommunication Standards Institute
EU	European Union
FBI	Federal Bureau of Investigation
FISC	Foreign Intelligence Signals Court
FXI	Freedom of Expression Institute
GCHO	Government Communication Headquarters
GDP	Gross Domestic Product
GNU	Government of National Unity
HANIS	Home Affairs National Identification System
ICT	Information and Communications Technologies
ID	Identity Document
IMEI	International Mobile Equipment Identity
IMF	International Monetary Fund
IMSI	International Mobile Subscriber Identity
INCM	Autoridade Reguladora das Comunicações
IP	Internet Protocol
IT	Information Technology
JCPS	Justice, Crime Prevention and Security
JSCI	Joint Standing Committee on Intelligence
LHR	Lawyers for Human Rights
MDC	Movement for Democratic Change
MI5	Military Intelligence Section Five

MICC	Monitoring of Interception of Communications Centre
MK	Umkhonto we Sizwe
MPDP	Media Policy and Democracy Project
MPLA	Popular Movement for the Liberation of Angola
NCA	National Constitutional Assembly
NCACC	National Conventional Arms Control Committee
NCC	National Communications Centre
NCIS	National Central Intelligence Service
NGO	Non-Governmental Organization
NIA	National Intelligence Agency
NICOC	National Intelligence Coordinating Committee
NIS	National Identity System
NIS	National Intelligence Service
NPA	National Prosecuting Authority
NPR	National Population Register
NSA	National Security Agency
NSO	National Security Organization
OAU	Organization of African Unity
OECD	Organization for Economic Cooperation and Development
OIC	Office for Interception Centres
OPEC	Organization for Petroleum Exporting Countries
PA	Palestinian Authority
POTRAZ	Posts and Telecommunications Regulatory Authority of Zimbabwe
PSIRA	Private Security Industry Regulatory Authority
RICA	Regulation of Interception of Communications and Provision of Communication-Related Information Act
SADC	Southern African Development Community
SAPS	South African Police Service
SARPCCO	Southern Africa Regional Police Chiefs Cooperation Organization
SDU	Self Defence Unit
SIGINT	Signals Intelligence
SIM	Subscriber Identification Module
SISE	State Information and Security Service
SMS	Short Messaging Service
SOCMINT	Social Media Intelligence
SSA	State Security Agency
SSR	Security Sector Reform
TIIT	Transport of Intercepted Internet Protocol Traffic
UJ	University of Johannesburg
UK	United Kingdom
UN	United Nations
UNDP	United Nations Development Programme
UNISA	University of South Africa

UNITA	Union for the Total Independence of Angola
US	United States
USAID	United States Agency for International Development
WOSA	Workers' Organization for Socialist Action
ZANU-PF	Zimbabwe African National Union-Patriotic Front
ZAPU	Zimbabwe African Peoples' Union
ZPSP	Zimbabwe Peace and Security Project

INTRODUCTION

Domingos da Cruz is an Angolan academic, journalist and activist. In 2015, the state charged him and sixteen other young people with threatening the country's national security by attempting to prepare a coup d'état, and attempted assassination of then-president José Eduardo dos Santos. The police arrested them after an unlawful intelligence operation that put them under surveillance (Verde 2021: 7–9). Their crime? Organizing a reading group seminar on non-violent dissent, discussing a book by da Cruz. The book was entitled *Tools to Destroy a Dictator and Avoid a New Dictatorship* (in Portuguese, *Ferramentas para Destruir o Ditador e Evitar Nova Ditadura*), which drew on Gene Sharp's work on non-violent resistance and assessed its relevance for Angola. Da Cruz's book also suggested strategies to challenge a government that had drifted away from the people and become more authoritarian, corrupt and unequal, despite having emerged from a heroic liberation struggle against Portuguese colonialism. Even though the youths were studying non-violent dissent as a means of expressing legitimate grievances, in 2016 the court found them guilty and sentenced them to between two and eight and half years in jail. Da Cruz received the harshest sentence as a supposed instigator, but the state granted them amnesty and released them after an international outcry about the case (Verde 2021: 7–9). Angola was one of many countries whose spy agencies overreacted to the potential for an Arab Spring-type uprising in the wake of the 2007–8 global capitalist crisis. In an interview, da Cruz explained the political context that led to the arrests and convictions, and the ways in which young people were attempting to use the political moment positively to imagine an alternative society:

> The Arab Spring influenced civil society in Angola, and it was a source of inspiration. In 2011, the people, particularly the youth from civil society and other groups worked without any form of organisation. The numbers of protests at that time, increased and also influenced me to see that a lot of people had concerns about the situation [and I thought] these guys need orientation, in terms of tools and foundations in order to fight . . . [My concern] was, okay, we need to organise this movement. We need to show, internally and externally, that we know how to fight, and we need to show that we have a vision for a future country, not [only] in terms of a political party [but] in terms of the new society that we want to build. That is why in my book, the last chapter is a draft of how we would like to build different sectors of society, like our vision of education,

about science, about health, about every essential sector. Yeah, the Arab Spring had influence in Angola, and of course, it influenced me too, to make contact with the people and try to organise the movement.[1]

Around the same time, intelligence operatives in the Special Operations Unit of the South African SSA set up a parallel intelligence agency to neutralize and impede trade unions and civil society organizations campaigning for then-president Jacob Zuma to step down from office. They put several trade unions and civil society organizations under surveillance and tried to stop a campaign within the ruling party, the African National Congress (ANC), to replace him as president of the party and the country (Mufamadi et al. 2018: 96–8). At the same time that these Angolan and South African agencies were busy chasing activists and journalists, corrupt elements in both countries were busy looting organs of state and enriching themselves. Unsurprisingly, Angola and South Africa share the dubious reputation of being among the most unequal countries in the world, with predatory ruling classes willing to resort to industrial-scale corruption, while governing and spying on desperately poor populations.

In this current age of global insecurity, governments and their spy agencies keep telling us that we need to live with increasingly invasive state spying for our own sakes. Bulk, dragnet surveillance, we are told, is a necessary evil, and we must be prepared to give up some rights to become safer. Yet, there is a disturbing pattern the world over in how national security surveillance agencies conduct themselves. They claim more and more power and bigger budgets on national security grounds, yet we never seem to become any safer. Repeatedly, they are exposed as having abused their powers, where the supposed protectors of national security become the very people who threaten it. Scandals about intelligence agencies spying on journalists, academics, civil society and opposition political parties have become frequent occurrences. In fact, we have become used to the spies sticking their noses where they do not belong, while not sticking their noses where they do belong. When the spies are exposed for abusing their powers and the public trust, it has become all too easy for them to blame rogue elements and commit to cleaning up their acts. Until the next time.

Even countries that claim to be serious about democratic controls over their spy agencies have failed to rein them in sufficiently. When former National Security Agency (NSA) contractor Edward Snowden leaked classified information that revealed massive abuses of the bulk surveillance capabilities of the US and British governments, public outrage spurred a global reform movement. However, according to the United Nations Special Rapporteur on Privacy, Joseph Cannataci, hardly any United Nations member states have actually done anything to reform state spying.[2] National oversight systems remain largely ineffective, while intelligence agencies get stronger and stronger. In fact, member of the European Parliament Sophie in 't Veld has likened national security to a huge black hole where fundamental rights and democracy are being swallowed up.[3]

The biggest surveillance scandal of recent times, as exposed by Snowden, has not forced governments to curb their spy agencies, which then raises the question, what will? The phenomenon of growing surveillance coupled with growing crime is a confounding one and raises the question, Why do these spy agencies even exist? Would we be any less safe if they did not? This book is about this issue. Using the region where I am based, namely, southern Africa, as a backdrop, I examine what is really going on under the hood of the spy agencies that conduct national security surveillance. I look at what we can do about these areas of the state if they aren't serving us, and if we are genuinely committed to a more just and equal society. For reasons that I will discuss in more detail in the next chapter, I will look at these issues from an anti-capitalist perspective. In other words, I adopt the view that in capitalist societies, state spying serves the capitalist system before it serves the public interest. This perspective is important because it points the way to more lasting solutions to the intractable problem of surveillance abuses: solutions that move beyond reforms that may work for a time, but are more often than not thwarted.

Typically, the anti-capitalist left has very ambiguous feelings about security powers as we know them under capitalism. Much of this has to do with the fact that the left often sees these powers (correctly) as being part of the repressive apparatus of the state, used to wield hard power against society. Assigning the state a monopoly on the carrying of arms and the use of violence is a central tenet of modern capitalist society, and the state is an instrument of class rule. Yet, the left often has very little to say on questions of how security powers should be organized in a classless society, or how to get there. Consequently, they struggle to offer a meaningful vision for whether these powers should even exist, and to what end. Calls to defund the police are growing around the world, in response to police violence against Black people in the US. Activists and academics have put a great deal of work into envisioning alternatives for policing, but for some reason there is no serious discussion about what to do with the state's intelligence and surveillance powers. Calling for these agencies to be de-funded and shut down is an option – but what then?

In this book, I grapple with these problems and how they manifest themselves in southern Africa, one of the most peripheral, exploited and oppressed regions of the world. I look at what an anti-capitalist perspective on intelligence and national security surveillance powers could look like. Are these powers even needed, and if so, what should they do and why? If societies should have surveillance powers, how far should they extend and what lines should they not cross? I have decided to confine my focus to intelligence-led surveillance rather than the broader gamut of security and policing powers, because I believe that there is a gap in the literature in this regard. Typically, intelligence is highly secretive, poorly understood and therefore particularly susceptible to abuse. Former spies–turned-academics tend to dominate intelligence studies, which means that they are more likely to take the normative foundations of these powers for granted. I focus on those aspects of state intelligence that claim to protect national security, as typically these powers are the most extreme. In fact, we can learn a great deal about the state of health of a society by how quickly its state rushes to invoke national security powers when responding to social crises.

The broader context: The global and regional expansion of security powers

Globally, national security powers have expanded since the terrorist[4] attacks on the United States on 11 September 2001, and surveillance[5] has become central to this expansion. Governments across the world justify increasingly invasive forms of surveillance as being necessary to fight serious crime and terrorism: social ills that, if left unchecked, could undermine attempts to make societies more just and equal. Intelligence agencies are also becoming increasingly reliant on intelligence obtained from electronic signals (an intelligence discipline known as signals intelligence, or SIGINT), underpinned by big data analytics. This is being done to increase efficiency and reduce the risks associated with human intelligence, or HUMINT, such as subjectivity in analysis and the risk of detection at the collection stage. Communications intelligence, or COMINT, is a sub-discipline of SIGINT and involves collecting intelligence from communication signals (Gill and Phythian 2012: 92–8). In this book, I will refer to the broader intelligence discipline of SIGINT as it covers a broader range of practices than COMINT.

As more intelligence agencies use data mining to generate intelligence, people risk becoming more resigned to an existence where no reasonable expectation of privacy exists. After all, the argument goes, if people are going to enjoy safety, security and prosperity, then they need to accept that an individual right (privacy) must give way to a collective right (security). This existence most likely involves the near-ubiquitous use of dragnet SIGINT surveillance, constant tracking in public spaces using 'smart' closed-circuit television (CCTV) camera systems and drones, mining social media for intelligence purposes, biometric forms of identification and increasingly securitized and militarized borders in the face of the migration crisis precipitated by the war on terror and the 2007–8 recession. Intelligence agencies are also exploring the possibility of exploiting 'smart' data-generating devices networked through the Internet of Things (IoT) for collection and analysis purposes. However, excessive secrecy is making it difficult for people to evaluate claims about the necessity for these powers. The technological capabilities of intelligence agencies have run far ahead of the oversight capabilities of the judicial, administrative and legislative bodies and the public. The 'law lag', where laws regulating spying powers fail to keep up with these capabilities, is a worldwide problem. To all intents and purposes, it is open season on peoples' data for criminal justice and national security purposes, and large carve-outs in data protection laws for the police and intelligence agencies make the problem worse.

When Snowden revealed the extent to which the capabilities of the major surveillance powers had become a tool of abuse of peoples' fundamental rights and freedoms, public and journalistic attention focused largely on the global North. However, national security surveillance is growing massively in the global South, where data protection rules and intelligence oversight are particularly weak, and southern Africa is no exception to this general rule. Some of the most egregious human rights violations are taking place in the region. In these countries, there is mounting evidence of governments and, in some cases, the private sector using surveillance to disassemble social movements, criminalize journalists, lawyers and other human rights defenders, and to reproduce inequality more generally.

Furthermore, there are signs that global superpowers are making the problem worse by contributing to a global transmission belt of security tools and practices, and globalizing intelligence-led policing practices and technologies like Automatic Number Plate Recognition, IMSI (International Mobile Subscriber Identity) catchers, and monitoring centres produced by major arms manufacturers, many of which are based in the global North. Recent reforms to the control of exports have failed to address the spread of dual-use surveillance technologies (technologies that have both military and civilian uses) to authoritarian and semi-authoritarian countries. In fact, the expansion of surveillance powers and the dangers this expansion poses to the peoples of southern African remain largely an untold story.

Why the focus on southern Africa?

When the 2007–8 global financial crisis wreaked havoc on peoples' lives, anti-austerity protests sprung up around the world in response. The most dramatic took place in the Middle East and North Africa. For a brief while, it seemed that what came to be known as the Arab Spring held out real possibilities of change to some of the world's most corrupt and autocratic regimes, and the global capitalist system more generally. Yet, less well known is the impact on southern Africa, which also experienced its own 'Arab Spring', and in fact continues to do so. Thousands of people have taken to the streets in protest against authoritarian governments, exploitation of the region's abundant natural resource and austerity. As protests spread across the region – fuelled by massive hikes in the prices of fuel, bread and other goods and services – and more young tech-savvy actors with no previous experience of struggle became involved, governments already panicked by the Arab Spring scrambled to acquire data-driven surveillance tools to monitor these protests. When affordability was an issue, many also continued to rely on old, tried and tested HUMINT. This expansion of surveillance capabilities is taking place in spite of the fact that the region faces no major terrorism threats and is largely at peace – with the exception of an unfolding crisis in the Cabo Delgado province of Mozambique, which could have a destabilizing impact beyond the province. Intelligence and security policies, practices and technologies are being imported wholesale from the major surveillance powers in the global North, such as the US, the UK and Europe, while China is also becoming an increasingly important supplier of surveillance tools to the region. The major surveillance superpowers claim that worldwide dragnet surveillance is necessary, given heightened security risks. China is using southern Africa as a surveillance commodity dumping ground, and exporting surveillance tools and practices with no due diligence or real concern about how the countries they sell them to are using them. In fact, there is a surveillance free-for-all in the region. Given the lack of controls on intelligence and surveillance powers, abuses are almost inevitable.

At the same time, southern African intelligence agencies are searching for anti-imperialist alternatives to the major intelligence powers of the global North, and Snowden's disclosures on the abuses of the Five Eyes alliance of countries have intensified this search. Tasked with sharing signals intelligence of political, military or economic value, the Five Eyes alliance incorporates the US, the UK, New Zealand/Aotearoa, Canada and Australia. It has assumed the character of a standing cooperation agreement on SIGINT collection and sharing. Many intelligence officials want to 'do' security differently, to the point where they have even looked to the BRICS (Brazil-Russia-India-China-South Africa) alliance of countries to provide alternative models and justifications for state security powers. However, researchers have not done enough to track the diffusion of surveillance tools and practices in the region, the emerging inter-imperialist rivalries between the established global security powers and the emerging BRICS superpowers, and the possible sites of democratic oversight and resistance to unaccountable surveillance. They have also not done enough to develop new concepts that effectively challenge dominant and conservative security discourses.

Unwitting publics are being caught between a rock and a hard place. Desperate for respite from crime, they look to the state to protect them. Yet, at the same time, those very states use security powers in ways that extend far beyond fighting crime and terrorism, and into social control and the maintenance of capitalism more generally. Moments of political ferment can be fertile ground for conceptual breakthroughs. However, because there is no tactical or strategic clarity about security powers, activist movements often engage in limited calls for intelligence reforms, and fail to provide alternative visions for intelligence. This lack of clarity is surprising, as southern Africa has a rich history of liberation movements organizing their own intelligence and security functions as part of their struggles against colonialism, capitalism and apartheid. Linking the struggle against the problem of unaccountable surveillance to broader anti-capitalist struggles should help to move the issue beyond elite non-governmental organizations (NGOs) focusing merely on privacy and data protection. Such a link could politicize the problem as being a broader problem of social control of increasingly restive societies, and create a mass base for the work that cannot be marginalized easily.

Why should an anti-capitalist security perspective on and from southern Africa even matter in the broader scheme of things? The continent has been largely peripheral to the global economy, but increasingly its raw materials are becoming central to productive activities. Currently, there is what Padraig Carmody (2016: 1–14) has termed a 'new scramble for Africa' in the form of attempts to commandeer the continent's natural resources. Africa has become increasingly important to the global economy as it is a major provider of the natural resources that make the current capitalist economy function. Southern Africa especially is rich in natural resources, and the region's commodities and land are at a premium. The BRICS alliance and local elites working in partnership with its governments are well placed to take full advantage of this scramble, but surveillance of whole populations will become more necessary. If the major surveillance powers are using surveillance to move beyond their intended purposes of fighting crime and terrorism, and take control of these resources for their own ends, then global stability and security are at risk. At the same time, the region provides a context to think more fundamentally about the necessity of security powers, as the conventional national security threat level is relatively low. If governments are using surveillance tools for legitimate ends, then there can be little argument against them. However, if they are using these powers for broader social control purposes, then it becomes easier to mobilize against these powers.

In the past, imperialism and colonialism politicized struggles in Africa and made them unsustainable. The struggles in the colonies reached far beyond their geographic boundaries, becoming explosive for the capitalist system as a whole. The youth-heavy nature of many of these societies, coupled with austerity measures imposed in the wake of the 2007–8 recession, has turned Africa, including southern Africa, into a powder keg of social instability. At the same time, struggles for liberation are still in the living memory of many older people in the region; consequently, many remain open to radical, emancipatory ideas. All these factors mean that the region is a weak link in the global capitalist chain. Struggles against more contemporary forms of imperialism and colonialism could resonate throughout the world once again and serve as inspiration for reshaping the world as we know it. That is why I think it is important to move beyond the 'usual suspects' in the North when discussing national security surveillance and what to do about it, and look at a region that could be far more damaged by unchecked surveillance than anywhere else in the world.

This book looks at what can be done to rein in national security surveillance powers and restructure how they are used beyond the limited and often ineffective reforms that have been attempted. This book is not just a complaining book; it is a call to action that includes a suggested programme that ordinary people and organized movements could consider to defend democratic spaces and open up possibilities for anti-capitalist alternatives. Unless social and political movements equip themselves with the knowledge and understanding of these practices, politicize them as being central to capitalist oppression and exploitation rather than relying on individualized defences of privacy, and develop collective programmes to rein in these practices, they will continue to be used to disassemble these very movements.

Methodology

In this book, I alternate between empirical research focusing on what actually exists, and conceptual, normative ideas about what could or should exist in the field of intelligence and national security surveillance. I adopted this approach because I believe that developing alternatives needs to be grounded in current realities and a diagnosis of current problems; otherwise, alternatives are likely to be abstract and fail to speak to real societal problems. For the empirical research, I used qualitative methods, and as the questions I had set myself were exploratory, my approach was inductive. However, I used a flexible analytical framework based around the following organizing concepts: actors, interventions or actions, relationships, and outcomes or impacts. I attempted to understand the different surveillance actors and their roles and responsibilities in southern Africa, the relationships (if any) between these different actors, how they were changing over time, and relationships between these actors and the broader political environment. I set out to understand what surveillance was taking place on national security grounds, why, how these capabilities were organized, who resourced them and why, and to what end. This framework allowed me to organize the research systematically, link the main questions I had set myself to the empirical research, and allowed me to explore issues that brought me back to the overarching question.

My main research methods for the empirical research were semi-structured in-depth interviews, transcribed but not coded, and document research and analysis, including documents that were leaked into the public domain, as well as to me specifically. I identified possible interviewees through snowball sampling, asking for references and recommendations as I went along, and starting with people who were in my immediate circle of influence, as inevitably trust was central to obtaining valuable data. I put particular emphasis on speaking to people who had direct experience of surveillance and/or anti-surveillance work, usually activists, as well as the lawyers and NGOs who defended them and the journalists and researchers who wrote about them. These interviewees, I felt, brought a level of experiential knowledge and authenticity to the issues.

Security practices are notoriously difficult to research at the best of times, and writing a book on national security surveillance during the global Covid-19 pandemic made things even more difficult. This is, of necessity, a 'Zoom book', where I conducted much of the research on digital platforms rather than through in-country research (although not always on Zoom). On the one hand, interviews were easier to organize as they did not involve travel, but on the other they also involved additional digital security risks (such as hacking). Consequently, it was important that my interviewees were comfortable with the relative security of the platforms used, the recording and transcribing of interviews, and the storage of interview material. These interviews lacked the intimacy of face-to-face interviews, and their virtual nature may have inhibited discussion. However, it was the choice between that and not being able to write this book. This is because regional travel may not be possible for some time to come, given the global inequalities in how the Covid-19 vaccines are being rolled out: southern African countries are likely to be the last in line in the vaccine race. Some interviewees participated on the basis of confidentiality, which I respected, and their interview notes have been scrubbed of personal identifiers. There were other challenges attached to conducting empirical research in the middle of a global pandemic. The pandemic and its effects weighed people down; some became infected, or their family members became infected, and others lost loved ones. In fact, just about everyone was either infected or affected. At times, it felt like a real imposition to ask people to focus on these issues. I, too, had my challenges.

In addition to the interviews, I drew on a diversity of sources of information. These included the Snowden disclosures, Wikileaks leaks, import and export data on the global trade in surveillance (including reporting in terms of the Wassenaar Arrangement on Export Controls for Conventional Arms and Dual-Use Goods and Technologies), network surveillance data produced by Citizenlab (University of Toronto) and information released in response to the freedom of information requests I made.

I sourced the leaked Snowden documents from The Snowden Archive, an online archive of documents established as part of a joint research project between the Canadian Journalists for Free Expression and the Politics of Surveillance Project, Faculty of Information, University of Toronto.[6] I selected the documents by searching on 'Africa' and 'Five Eyes', and then narrowed the searches to different southern African countries that are particularly under-represented in the literature. I also conducted similar searches on the Wikileaks and Surveillance Industry Index site, which is a project of the international non-governmental organization Privacy International. They also run a global network of privacy advocates and researchers, which I participate in. From 2011 onwards, Wikileaks published the 'Spyfiles', containing largely classified or commercially confidential documents about the typically secretive mass surveillance industry. Wikileaks published these documents out of concern that the industry was 'practically unregulated' and yet providing highly invasive surveillance equipment that was open to abuse (Wikileaks 2011). The Surveillance Industry Index is a publicly available database of documents on and from the global surveillance industry (Privacy International 2016b). I did not conduct content analysis of the documents, as I was not interested in the documents as texts or bearers of overt and latent meanings, but rather as pointers to surveillance practices.

There are ethical and practical risks in relying on leaked documents for academic analyses. The documents present only a partial picture of the SIGINT activities of the Five Eyes countries and the industry linked to their surveillance activities. This is especially so with regard to the Snowden leaks, which consisted of NSA documents in the main, and which therefore risks skewing the analysis towards the NSA's perspectives and priorities. Drawing on journalism ethics, it is possible to argue that using these documents is justifiable in situations where there is an overwhelming public interest in doing so, and where the public interest outweighs the potential harm to the document originators (Poor and Davidson 2016: 3–5). Government surveillance practices and the surveillance industry are notoriously secretive. Leaks are one of the few ways that their activities enter into the public domain, as there are hardly any other ethical alternatives to collect the information, and unexamined surveillance practices lend themselves to abuse.

Leaked documents may be drafts. They may not enjoy official status in their originating organizations or may provide incomplete information or may even be fakes. As leaked documents are unlikely to be comprehensive, they may present fragments of a complex picture, leading to incomplete and incorrect conclusions being drawn. I mitigated these risks by using the explanatory journalism linked to the leaked documents in the Snowden archives. The journalism provides important context for the documents and considers their relevance, gaps and silences. Furthermore, as journalists screened and prepared the documents for publication, they redacted any personal identifying information before publication, which reduced the ethical risks of using them. Journalists have not mediated the Wikileaks documents, so the risks of relying on them are higher. However, Privacy International's analysis of some of the documents in the Surveillance Industry Index provides an additional layer of scrutiny by an organization that is indisputably a specialist in the field.

Outline of chapters

The book is divided into seven chapters. I provide brief descriptions of these chapters here.

Chapter 1 is entitled 'National security surveillance and anti-capitalism: A theoretical discussion'. In this chapter, I set the context for the rest of the book by discussing the key terms used in it, such as national security, surveillance, anti-capitalism and imperialism. I also discuss why an anti-capitalist perspective on national security surveillance matters, and particularly one that is informed by the theory of racial capitalism. I discuss how national security surveillance is a form of imperialism, how the main features of imperialism apply to surveillance and how surveillance practices travel around the world.

Chapter 2 is entitled 'Doing security differently? National security surveillance in southern Africa'. Here I examine the legacies of imperialism and colonialism in how post-colonial national security surveillance is practised. Focusing particularly on three Anglophone countries, namely Zimbabwe, Botswana (both former British colonies) and Namibia (a German colony, replaced by South African colonial rule until independence), I focus on how their intelligence agencies have or have not broken with the practices of their former colonizers. I also look at the common trends in how these agencies are set up and run, whether alternative intelligence capabilities are needed to ones that exist and, if so, what they could look like.

Chapter 3 is entitled 'Lawful interception as imperialism'. In this chapter, I examine the spread of targeted communication surveillance throughout southern Africa, focusing on those used for national security purposes (known as 'lawful interception'). I explore how such targeted surveillance has functioned as a form of imperialism, having absorbed interception standards from the US and the UK that are not in the best interests of digital security. I also look at how lawful interception is not necessarily a panacea for the kinds of untargeted SIGINT surveillance abuses that Snowden revealed, whether these powers are needed and what alternatives exist to a form of surveillance that makes communications less secure for everyone.

Chapter 4 is entitled 'Mass surveillance and national security imperialism'. In this chapter, I examine untargeted mass surveillance practices of the Five Eyes alliance, and the ways in which SIGINT is being used to continue imperialism by other means. I also look at the diversity of mass surveillance practices in southern Africa, given that the many countries in the region lack the capabilities to rival the

Five Eyes. I also look at what an anti-capitalist perspective on mass surveillance could look like.

Chapter 5 is entitled 'The global trade in spyware'. In this chapter, I examine how the global trade in surveillance technologies, or spyware, reproduce and reinforce neocolonial and imperialist relationships cemented during southern Africa's colonial and apartheid past. I examine what should be done about the global trade in spyware, and how tactics and strategies used by anti-war and disarmament movements could be applied to activist work in this area.

Chapter 6 is entitled 'Police as spies: Securitization of protests and intelligence-led policing'. In this chapter, I examine the expansion of intelligence-led policing in southern Africa, as an example of the global conveyer belt of security practices running from the North to the South. I use the South African police's responses to the recent student protests at tertiary institutions, organized around the hashtag #feemustfall, as a case study of what intelligence-led policing does and doesn't deliver, as a form of policing that blurs the lines between law enforcement intelligence and national security intelligence. I then ask what political and ideological stance anti-capitalists should take towards intelligence-led policing: who should be policed, how and why?

Chapter 7 is entitled 'Fortress South Africa: Securitizing identity and border management'. In this chapter, and again using South Africa as a case study, I explore the global trend towards securitizing and militarizing civil functions that typically fall under 'Homeland Affairs' departments, such as national identity systems and the management of immigration. Then, using the case of Mauritius and its response to the rollout of a biometrically based smart ID card system, I explore what an anti-capitalist perspective on border control and identity management could look like.

Chapter 1

NATIONAL SECURITY SURVEILLANCE AND ANTI-CAPITALISM

A THEORETICAL DISCUSSION

Introduction

Why do we see activist movements, especially anti-capitalist movements, the world over being targeted by intelligence agencies on the basis of them being national security threats? What is national security in the first place? What is intelligence? In this chapter, I set the context for the rest of the book by examining some of the key terms used and their relevance for national security surveillance in southern Africa. In particular, I look at how national security and intelligence have expanded their meanings to encompass a broader range of threats to the capitalist system. I also look at why an anti-capitalist perspective matters. Explaining the expansion of the surveillance industry through the lens of capitalism, and particularly racial capitalism, helps us to understand the real-world uses of national security surveillance as opposed to its purported uses. This analytic lens helps us to identify the mechanisms of surveillance that sees its uses moving far beyond concerns with serious crime and terrorism into maintaining existing social orders.

Given that the historical period of foreign domination and colonization in the region has largely passed, how relevant are key anti-capitalist concepts of colonialism and imperialism to global surveillance relationships today, and southern Africa's place in those relationships? I argue that, far from being anachronistic, they are crucial to understanding the expansion of national security surveillance, as they help us to understand the contributions of these capabilities to global inequalities within and between nations, and global insecurity more generally. More specifically, I discuss the usefulness of Lenin's five features of imperialism for understanding the diffusion of surveillance practices across the globe, including in southern Africa. I also look at how we can interpret, augment or update these features for the current period. I examine how national security surveillance has become a manifestation of imperialism, as extreme practices designed mainly for fighting terrorism have diffused across the world, including to countries that face no significant terrorism threats. In the process, governments, including those in southern Africa, have used national security surveillance not just as a criminal justice and intelligence-collection tool but for social and political control within the context of a global capitalism that is increasingly destructive and extractive.

From threats to interests: Defining and redefining national security

National security surveillance is a slippery concept that is notoriously difficult to define. Surveillance is very different from monitoring, which involves the intermittent observation of people and events without specific objectives in mind. Surveillance involves routine, systematic monitoring to meet pre-determined objectives, such as to uncover evidence of a crime. Surveillance can take many forms and can be undertaken by humans or electronic devices programmed to collect, store and possibly analyse the data collected. Intelligence agencies use national security surveillance to generate intelligence information, either for strategic intelligence purposes, where intelligence agencies map out longer-term threats and trends, or for counter-intelligence, where agencies defend a country against threats.

'National security' is an extremely elastic term, which is dangerous as courts generally punish national security crimes much more severely than ordinary crimes, due to their perceived seriousness. Southern African governments across the board have defined national security in very broad terms (more details in relation to specific countries are discussed in the next chapter). They are not alone; governments the world over tend to stretch their definitions of national security to include all manner of threats and interests, although some do not to define the term at all, and to leave it deliberately unclear, preferring to let the courts define it through case law. Security could be understood as the absence of threats and fear about such threats, but national security, or the prevention of threats to the stability and sovereignty of a nation-state, has taken on increasingly complex layers of meaning. Since the end of the Second World War, ushering in a period of unprecedented world peace, governments have moved away from focusing on conventional national security threats that equate national security with military security, or the protection of a country from external threats using military means. Increasingly, they have included within its ambit a range of non-military threats that relate to both domestic and foreign policy; these may include threats to vital economic and political interests, the loss of which could undermine the very existence of a country. Threats can also include those that have the potential to undermine the security of the state or society and the protection of citizens at home and abroad, while ensuring that the country does not become a base for threats to other countries. National security can encompass a broad range of threats, some of which are vague, like domestic extremism, espionage, critical infrastructure, defence of a country and its sovereignty, terrorism, proliferation of weapons of mass destruction, failed states, natural disasters or health emergencies that may cause instability, and organized crime that is so serious that it threatens national stability.

Despite the vagueness of key concepts, what is clear, though, is that national security is a higher-order form of security than personal security, in that it requires a national rather than a personal or local response. However, it is also a lower-order form of security than international security, which usually requires a coordinated response by nation-states (Privy Council Office of Canada 2004: 1–8). Some countries have also included activities that threaten their constitutional order in their definitions. This is especially so when it comes to criminal threats, as ordinary crimes cannot be considered national security threats unless they are of such seriousness that they threaten the very existence of a nation-state. Some countries also consider the protection of senior officials like presidents or prime ministers to be national security matters, as attacks against them can destabilize a country, and some have expanded their definitions even further to include protection of military capabilities, maintenance of foreign relations, threats to health and economic well-being and border security (Mendel 2013: 12).

However, a normative 'ideal' definition for a liberal-democratic society would most likely try to narrow national security down as much as possible, to prevent governments abusing the term to spy on political opponents or cover up corruption. It may to restrict its definition to material harms: in other words, harms that are likely to be extremely serious and demonstrable if they occurred rather than being speculative or difficult to prove. These harms are most likely to be directed at a country's critical infrastructure through violent attacks of an ideological nature, or attacks that are so serious that they require a national response, including through military action (Mendel 2013: 12). Another option to lessen the potential for abuse is offered ostensibly by the human security definition of national security, which focuses on the need to protect the individual from harm, rather than the state. I will discuss the human security definition of national security, its strengths, weaknesses and pitfalls in the next chapter.

Less well debated are the ways in which state intelligence has expanded down the years: in fact, in the same way that national security has become elastic, so intelligence has too. Having focused mainly on foreign threats to national security before the Second World War, intelligence has come to encompass a range of fields and disciplines, both foreign-focused and domestically focused. This expansion has led to considerable disagreement even within the intelligence establishment about how it should define and practice intelligence. The most frequent characteristics that emerge from conventional intelligence definitions, though, are that it is both a process and a product, as well as an organized system for collection and analysis. These definitions maintain that intelligence is security-based, state-sanctioned and state-driven. Intelligence seeks to provide government policymakers with competitive advantages over other governments, especially their adversaries, by forewarning them about possible threats and opportunities. These forewarnings allow them to gain or expand their power. Intelligence is not confined to information collection, analysis and dissemination, though: it also includes counter-intelligence or even covert actions to further foreign policy objectives. Covert action could extend to operations the agencies undertake on the basis of plausible deniability, or operations that cannot be traced back to the responsible government. Some countries separate analysis and operations, to prevent analysis from being talked up to justify operations, but others do not (Warner 2002: 1522). Intelligence agencies are putting a growing emphasis on open-source intelligence, obtained from publicly available or 'grey' sources that are not necessarily classified, but that require more effort to obtain than public information. The agencies also use intelligence to provide governments with an element of surprise over their adversaries: important when intelligence is used to further the ongoing struggle between nations (Warner 2002: 21). Offering a more succinct definition reflecting the US focus on foreign intelligence, Michael Warner from the Central Intelligence Agency (CIA) defined intelligence as 'secret, state activity to understand or influence foreign entities' (Warner 2002: 21). However, in reality, intelligence, even in the US system, encompasses a range of foreign and domestic threats and interests.

It should be apparent from these definitions that national security and the intelligence activities designed to protect it are state-centric and nation-centric, even nationalistic: that is, they focus on protecting the state as the supposed guardian of the general interest. Furthermore, the nation-state is the main focus of national security protections, even if they are at the expense of other nation-states. The dominant definitions of intelligence do not even consider that intelligence activities could take place in social movements or civil society. Several southern African national liberation movements had intelligence capabilities, which were essential to them being able to protect themselves against apartheid and colonial infiltration (to be discussed in the next chapter); yet according to these definitions, these activities do not even qualify as intelligence.

To make things even more complex, national security has come increasingly to encompass a country's national interests and not just threats, which can lead to a situation where national security encompasses every major problem a country faces. Governments have used the term's elasticity to shoehorn all manner of activist activities that threaten capitalist class interests into it, leading to them justifying the disruption and impeding of activist movements on the pretext of countering terrorism, subversion or domestic extremism, and using political intelligence gathering as the basis to do so (Choudry 2019: 3–16). While probably being the most well-recognized field of intelligence that is particularly susceptible to abuse, political intelligence is not the only one; intelligence relating to a country's economic interests can be abused, too. In fact, economic intelligence has morphed into a new field since the end of the Cold War, and agencies have justified focusing on it on the basis that espionage has become an unavoidable reality of modern international relations. They also argue that in an increasingly competitive global economy, economic security is an important dimension of national security (Gill and Phythian 2012: 26–7).

When it comes to national security surveillance, overbroad definitions of national security can and do lead to massive over-collection of personal information. For instance, bulk SIGINT surveillance, which governments usually use for national security purposes, is so invasive not only because SIGINT capabilities are so great – although not to the extent where even the Five Eyes alliance can operate on a 'collect it all' basis – but because the national security mandates given to these agencies are so broad. In the UK, for instance, the intelligence agencies can apply for warrants to intercept communications on national security grounds. Although the government has not defined the term, in practice it does encompass serious crimes or in the interests of economic well-being of the UK, in so far as those interests are also relevant to the interests of national security (Government of the United Kingdom 2016). In other words, this mandate allows the collection of intelligence that relates not only to threats facing the UK, but its interests, too. Collecting data on threats to the UK may be less controversial and easier to defend. However, who decides what the UK's interests are, and on what basis?

Other countries have expanded their bases for communication surveillance in similar ways. For instance, New Zealand/Aotearoa also collects SIGINT that focuses on the country's 'economic well-being' (Hager 1996: 241–3). South Africa has a slightly narrower formulation for targeted communication surveillance, though, which allows for interception directions (or warrants) to be issued if the 'the gathering of information concerning an actual threat to the public health or safety, national security or compelling national economic interests of the Republic [of South Africa] is necessary'.[1] While this formulation requires the spies to demonstrate that the intercept information they collect is both necessary and compelling, nevertheless, it remains vague. So, these countries have endorsed expanded mandates for their spy agencies to include economic intelligence, which they collect ostensibly to provide policy- or commercially relevant economic information to assist policymakers to make better decisions. If they do not, then a country may argue that it is not able to maintain its competitive advantages, or prevent itself from having its economic or technological secrets stolen.

However, as economic intelligence can lead to the over-collection of intelligence, it can exacerbate international tensions. This is because countries use state spying to gain unfair advantages in trade negotiations and commercial deals, and they can and do resort to stealing the trade secrets of other countries. Economic competition becomes less about which countries have genuine competitive advantages, and more about which have the most powerful spying capabilities. Furthermore, governments tie intelligence more explicitly to the defence of the capitalist system, where anti-capitalist and eco-socialist critics become natural enemies of national security. This form of intelligence can also lead to state agencies being repurposed to serve the interests of private actors, and secrecy may prevent information from emerging publicly that corrupt relationships have formed in the process (Seiglie and Coissard 2008; Duncan 2020). In view of the dangers, the Council of Europe's European Commission for Democracy Through Law (or the Venice Commission) has warned that national security intelligence collected for 'the economic well-being of the nation' should be prohibited (De Capitani 2015). It has also argued that economic intelligence should be narrowed to clearly defined areas such as the prevention of the proliferation of weapons of mass destruction (and violation of export control conditions generally), the circumvention of sanctions and major money laundering. However, rather than narrowing or clarifying their definitions of national security, the general trend has been towards countries expanding and muddying their definitions of national security to justify intelligence collection, analysis and covert action against a whole range of actors that may threaten capitalist class interests and the capitalist system more generally. This is why an anti-capitalist perspective is so important on national security powers: it enables us to unmask the system-maintaining nature of national security powers (Choudry 2019: 17).

Anti-capitalism: Politics, programmes, practice

Anti-capitalism is an enduring current of political thought with a long history that is beyond the scope of this book to explore. While there have been right-wing critiques of capitalism, anti-capitalism is most closely associated with the political left who believe that the system of private ownership of production, the exchange of goods, services and labour through the market, lies at the root of so much misery and hardship in the world today. Since the 2007–8 global recession wreaked havoc on peoples' lives worldwide, anti-capitalism has enjoyed even more popularity, to the point of becoming central to the political thought of social and political movements the world over. Capitalism means that society's basic resources such as land and the products people make are owned and controlled by private companies, turned into commodities to be bought and sold, and to make profits that remain in private hands. Anti-capitalism, on other hand, means that these resources should revert to public, collective ownership, or even no ownership at all: whichever ownership models benefit society as a whole. Such public ownership would free people up from having to sell their labour power for money, often for less than what it is worth. Instead, they could produce goods and services for the benefit of broader society, and people could lead more balanced and fulfilling lives not dominated by their need to survive. However, despite its huge popularity, anti-capitalism lacks a unified programme or ideology, with competing ideas of how capitalism is to be changed (Tormey 2004: 73).

Anti-capitalists are suspicious of arguments that portray the state as a politically neutral institution and instead tend to see it as an instrument for the protection of private property. When the capitalist system is threatened, the state's security institutions, including the military, the police and the intelligence services, will most likely act to defend it and prevent a new society from coming into being. However, anti-capitalists can be radicals or reformers. They can oppose corporate power more generally, or its more specific manifestation since the 1970s, namely, neoliberalism, but not be anti-capitalist in the strict sense of the term, as they may not support the abolition of private ownership and wage labour (Tormey 2004: 107). At the same time, anti-capitalists are also likely to be suspicious of arguments that encourage people to strive for achieving individual rights, such as freedom of expression or privacy, as the ultimate objective of their struggles. While, undoubtedly, there are merits in struggling for these rights, anti-capitalists will recognize that these rights will never be enjoyed on a universal basis for as long as capitalism exists, as the system inevitably leads to oppression and exploitation. In fact, oppression is necessary for exploitation, as people need to be controlled and repressed when they rise up against their poor living and working conditions.

Why is an anti-capitalist perspective important at all? As a political idea, it allows people to imagine and work towards a society that is just, equal and fulfilling. However, it does not impose a single programme on how this emancipatory vision should be achieved. To that extent, anti-capitalism is broader than a Marxist or socialist perspective. Potentially, it offers a programme for organizing opposition to capitalism and can bring together a broader range of social forces than Marxism, providing a more inclusive foundation for movement building. This is especially important in a political moment when classical Marxist parties lack the mass support needed to change the balance of power. However, the broadness of anti-capitalism can be both a strength and a weakness. According to Erik Olin Wright, there are four possible types of anti-capitalist resistance: smashing capitalism, eroding capitalism, taming capitalism and escaping capitalism (Wright 2015). The first two involve transcending the structures of capitalism and replacing them with structures that enable a free and equal society, while the second two involve neutralizing the harms caused by capitalism, without necessarily trying to replace it. These forms of resistance offer very different approaches to the problem of capitalism, and ones that can lead to significant strategic and tactical differences in anti-capitalist movements. Forms of resistance will be determined by the possibilities offered by the political moment they find themselves in, the extent of political space, the strength of anti-capitalist movements and their ability to win significant concessions from the capitalist class.

Anti-capitalists have long recognized that those who are the most oppressed and exploited by capitalism should be at the forefront of struggles against it. Overwhelmingly, they are likely to be members of the working class, defined broadly as the class of people who have to sell their labour power in order to survive. However, capitalism's genius has been to divide the working class against itself, including along the lines of race (or colour) and gender. Capitalism has pitted Black and white workers, and men and women, against one another, using ideologies that put white male workers at the top of a social hierarchy. Since the 1970s, anti-capitalism has been enriched by a theory of liberation – namely racial capitalism – that recognizes the interrelatedness of race and class as different forms of oppression used by the capitalist class to differentiate some elements of the working class from others. The term emerged to explain the specificities of the South African struggle against apartheid, when a racially divided working class was the biggest obstacle to the liberation movement, and was developed further by Cedric Robinson (2000).

Racial capitalism recognizes that racism is not just a set of prejudiced ideas, but a systematic form of oppression used to extract surplus from Black people by differentiating and dividing Black from white members of the working class. Race and capitalism are inseparable analytical categories, in that the capitalist class uses racism not just to fuel societal prejudice, but to justify the particularly vicious exploitation of Black people, and the marginalization and plunder of whole nations on the basis that they are majority Black countries. Racial capitalism posits that it is impossible to arrive at true national unity under capitalism; neither is it possible to end the exploitation of peripheral countries by dominant ones through colonialism and imperialism. In order to overcome these divisions, anti-capitalists and anti-racists need to unite as their struggles are indivisible. Racial capitalism challenges the left to broaden anti-racist struggles to include struggles for redistribution of wealth and avoid race essentialism, where struggles are reduced to being about race, while it challenges anti-capitalists to avoid the dangers of race-blind class reductionism, where the struggle is all about class struggle and where anti-racism is considered to be false consciousness. While it recognizes that race does not exist as a scientific fact, as all human beings are the same race and racial identities are socially constructed, the social reality of race is ever-present in contemporary societies and continues to be used by the ruling class to justify many oppressive and exploitative practices. Neither does it attempt to assign causal primacy to forms of differentiation, be they race, class, ethnicity or nationalism, as doing so inevitably leads to repetitious and circular arguments (Alexander 1985: 128). Any genuine, aspirational liberation movement needs to be anti-racist, anti-capitalist and anti-imperialist, and nowhere is this insight more relevant than in the region that gave birth to the idea of racial capitalism, namely, southern Africa.

Racial capitalism is not mechanistic; as a theory, it recognizes that there is a contingent, but not a necessary, relationship between racism and capitalism: in other words, in some historical periods, racism may be functional to the reproduction of aspects of the capitalist system, and at other times it may be contradictory (Alexander 2002: 24). Racism provided the colonial powers with the ideological justification to divide the world up into superior and inferior nations. They ended their direct occupation of territories not because they saw the error of their ways but because colonialism was too costly for them to maintain, both in terms of the increasingly international unacceptability of the system and because of struggles against it that were gaining ground. The apartheid regime dispensed with its formalized system of racial oppression and exploitation, known as apartheid, because it was eroding the competitiveness of South African capital, and so had to end it to allow the country to renew its economy along neoliberal lines. However, both the colonialists and the apartheid regime were confident that the nature of the post-colonial, post-apartheid state would remain essentially the same, as class relations would be largely unaltered. Hence, a new class of political elites, represented by former liberation movements that could rule into perpetuity, were promoted by the colonialists to prevent a power vacuum from emerging that could create political space for more radical oppositional movements (Alexander 2002: 64). Nevertheless, racism remains intrinsic to capitalist accumulation in the region, in that as a form of difference it can still be used by the former colonial powers to justify extractive practices through unequal terms of trade.

Why an anti-capitalist perspective on security powers?

As mentioned in the introduction, scholars and activists on the left have put considerable efforts into developing alternative visions for policing, especially in the wake of police violence against Black civilians in the US. However, perhaps because of its relative invisibility, less work has been undertaken on developing alternative visions for national security surveillance and intelligence, whether these areas of the state are even needed, and if they are, how they should be organized beyond capitalism. Where there has been critical questioning of the necessity for security powers, much of the thinking, writing and activism tends to lapse into calls for reforms or greater oversight, which predictably never keep up with the abuses they are meant to prevent. Global North countries facing terrorism threats have become trapped in counterproductive downward spirals, where military and intelligence aggression foments resentment and alienation, which in turn fuels even more terrorism, inevitably followed by the expansion of surveillance powers. Scholarship on these issues faces an additional challenge in that security and intelligence studies, and especially the latter, are dominated by scholars who accept the arguments that these security powers are a necessary evil that are needed to keep people safe. This is particularly unsurprising for scholars who were intelligence or police officers in their previous professional lives. The information asymmetries between them and other scholars, and overall secrecy more generally, give them a competitive edge in the field.

The growing field of surveillance studies incorporates a diversity of intellectual traditions, though. Possibly the most recent trenchant critique of the power of big technology firms and the ways in which they enable bulk surveillance has been offered by Shoshana Zuboff. She can be credited with making the term 'surveillance capitalism' part of popular debate and critique. Her explanation of how firms such as Facebook and Google have developed illegitimate business models that expropriate peoples' data, accumulating huge power and wealth for their owners, and her identification of the prediction power of these companies as being anti-democratic, is a major contribution to the literature. However, Zuboff's critique is not anti-capitalist. It critiques what she considers to be a new and distinct form of rogue capitalism, and not capitalism per se, as though capitalism isn't always rogue. Consequently, she does not really posit alternatives beyond capitalism, instead falling back on vague references to replenished democracy bolstered by healthy democratic institutions (Zuboff 2019: 519–21). Surveillance capitalism still posits a form of technology exceptionalism, where technological developments are assigned causal primacy in periodizing capitalism. This concept contains problematic assumptions that cannot and should not be universalized, as a region like southern Africa still has a relatively low level of internet penetration. Furthermore, as will be discussed, much of the surveillance taking place in the region is decidedly low-tech or even no-tech, in that physical surveillance is still very integral to intelligence practices.

If national security surveillance has expanded in unaccountable ways, then what precisely is the fight against? Someone who accepts the need for these security powers would argue that the fight is against rogue police or spies, and that greater controls and oversight over their powers would cure these problems. An anti-capitalist, on the other hand, would shift the analysis of the problem from the episodic problem of spies abusing their powers to the systemic problem of capitalism, and how it needs surveillance to survive. An anti-capitalist would identify the true nature of the problem with clarity, and point society towards lasting solutions. So, if the problem is one of spies going rogue, then the solution is to reform the spy agencies and ensure better oversight. But, if the problem is capitalism, it can be anticipated that spies will continue to go rogue until the system they truly serve and protect is dismantled. In other words, seeing the expansion of security powers through the lens of anti-capitalism allows us to politicize these security powers, and makes it clear that activists need to link any struggle against them to a political struggle about how power is organized in society.

We could understand expanding security powers as a response to the September 11 attacks, as well as subsequent terrorist attacks. However, doing so lets the spies and their political overseers off the hook, as it allows governments caught in the act of allowing security overreach to attribute it to a well-intentioned, if overzealous, attempt to protect their citizens. Of course, there is some merit in this argument. But, this explanation does not account fully for the problem. Instead, placing the problem in the broader context of the crises of capitalism in the wake of the 2007–8 global recession provides us with a more complete explanation. In the wake of the recession, thousands of people took to the streets to protest against austerity imposed by governments to stabilize and renew the capitalist system. Governments enabled the take-up of technologies developed for war – including the war on terror launched in the wake of the September 11 attacks – by civilian institutions of state to contain and disassemble protests. The post-recessionary capitalist system needed surveillance for it to survive, as outright mass repression was likely to escalate rather than dampen protests.

An anti-capitalist perspective allows us to explain the evolution of security powers historically, and relate it to the evolution of capitalism more generally. It seeks to explain how modern intelligence has enabled the worldwide spread of neoliberal capitalism, especially political and economic intelligence. It allows us to show that spying has become increasingly important to the concentration of wealth. Capitalism needs democracy to make the system palatable; yet, more recently, governments have been less concerned about mitigating the disastrous effects of capitalism, and more willing to pursue undemocratic methods of containing resistance. The expansion of security powers is linked to the crisis of liberal-democratic politics, which offered limited incorporation of sections of the working class into the capitalist system and included the official recognition of basic democratic rights such as freedom of speech, assembly and privacy. However, in the wake of the recession, governments were willing to dispense with even limited incorporation.

An anti-capitalist perspective on national security surveillance would also push the question of agency to the front of any strategy on how to limit these powers, and focus on the potential change agents in the struggle against these ever-expanding powers. As the capitalist system becomes more unstable, then resistance to it becomes more likely; this double-movement creates a potential for activists to roll these powers back in meaningful ways. Anti-capitalist politics are broad, but all anti-capitalists are likely to look to unofficial politics, especially mass movements, to provide surveillance counter-power rather than the familiar reforms often demanded by security watchdogs (like greater judicial and parliamentary oversight, for instance). Then the analysis would shift to how strong or weak social and political movements are. Social and political movements may also have experiential knowledge about the true nature of security powers if state spies have infiltrated and disrupted them. By using a united front approach, they are also more likely to move the struggle away from single-issue politics, generalize it across society and link it to the broader struggle against capitalism. By challenging us to think about how society should be organized in future, an anti-capitalist politics makes us move beyond everyday surface reactions, and helps us to think more deeply about how much security we actually need, what kind, who should enforce it and how. They could help us to see that a different form of social organization to capitalism could resolve the fundamental problems of society, leading to the need for many security powers fading away.

How national security surveillance travels around the world

Anti-capitalism provides a framework for understanding the global architecture of national security surveillance, and southern Africa's place in it. Intelligence and surveillance practices have become increasingly similar across the world: more and more governments spy on their citizens' phones and internet usage, use similar justifications to one another, pass similar laws and seek similar technological capabilities. As will be discussed in subsequent chapters, southern African countries are no exception to this general rule. While there are undoubtedly variations in these practices, countries do learn security practices from one another, and these similarities are enabled by the global trade in surveillance. According to Privacy International (n.d.), this global trade picked up pace in the 1990s, and comes in at least five forms:

Direct equipping of foreign intelligence and security forces

Companies or state agencies may sell or even donate surveillance equipment to the intelligence and security agencies of other countries. This they may do partly as a business opportunity, and partly to expand their own surveillance capabilities in those countries, as the deployment of domestic equipment in foreign communication networks could allow the manufacturers to gain remote access to those networks through exploitable vulnerabilities or even 'backdoors'. These are security flaws that are built deliberately into surveillance equipment to enable a third party to extract data from communication networks illicitly, and without the consent either of the service provider or of its users. The global trade in surveillance equipment has become big business in recent times, which will be discussed in more detail in Chapter 5.

Training of foreign intelligence and security forces

When surveillance equipment is diffused across the world, so is support training. This training can help to normalize surveillance practices by making them appear to be an everyday and even necessary part of societal functioning. Surveillance practices, too, can be diffused around the world as 'best practice'; so in other words, as practices that countries should not only implement, but aspire to emulate. For instance, surveillance-intense intelligence-led policing models have been diffused across the world through training programmes as policing best practice, which will be discussed in more detail in Chapter 6.

Financing of their operations and procurement

Overseas development assistance may include financial assistance, either as donations or as loans, for security sector activities generally, or surveillance activities specifically. Much of this financial support, especially in the security realm, is unlikely to be benevolent, though, but is most likely intended to further the strategic interests of the donor country or institution. Security funding is a highly sensitive area, as it can be used to influence, control and even compromise the sovereignty of a country. The European Union (EU) has provided support to non-EU countries to tighten border controls through, for instance, increasing surveillance of their borders to reduce migration to EU countries. Increasingly, China has become involved in supporting intelligence training and the procurement of surveillance equipment in southern Africa (Privacy International 2018a). These issues will be discussed in more detail in Chapters 5 and 7.

Facilitation of exports of surveillance equipment by industry

The surveillance industry is always looking to open new markets around the world and use various methods to facilitate these exports, such as security-related trade fairs. They have a vested interest in ensuring that governments facilitate exports as well, and governments also have a vested interest in growing their export bases. However, simple facilitation is tricky, as surveillance equipment can be easily abused, leading to exporting countries becoming embroiled in politically costly controversies. The global drive to control the flow of weapons to countries experiencing armed conflict and the need to control weapons of mass destruction such as chemical or nuclear weapons have led to countries cooperating to develop global baseline standards for the banning or the controlled exporting of such equipment. As surveillance tools are typically highly sensitive, and governments often classify the most invasive as weapons, they may be subject to export controls. The Wassenaar Arrangement on Export Controls for Conventional Arms and Dual-Use Goods and Technologies is an example of a multilateral export control regime that applies to certain surveillance tools (The Wassenaar Arrangement u.d.). This Arrangement facilitates the export of surveillance equipment, but within a controlled framework that requires exporters to consider the potential for abuses of the equipment. However, its vagueness facilitates the relatively easy exports of surveillance equipment, including to semi-authoritarian and even authoritarian countries. These issues will be dealt with in more detail in Chapter 5.

Promotion of legislation enabling surveillance

Countries can promote security and intelligence laws that boost their foreign policies abroad. For instance, encouraged by the US Federal Bureau of Investigation (FBI), many southern African countries have adopted what have become known as 'lawful interception' laws, requiring public and private communication service providers to make their networks intercept-capable and outlawing those that are not.[2] Many countries updated existing surveillance laws, or introduced new laws, including in southern Africa, in the wake of the September 11 attacks on the US and the July 7 attacks in London. In the rush to legislate against terrorism, some countries adopted a 'cut and paste' approach towards legislation, at times borrowing heavily from laws elsewhere, usually from the US, Europe, Canada and Australia. These borrowings were not politically neutral, but carried with them many ideological assumptions about intelligence, security and social control more generally. This issue will be discussed in more detail in Chapter 3. At the other extreme, the major surveillance countries also export surveillance practices that are poorly controlled through legislation, in order to keep them away from public scrutiny. Bulk SIGINT surveillance is one such practice, which will be discussed in Chapter 3.

However, national security surveillance practices have not diffused equally around the world. Some countries have become net manufacturers and exporters of equipment, or provided more external funding or exerted more influence on laws and policies, than others. In other words, these relationships have become asymmetrical, with a few major surveillance powers controlling the pace of developments in the field to their benefit and at the expense of recipient countries. Controlling the means of intelligence and surveillance of another country could be dangerous, as a hostile actor in an exporting country could use this control to compromise the national security of a recipient country as that country would not be able to protect itself. Yet, this is precisely the danger that many countries face as they participate in the arms race for surveillance technologies: it is a race whose rules are written by the few and imposed on the many. The pattern of these asymmetrical relationships become easier to understand through reference to the Marxist theory of imperialism, which still remains so relevant to anti-capitalist politics despite the historical period of classical imperialism having come to an end.

Features of classical imperialism

Understanding how national security surveillance builds on exchange patterns of imperialism necessitates identifying some of the main features of classical imperialism. Imperialism cannot be equated simply with capitalist expansion to other countries, and the domination of those countries, through either direct or indirect control. In Marxism, the term has a much more precise historical meaning, and refers to the period of capitalist expansion that occurred towards the end of the nineteenth century. Imperialism at that stage involved a fundamental restructuring of how the most powerful capitalists operated, where competition was replaced by monopoly capital, and governments engaged in aggressive colonial expansion and wars to expand monopoly capital's reach into non-market economies (Mandel 1955). Possibly the most influential theory of imperialism was developed by Vladimir Lenin, who understood it as the practice of one country or group of countries extending control over others during this period. For Lenin, imperialism was a stage of development of capitalism dominated by monopolies and finance capital, where capital was exported to renew profitability in new terrains, and where the world was divided up into territories controlled by the biggest capitalist powers to enable this renewal.

Lenin's definition of imperialism included five features. The most important feature of Lenin's definition was the concentration of production and capital, to the point where competition was eliminated in key markets; consequently, monopolies came to dominate economic life. In fact, Lenin referred to imperialism as the monopoly stage of capitalism. Monopolies used predictable methods to secure their dominance, including establishing monopolistic associations like cartels, trusts and syndicates to lock their competitors out. According to Lenin, monopolist associations used several methods to secure their dominance. For instance, these associations manipulated competitive markets by stopping supplies and deliveries of raw materials to their competitors, monopolized labour through alliances and closed trade outlets. They also established agreements with buyers where they agreed to trade only with the cartels, cut prices to undercut their competition and raised their prices once they eliminated competition, stopped credit supplies to their competitors and boycotted them (Lenin [1916] 1963).

Concentration was also enabled by the merging of banks and industries to create a new form of profit-making, namely, finance capital. These mergers increased concentration, as a few companies used cartel behaviour to lock out competitors. They did so by drawing on the banks to finance their expansion, cooperating with one another to prevent competition and raising barriers to entry for smaller companies, as financiers withheld capital from these companies. Monopolist companies used the holding system, where even if the parent company did not hold shares in a subsidiary, it could still multiply its profits through holding a controlling stake in the shares, which increased the power of the monopolists (Lenin [1916] 1963).

As home markets became saturated, companies began to export capital and not just commodities. Financialized capitalism expanded outside their home territories, and monopolist capitalist associations carved the world up among themselves into different spheres of influence. Citing examples from the electricity and oil industries, Lenin showed how, using finance capital, monopolist companies in these areas expanded throughout the world. In pursuing their expansionist aims, these companies promoted uneven development of infrastructure in the countries they dominated, where the railways and communication infrastructure, for instance, was developed not to raise the living standards of the masses, but to enable profit-extraction. This process of financialized capitalist expansion led to territorial division of the whole world among the biggest capitalist powers. This division provided new markets and raw materials for them – including through direct colonial rule in other countries – and divided the world up into creditor and debtor countries. Disagreeing with Karl Kautsky, Lenin argued that these territorial divisions were not necessarily peaceful in nature, but periodically involved wars among the imperialist powers to re-establish territorial boundaries (Lenin [1916] 1963). However, uneven development across the globe led to decay and resistance in the colonies. Consequently, imperialist powers like Germany used intelligence to track the struggles of national emancipatory movements in the colonies, to understand the extent of the threat.

Rosa Luxemburg also made significant contributions to our understanding of imperialism by focusing on one of the internal contradictions of capitalism, namely, that workers could not afford many of the commodities they produced. This problem of under-consumption drove the need for capitalists to expand into non-capitalist territories and dissolve their indigenous modes of production. Doing so allowed these capitalists to take advantage of other nations through exploitation, while creating new markets for their products: hence the utility of imperialism for capitalism. Imperialism also created what she referred to as 'compensating outlets' for capitalism, such as the armaments industry, which governments established to absorb excess capital, while facilitating the expansion of this industry by allowing them to export to non-market economies (Mandel 1955). However, for Luxemburg, there were limits to the abilities of capitalists to exploit the non-capitalist territories, as once they became marketized they were likely to suffer from the very same problems of under-consumption and declining profits afflicting their home countries, leading to the breakdown of capitalism. At that stage, the major imperialist countries were more likely to engage in (and did engage in) more violent forms of exploitation, including through war (Luxemburg 1951). Her arguments inevitably led her to positions that were both anti-imperialist and anti-militarist.

Lenin reloaded:[3] *Colonialism and imperialism today*

How relevant are imperialism and colonialism as explanatory terms today, as the major imperialist powers have largely ended their direct control of 'their' colonies? Answering this question would require us to establish whether Lenin's five features of imperialism remain features of contemporary capitalism.

It could be argued that Kautsky has been proven correct and that after the Second World War the world entered a period of what he called 'ultra-imperialism', or a relatively peaceful period of post-imperialist competition among the major superpowers. However, given the conduct of the US in the wake of the September 11 attacks, ultra-imperialism does not appear to be an appropriate descriptor. As David Harvey has argued, the US achieved its dominance in the wake of war through what he describes as 'the new imperialism', where neoliberal capitalism has expanded across the globe. For Harvey, imperialism in the contemporary world is a distinctively political project on the part of actors whose power is based on the command of a territory and a capacity to mobilize its human and natural resources towards political, economic and military ends. Harvey has updated Luxemburg's account of capitalism's need to corrode non-capitalist relations as 'accumulation by dispossession', where capitalists accumulate wealth through depriving people of their rights and possessions. This form of accumulation differs from accumulation through production, where capitalists create wealth through productive activity (Harvey 2003).

For Harvey, the global economy has become too large for the US to manage, leading to a need for it to accumulate political power differently, and surveillance provides it with a means to do just that. Consequently, the US preferred means of accumulating power in the current period is through the exercise of global hegemony. This the US exercises by claiming that it is acting in the general interest to secure a global environment where other countries could benefit through the mutual gains from their own interactions (such as trade) or through their enhanced collective power (Harvey 2005: 36–8). The US has also successfully harnessed resurgent nationalism after the September 11 attacks to justify routine rights violations abroad, on the pretext that they are necessary to protect domestic security (Harvey 2003: 196). Hence, many countries have decided that that foreign communications are not subject to the same privacy protections as domestic communications. Even in the post-war period, the US has shown that it will resort to military means to assert its dominance where less violent means fail (Harvey 2003: 26).

Harvey provides useful pointers to understanding the utility of national security surveillance to the new imperialism. The global surveillance network provided by the Five Eyes alliance allows the US to extend its capabilities to keep a watchful eye over large parts of the globe, mainly by spreading the burdens, the risks and the benefits of dragnet surveillance to trusted allies, while maintaining overall control of the means of surveillance. He has attempted to understand surveillance in the context of the contradictions of capital; in doing so, he has focused on how surveillance has become integral to neoliberal state formation. For Harvey, technological innovation is central to capitalism, in that it develops the productive forces necessary to drive profit; but at the same time, the fruits of innovation tend to be spread unevenly across society. As a result, capital also has an interest in using innovations to control surplus populations that have become redundant to the production process, and surveillance provides it with the technological means to do just that. Surveillance has also become an increasingly important political technology for imperialism. The US has used freedom and democracy as legitimizing discourses to justify a neocolonial expansion into other territories, and this warped understanding of freedom is being used to curtail communications freedom (Harvey 2015: 91–130; 264–6).

More recently, Harvey has argued that the classical imperialism of Lenin has been superseded by a more multipolar world characterized by growing inter-imperialist rivalry. Considering the rise of China as a global superpower, Harvey argues that there is a more complicated and bidirectional flow of value in the contemporary period, to the point where economic value that has been drained from the East to the West has been reversed (Harvey 2015: 169). There are also a growing number of middle powers, which are still dependent on the major imperial powers and protect their interests. Nevertheless, they exercise considerable regional dominance over their less powerful neighbours. These are countries that are not as powerful as the major imperialist powers, but nevertheless exercise considerable influence in their regions, to the point of dominating weaker countries in these regions by replicating imperialist relationships with these countries to establish regional platforms for accumulation: a process that has been termed sub-imperialism (Bond 2015; Çağlı 2009). According to Patrick Bond, sub-imperialist states extend imperialism by providing the major imperialist powers with a means of maintaining regional control over different countries. This they do by using proxy states to exercise domination on their behalf and ensure that capitalist accumulation to their advantage continues unhindered by any local resistance: South Africa, Israel, Indonesia, Taiwan and Turkey are some of the countries that could be said to play this role (Bond 2015: 15–16). Thus, the sub-imperialist powers could be understood as the regional 'policemen' of the major imperialist powers, using their coercive capacities (including their surveillance capabilities) to contain local struggles or opposition.

This does not mean to say that sub-imperialist countries cannot exercise autonomous power on some issues, but these are typically issues that are not particularly relevant to the maintenance of global neoliberalism (Bond 2015: 15–16). However, local elites in their respective countries may not be playing a comprador role only. They can and do exercise autonomy from the major imperialist powers and practice resource nationalism by acting in their own interests, rather than those of an external actor: much depends on the space they enjoy to resist imperialism and shape their own growth paths. Security powers often are highly relevant, though, as they are central to the maintenance of social control in countries that may become destabilized by inequality, which means that they remain particularly susceptible to imperialist domination and control.

The most significant organized sub-imperialist force in the global South today is the BRICS alliance of countries. After the Second World War, the US established its hegemony over the rest of the world very effectively; however, its hegemony is being challenged, not least by the BRICS countries. The former president of Brazil Lula da Silva even went as far as celebrating this new alliance as an important counterweight to the dominance of the imperialist powers, and, through BRICS in Da Silva's words, 'a new global economic geography is being born'. However,

BRICS stands accused of providing a platform for sub-imperialism, where the BRICS countries use the partnership as a cartel-like association to externalize their accumulation strategies to weaker countries in their respective regions. In doing so, they reinforce the very neoliberal practices that allowed the major imperialist powers to continue dominating global affairs, and in the process contribute to neoliberal regime maintenance. China, Russia and South Africa are particularly susceptible to exhibiting sub-imperial behaviour. These countries use what David Harvey (2003) has called spacio-temporal fixes to carve out regional territorial spheres of influence to solve their own internal accumulation problems (Bond 2015).

However, this reading of BRICS as a sub-imperial conveyer belt has been contested for being overly pessimistic 'BRICS-bashing', in that it leaves no room for regional struggles against the major imperialist powers. In doing so, it ignores the progressive, even anti-imperialist, potential of a regional hegemonic bloc located in the global South, that addresses the most pressing issues faced by the hemisphere (Tandon 2014). Yet, approaches that emphasize global South solidarity while glossing over the sub-hegemonic activities of middle powers can lend themselves to authoritarian national developmentalist projects.

While it cannot be denied that the character of imperialism has changed somewhat since the days of Lenin, it also cannot be denied that the essential features of imperialism remain intact in the current period. In fact, global economic flows are strongly suggestive of a deepening of exploitation by the legacy imperialist powers, and there is little empirical evidence of China catching up to them. The major imperialist powers have intensified their effort to drain wealth from Africa through primary commodity exports on terms that are not advantageous to the continent: to this extent, Harvey's denial of imperialism amounts to a denial of contemporary realities. Consequently, it is necessary to acknowledge the continued existence of inequalities between countries, whether they are characterized as developed versus developing, imperialist versus oppressed, or core versus periphery countries. These realities require not a dismissal of Lenin's theory of imperialism, but an extension of the theory which takes into account the existence of middle powers and nation-states that may well act in their own interests while acknowledging the existence of global hierarchies of dominant and subordinate nations.

Other scholars have been more robust in their assertions that imperialism is alive and well in the contemporary period, albeit in a slightly altered form. For instance, Marxist media and communication scholar Christian Fuchs has argued that there is abundant information that most of the major indicators of imperialism are still in evidence today, with the exception of direct colonial domination of other territories. However, the world's major powers do not need to exercise control directly through colonialism, or through the occupation of land by military force; rather, they can (and do) exercise indirect political, economic or cultural influence over other territories. The concentration of capital and monopolization of industries remains extreme, with the most dominant companies headquartered in the US. Finance capital has become central to the workings of the global economy, and the export of capital has intensified under 'globalization'. A small number of countries continue to dominate the global economy and exercise undue influence over particular parts of the world, mainly the US and the European trading bloc. A major shift in the structure of global capitalism, though, involves the rise of Asia as an economic power, especially China; however, it remains incontestable that the US still dominates the globe militarily (Fuchs 2010b).

Media studies scholar Dal Yong Jin (2015) has argued for the continued relevance of imperialism as a descriptor for contemporary cultural and communication relationships. While he acknowledges that the Leninist definition of imperialism cannot be applied easily to today's world, he argues that the world is experiencing a new form of imperialism where some countries exercise political, economic and cultural domination over others, focusing particularly on the role of big, monopolistic media corporations in controlling the media landscape globally. These dominant companies, emanating largely from the US, increase inequalities in access to media and communication across the globe.

The cultural imperialism thesis has been criticized for assuming a one-way flow of cultural goods from the global North to the rest of the world, where the reality has been somewhat more complex with Southern countries also contributing to media and communication counter-flows (Wasserman 2010: 52–5). For Dal Yong Jin, though, criticisms of cultural imperialism are somewhat dated as they fail to reflect more recent realities where a small number of internet-based companies, mainly from the US, have come to dominate media and communication flows once again: a phenomenon he refers to as 'platform imperialism'. This dominance is not territorial, but it does not need to be: so much of peoples' lives are lived online, and dominating the means of communication allows these platforms to achieve levels of penetration in new markets that far surpass the traditional forms of domination during the period of classical imperialism. Platforms such as Facebook and Google commercialize the labour of their users and on-sell it to advertisers using opaque data-sharing arrangements, and contribute towards capital accumulation to the benefit of the US. Lax government competition and privacy rules facilitate the global growth of these internet companies, and consequently, both have expanded their worldwide reach by gobbling up other platforms and turning themselves into near-monopolies in their respective domains (Yong Jin 2015: 22–41).

'Imperialism' is not the only Marxist term enjoying renewed relevance; 'colonialism' has become a term that media and communication scholars have become much more familiar with, through an emerging body of scholarship called critical data studies. These scholars argue that the field needs to be decolonized and de-Westernized, and opened up to global South perspectives. Doing so means using conceptual frameworks that speak to these experiences, and data colonialism combines an acknowledgement of the extractive practices of historical colonialism with the contemporary appropriation of data for commercial and political purposes (Milan and Treré 2019; Couldry and Meijas 2019: 337). Data colonialism as a concept calls attention to inherently unequal relations of data exchange, and highlights the practices of governments and commercial companies in surveilling and exploiting the data of marginalized groups, Black people and women disproportionately, while imperialism could explain the strategies and ideologies they use to dominate particular populations (Mann and Daly 2019).

Data colonialism could be seen as a metaphor for the ways in which the big technology companies expropriate peoples' data for the purposes of capitalist accumulation (Thatcher, O'Sullivan and Mahmoudi 2016: 990–1006). In the process of doing so, these companies are ensuring that more and more aspects of everyday life are colonized by capital, which expands into more and more non-market areas. For instance, according to Mann and Daly (2019: 379–95), Australia has used SIGINT to disadvantage the impoverished nation of Timor-Leste in trade negotiations and 'blacklisted' individuals considered at risk of recidivism, who consisted disproportionately of first-nation Australians. Hence, they concluded that Australia's uses of big data-driven surveillance 'assume a specific colonial character, targeting marginalized and minority groups internally and at the border, and poorer neighbours in the region' (Mann and Daly 2019: 387). So, while dispossession of data is experienced across the board by many people, it takes on a particularly pernicious character when it comes to the data of Black and poor people.

However, imperialism could have even more explanatory value than colonialism when it comes to global surveillance relationships. As Edward Said has explained, the former involved 'the practices, the theory and the attitudes of a dominating metropolitan centre ruling a distant territory', while the latter involved 'implanting of settlements on a distant territory' (Said 1993: 9). In other words, focusing on data colonialism may lead us to focus narrowly on the technicalities of extracting value from data in the service of capitalism, at the expense of the broader ideological justifications and political objectives of these practices. Data colonialism can also become a vague concept that is too metaphorical to have much explanatory value and empties colonialism of its political content. According to María Soledad Segura and Silvio Waisbord, data colonialism is a muddy idea that diminishes the centrality of violence in colonialism (Segura and Waisbord 2019: 416–17). There are major differences between the colonialism of old and now: the brute force used to commandeer the resources of southern Africa is no longer possible or politically acceptable. Imperialism, on the other hand, describes an ideology whereby a country extends control over others through political, economic and cultural means, and which may involve violence and colonization, but does not have to.

In spite of the empirical evidence pointing to the continued existence of imperialism, albeit in altered form, some scholars remain reluctant to use the term 'imperialism' to describe the current moment as they feel that it de-historicizes the term. While rejecting the term 'globalization', they prefer 'neocolonialism' and 'neo-imperialism' to describe the incorporation of the former colonies into the global economy. Neocolonialism is a form of indirect control that allows for the former imperialist powers to maintain global hegemony by continuing to exploit weaker countries without having to resort to the politically damaging practice of direct colonial rule. Neo-imperialism describes the political justification for doing so. Through these practices, the former imperialist powers continue to assert imperialist power through the exploitation of unequal economic relations. This exploitation can lead to subordinate countries being nominally independent and sovereign, but not substantially so. I think there is a strong argument to qualify the term 'colonialism' to describe countries that are not colonized physically by other countries, and rather to use the term 'neocolonialism' to refer to indirect control. However, the arguments for maintaining the term 'imperialism' to refer to global hegemonic practices are strong enough for me to continue to use it without qualifying it.

National security surveillance and Lenin's five features of imperialism

When analysing the expansion of national security surveillance practices and industries, it becomes apparent that they follow a well-recognized economic geography, reproducing and reinforcing patterns of global power established during earlier periods of imperial conquest and colonization. We can understand these patterns as imperialist through reference to Lenin's main features of imperialism, updated and augmented for the contemporary period. In other words, the growth of surveillance manifests the main features of imperialism, and is an indicator of the continued existence of imperialism. This is not to say that some features have not changed, but we can gain much from understanding the structure of capitalism in the twenty-first century as being imperialist. Most significantly, it focuses the mind on the highly unequal, extractive and crisis-ridden nature of the system, and, despite an unprecedented period of world peace, the dominant players may resort to war in future to re-stake their claims on parts of the globe. While I discuss the relevance of the main features of imperialism for national security surveillance in subsequent chapters, I provide a brief summary of the main trends below:

Monopolization of the means of surveillance

The Five Eyes alliance of countries is the most significant known SIGINT liaison network in existence. As the intelligence alliance of the Anglosphere, the Five Eyes alliance could be described credibly as a cartel as understood by Lenin, namely, an organization that regulated the production of goods (in this case SIGINT) and locked other competitors out by virtue of its monopoly power. The major imperialist powers and some of their most influential former dominions agreed to cooperate with one another to gain comparative advantage over other potential competitors, notably China and Russia (two major targets of Five Eyes surveillance). Even countries that have not aligned themselves to any of the major superpowers have entered into third-party agreements with the NSA, effectively turning them into surveillance allies of the Five Eyes (Madsen 2014). The surveillance industry has become more concentrated, too, with the most powerful manufacturers of surveillance equipment being based in Europe and the US, and particularly in the two most powerful Five Eyes countries, the US and the UK, giving them considerable control over the means of surveillance. The Five Eyes as a near-monopoly is discussed in more detail in Chapter 4, and the concentration of the surveillance industry is discussed in Chapter 5.

Convergence of the surveillance and armaments industries

The convergence of the surveillance and armaments industries has enabled global communication surveillance, as has the convergence between military and civilian uses of surveillance. Consequently, dual-use surveillance technologies have proliferated. As military spending has declined, the most powerful arms manufacturers have diversified away from conventional arms and into the manufacture of surveillance hardware and software, and overwhelmingly these manufacturers are based in the US and Europe. They leveraged their dominance of the conventional arms industry to enter into the surveillance market. This market is lucrative, as can they sell their wares not only to the defence industry but to police and intelligence agencies as well. As 'theatres' of war such as Iraq and Afghanistan wound down, and state arms budgets contracted, the arms industry was forced to seek new, domestic markets for their wares. Police militarization has also allowed them to market their wares to police agencies.

However, arms companies would not have been able to exploit these markets without governments reframing those who are considered 'enemies', by not confining themselves to the traditional targets of warfare only (such as hostile countries), but including non-traditional ones as well (such as internal populations that threaten existing social 'orders'). In the process, the boundaries between law enforcement concerns and national security concerns have become porous (Andreas and Price 2001: 31–52; Kraska 2014). As John Bellamy Foster and Robert McChesney have argued, those state actors who have the most tanks and guns are ceding their positions of power to those who have the most intelligence, creating an industrial base for surveillance, and even its universalization (Bellamy Foster and McChesney 2014). The trends in the global trade in spyware, which follow imperialist and even sub-imperialist patterns, are discussed in more detail in Chapter 5, and some of the implications of the convergence of policing and national security intelligence are discussed in Chapter 6.

Financialization and surveillance

The expansion of surveillance is connected intimately to financialization. Wars create demand for armaments and industrial output more generally: an industrial strategy that they call 'military Keynesianism' (Bellamy Foster and McChesney 2014). However, wars involve bodies, raising the cost of involvement in theatres of war politically and socially. Ordinary citizens may begin to push back against warfare economies as the true human cost becomes visible. The lack of visible victims of surveillance makes it a much more difficult problem to raise public consciousness about, and consequently to organize around. Small wonder that key arms-producing countries have begun to orientate their economies away from traditional industrial capitalism to what Bellamy Foster and McChesney have called surveillance capitalism, or a form of capitalism that has new, distinct characteristics (Bellamy Foster and McChesney 2014).

These characteristics include the creation of huge, but unstable, financial surpluses, generated by financial speculation, which need to find investments but cannot turn to a favoured outlet like arms. Financialization has also created a huge appetite for data, and these databanks themselves have offered new revenue streams to companies which can profile and target potential customers with products. They have also provided troves of information to intelligence agencies for both criminal investigations and broader social control purposes. More intense public–private collaboration in an industry that was dominated traditionally by governments cannot be underestimated as a key factor: as Snowden himself has observed, surveillance is the business model of the internet.[4] This model has allowed unprecedented cooperation between communications companies and governments, as the former has the resources to develop and maintain huge databanks that the latter can plunder at will (at least until recently).

Uneven development of surveillance capabilities

The global production and consumption of surveillance technologies tend to follow global patterns of production and consumption more generally. These patterns were forged during the imperialist stage of capitalist development, where the colonies were used as sites for cheap labour and resource extraction, and to open up new markets for consumption. But doing so also involved commercial enclosure of areas of life that fell outside the market. Indigenous intelligence capabilities were deliberately underdeveloped by the major colonial powers during the colonial period, and systemic weaknesses in intelligence agencies in the post-colonial period need to be understood in this historical context. The major economic imperialist and sub-imperialist powers have become the major surveillance powers, and they have used surveillance to pursue imperialism by other means. These issues will be discussed in more depth in Chapters 2–5.

Global territorial divisions and surveillance imperialism

In the same way that the major imperialist powers divided the globe up among themselves, so it has been with communication surveillance, too. Snowden's disclosures revealed the worldwide reach of the NSA and its surveillance partners. However, state surveillance by the major surveillance powers is not a free-for-all. Different actors in the Five Eyes alliance have been 'tasked' with undertaking surveillance on particular regions of the globe, based on the legacy of certain regions being the dominions of certain colonial powers. The territorial division of surveillance responsibilities will be discussed in more detail in Chapter 4.

Chapter 2

DOING SECURITY DIFFERENTLY?

NATIONAL SECURITY SURVEILLANCE IN SOUTHERN AFRICA

Introduction

In his historic account of intelligence liaison between the major imperial powers, Adam Svendsen argued that after the huge costs of having engaged in two world wars, the UK pursued an 'end of empire' approach towards intelligence, withdrawing from direct control of the activities of former colonies (Svendsen 2012). As part of its exit strategy, the UK assisted its dominions to form sovereign intelligence agencies, preferring liaison as a means of exercising global influence instead of control (O'Brien 2011: 16–72; Svendsen 2012). This account suggests that in the post-colonial[1] period, intelligence agencies in the former colonies were able to develop on their own trajectories without being dominated by the major imperialist powers, and particularly their former colonizers. But to what extent have empires, in fact, ended?

In this chapter, I explore the legacies of classical imperialism and colonialism in relation to national security intelligence and surveillance. I also look at how these legacies make themselves visible today. National security intelligence agencies in southern Africa are susceptible to state capture, often protecting the sitting head of state rather than the citizenry as a whole, and resorting to persecution, harassment and even violence against political critics of the incumbent political party (or faction of the ruling party). Intelligence scholars may understand these weaknesses as institutional weaknesses in the governance and oversight of intelligence; but rarely are they understood in the context of their colonial history. In this chapter, I assess some of the key trends in relation to civilian intelligence in Anglophone Africa, as examples of how colonial legacies still shape intelligence doctrine and practice. It is beyond the scope of this assessment to provide a comprehensive picture; rather what I aim for in this chapter is an indication of some of the major trends. I confine my focus to the intelligence agencies of Zimbabwe, Namibia and Botswana. These countries have different colonial histories, with Zimbabwe having been colonized by the British, and then taken over by an indigenous white minority, Namibia having been colonized by the Germans initially, followed by the South Africans, and Botswana having remained under direct British administration until independence. However, these countries also have a shared history of intelligence having developed out of colonial policing, and they retain highly problematic policing capabilities to this day, targeting domestic dissent. I also look at attempts to reform intelligence agencies in the context of Security Sector Reform (SSR), the successes and failures of these efforts, and whether SSR offered genuine alternatives to state-centric definitions of national security. Lastly, I touch on one attempt to develop a much more bottom-up approach towards security in Zimbabwe, and the results.

The intelligence and surveillance status quo in southern Africa

Southern Africa is inserted into the global economy in ways that are largely unfavourable to the region. Terms of trade are skewed against it, but the biggest problem by far the region faces is peripheralization. In other words, until recently, the most powerful nations have not even considered it important enough to exploit, and, consequently, it has been marginal to, and delinked from, global production. Colonial state structures were geared towards facilitating extraction of agriculture, minerals and other raw materials, which meant that they were highly centralized and bureaucratized. When neoliberalism swept through southern Africa in the 1980s, the ensuing democratization amounted to little more than liberalization. Consequently, any more substantial democratic gains were susceptible to reversal as they failed to bring about a genuine incorporation of the masses into the political system (Saul 2005: 17–31). These problems worsened with the collapse of commodity prices, reducing foreign assistance and strengthening Northern protectionism as the region's economies declined and outbound migration picked up (Saul 2005: 258).

However, the continent's relationship to the global economy is changing, with heightened global interest in the abundant natural resources it has to offer, this time not limited to Europe but including China. That country's practically insatiable appetite for raw materials has been driven by its spectacular growth over the past two decades, necessitating it to become much more externally orientated to maintain the pace of its expansion. As this new scramble for (southern) Africa, like the old one, remains premised on the extraction of natural resources, the economic structures of many African countries have not changed significantly from the classical colonial period. Mozambique's timber, Angola's oil and Zambia's copper have become increasingly important to China, and the Democratic Republic of the Congo (DRC) is a key provider of several minerals crucial to the information economy. China's strengthening ties with Africa notwithstanding, the continent, and particularly South Africa, remains of interest to the EU and the US, with the latter becoming increasingly concerned about China and Russia's expanding influence in Africa, leading to it ramping up its military presence on the continent (Carmody 2016: 1–14).

Unlike the US, China has avoided engaging in flashy displays of hard power on the continent, preferring diplomatic interventions to build economic ties ('resource diplomacy'), while maintaining tight control over its populace at home. As will be touched on elsewhere, China's interventions in southern Africa's intelligence and surveillance activities complicate arguments that it is devoted purely to a 'soft power' approach towards pursuing its interests. Neither does it conform to the model of 'flexigemony' that Padraig Carmody has asserted China uses in Africa, or a differentiated method to build China's influence on the continent under the radar, without incurring the wrath of the world's main military hegemon, the US (Carmody 2016: 72–87).

The region's peripheralization explains why it has faced few conventional national security threats, such as terrorism or armed invasion by other countries: it has been of little geostrategic importance to the global superpowers, which has meant that most countries have managed to stay non-aligned in the war on terror. Countries that produce minerals that are more strategic to the global economy have experienced more strife, though. With the exception of an unfolding problem in Cabo Delgado province the north of Mozambique – where armed Islamist groups have struggled for control of territories rich in natural resources – the region has largely been at peace since the wars of destabilization waged by apartheid South Africa came to an end. Beyond being a conflict driven by the desire to establish an Islamic state in the region, the discovery of natural gas deposits triggered the actions of the Ahlu-Sunnah Wa-Jamo group in Cabo Delgado, prompting them to seek greater armed control of these territories through a series of attacks. The growing presence of Islamist forces in the region, including the Islamic state, represents a backlash against government attempts to control the region's natural resources and their potential for exploitation by foreign investors. The military has responded to the conflict in a heavy-handed manner, leading to civilians being killed and injured and journalists reporting on the insurgency being harassed, threatened and arrested, and fuelling resentment in the local population (Amnesty International 2020; Brincat 2020).

Understanding the roots of the conflict is important, as it points to terrorism having been triggered not by Islamist ideological contagion but by the Mozambiquan government's mishandling of its own natural resources. The Central African Republic and the DRC still remain major flashpoints of conflict, but further south, the region has remained free of major armed conflicts (Stockholm International Peace Research Institute 2019b: 3). Madagascar also experienced a period of destabilization, with a 2009 coup ousting its then president, and Zimbabwe and Lesotho are particularly susceptible to internal political, economic and social crises. Yet, despite there being relatively few conventional threats to national security such as armed conflicts and military invasions, there is little evidence of intelligence agencies in the region rolling back their powers. On the contrary, largely they have embraced even more expansive definitions than the ones discussed in the previous chapter, and grown their capabilities to meet these purported threats.

Colonialism's bitter legacy: Zimbabwe's intelligence architecture

In a preliminary study of intelligence agencies in Africa, Roy Pateman concluded that 'there seems little doubt that, on the whole, intelligence agencies have worked considerably to the disadvantage of Africans' (1992: 585). While acknowledging that intelligence across the globe was facing turbulence, his assessment revealed particularly unhealthy trends in how African agencies conducted themselves, including offering routes to power for aspiring politicians, lacking controls and oversight, and, consequently, suffering scandal after scandal, and being riven with internal conflict (Pateman 1992: 569–85). Nearly three decades after this unflattering assessment of the continent's agencies, to what extent does it still hold relevance? Have the region's agencies transcended politicization and factionalization, and become professional, impartial protectors of national security?

Missing from Pateman's account are the contributions of colonialism to the weakening of intelligence on the continent, as though the original sins of these agencies should be blamed on post-colonial misrule only. In reality, though, the colonial powers deliberately underdeveloped indigenous intelligence capabilities in the colonies, using their own agencies coupled with local sources to monitor anti-colonial movements. Largely, intelligence agencies in Anglophone southern Africa emerged out of the colonial police, and particularly Special Branches, as the police were responsible for maintaining colonial power. In countries where military coups took place, post-colonial intelligence capabilities emerged largely in the military. Where civilian intelligence agencies emerged independently of the police or the military, almost all agencies were centralized in the presidency, operating as tools of the executive arm of government with limited to no independent oversight (Hutton 2009: 1; Thomas 2008: 1–3; Kwadjo and Africa 2009). This means that intelligence agencies suffer from legacy weaknesses from the colonial era as protectors of domestic political power, as well as entanglements with enforcement agencies to different extents, and these weaknesses set the context for how they function in the post-colonial period.

South Africa played a major role in destabilizing the entire region under apartheid. Yet, even while apartheid was at its height, the balance of forces shifted inexorably towards liberation movements. Anti-colonial struggles in the region also led the major colonial powers – namely Belgium, Germany, the UK and Portugal – to rethink their continued occupations. The apartheid regime in South Africa responded to these growing movements by seeking to establish itself as a dominant force in the region, which it hoped would be buoyed by a constellation of regional states that had resigned themselves to the 'reality' of white rule. One of their key strategies to achieve this objective was to sponsor vigilante movements to mount counter-revolutionary guerrilla warfare against liberation movements that had achieved independence, and that provided support to South Africa's anti-apartheid movements. Key to the regime's strategy was to paint resistance to apartheid nationally and regionally as being Marxist-inspired and underwritten by Russia and Cuba (Murray 1987: 35–7). These wars destabilized the entire region and became the major focus of the intelligence agencies in newly liberated countries.

Despite formal apartheid having been dismantled, and the region remaining largely at peace, post-colonial, post-apartheid intelligence agencies remain highly centralized, executive-orientated and predisposed towards abuse, as typically oversight and control measures are lacking. For instance, possibly the most notorious intelligence agency in the region is Zimbabwe's Central Intelligence Organization (CIO). The CIO was a creature of the white minority Rhodesian government, having been established in the early 1960s to collect intelligence for the British-South Africa Police Special Branch, one unit among several that were responsible for the protection of national security in British and Commonwealth police forces. The agency has remained relatively untransformed since then, despite the liberation movement, the Zimbabwe African National Union-Patriotic Front (ZANU-PF), having won the majority of seats in an independence election following a negotiated agreement in1980, and based on, a fairly moderate election platform. The other major liberation movement, the socialist Zimbabwe African Peoples' Union (ZAPU), also contested the elections as the Patriotic Front. According to a researcher on intelligence in Zimbabwe who requested anonymity:

> [The CIO] was founded back in the 1960s. It really functioned to counter the emerging African nationalists. That's the easiest way to know the spirit of what it is, is when it begins. So it actually functioned to protect the colonial order against the anti-colonialists. And I don't think enough was done at the point of the 1980 independence to undo the old legacies. So, now we had a body that functioned to protect the colonial order from the anti-colonial nationalist interests. Now, with the take-over, you're dealing with the opposite. In thinking about it, why it is the way it is, I think one can actually understand it by knowing what it did from the 1960s and 1970s. And in 1980, there is no reform process to say the CIO did all the dirty work to protect the colonial regime. They didn't say, let's undo what they [the Rhodesian government] did. No, they just carried on. In fact, the same people, [the founding head of the CIO] Ken Flower, remained until the late 1980s . . . [It's a relic] of that old colonial Rhodesian order that just wasn't ever reformed because those who took over parliament immediately realized, this is very useful. Yes, we can deal with our own, you know.[2]

The manner of integration meant that former liberation fighters were absorbed into the CIO, with many top positions being retained by white former Rhodesians, some of whom acted as double agents. Had the CIO been closed down and started up again and staffed with former fighters who then absorbed ex-Rhodesians carefully, it is likely that the organization would have made more decisive breaks from its old doctrines and practices. However, ZANU-PF had largely the same needs as the Rhodesian government – namely the maintenance of power and a focus on security rather than an intelligence-driven approach of focusing on the future and how to achieve a transformed Zimbabwe.[3] The post-independence CIO has been put at the full disposal of the sitting president, as national security matters fall under the president's office. This direct political control exists in spite of the fact that rightfully, in terms of the 2013 constitution of Zimbabwe, the CIO should report to a separate minister (Constitution of the Republic of Zimbabwe 2013: 107), which would dilute presidential control somewhat. Also, in terms of the constitution, Zimbabwe's civilian intelligence agency should be established in terms of either a law or a presidential or cabinet directive or order. This constitutional provision is highly problematic, as laws are subjected to parliamentary processes that are usually open to public scrutiny, whereas directives or orders are executive instruments that can be developed in secret. In contrast, the South African constitution states that national legislation must regulate the objects, powers and functions of the intelligence services, which leaves no room for the country's agency to be established in secret (Constitution of the Republic of South Africa 1996: 103). As a result of this unsatisfactory situation in Zimbabwe, very little is known publicly about the structure, powers and functions of the CIO, although in practice it has become clear that the CIO does enjoy the powers of arrest and detention. Ironically, though, when the CIO fell out of favour with the current president Emmerson Mnangagwa – a former Minister of State Security who oversaw the CIO – for supporting former president Robert Mugabe, the government began to consider a CIO Bill to place the entity on a statutory footing.[4] What has been documented about the CIO points to a highly factionalized organization that has become embroiled in internal battles in the ruling ZANU-PF, in spite of a constitutional injunction for it to remain non-partisan. The available evidence also points not to a cooperative intelligence ecology with effective coordination but to a competitive one where intelligence is used to bolster or destroy factions in the ruling party vying for political power (Tendi 2016: 203–24; Anonymous author 2020: 15).

What has helped ZANU-PF – which has ruled Zimbabwe since 1980 – to maintain a highly militarized and securitized state is that it has left national security doctrine, strategy and prescripts unclear. The party has portrayed itself as being anti-imperialist and highly critical of the West and perceived Western attempts to subvert the country's sovereignty. Yet, in reality, it is unclear about what definition of national security the government is operating with. This lack of clarity allows the ruling party to politicize intelligence and contrive threats to manage internal opposition and groups perceived to threaten ruling party interests.[5] According to Jeremy Brickhill – who was a senior intelligence officer in the Zimbabwe People's Revolutionary Army (ZPRA), the military wing of ZAPU, during the country's struggle for national liberation, and later a co-founder of the Zimbabwe Peace and Security Programme (ZPSP) – ZANU-PF was not a principled and consistent anti-imperialist party. Instead, the party has constructed national security threats to align itself to unlikely international allies and target domestic political challengers, while ignoring actually existing threats:

In 1980 to 1983, ZANU-PF and apartheid South Africa, and the Western world shared the perception of the threat, which was that the Soviet Union, ZAPU and the ANC/MK were the threat. As a result of which, ZANU, the apartheid state, and the west and America and the UK went along with the destruction of ZAPU and the Gukurahundi[6] because that was the perception of the threat at that time. So, ZANU at that time was aligned to western interests . . . it was not an anti-imperialist party. And how it framed its populist anti-imperialist rhetoric is therefore got to be seen in the context of the interests this political party has been pursuing. The state perception of our enemies is that it's sanctions and the West, the opposition and civil society, but in whose interest is it? Is that based on the fact that we're pursuing a radical transformation agenda? I don't think so. It's more about protecting an elite, or what was established at the time as a parasitical new black capitalist party that has captured the state . . . I mention it like that, because what we [the ZPSP] were engaged with was trying to move the discussion towards the threats that we saw, [which were] impunity, a breakdown of the rule of law, climate change, small arms crime, corruption, regional water conflict, which by the way, is one of the major threats . . . We were framing this discussion outside of that historic political contestation and the ZANU perception of who its enemy was.[7]

National security spies as police: Botswana's intelligence regime

Even when civilian intelligence agencies have been established after colonialism, they have been permeated by the culture of governments using these agencies as political police to target domestic opponents. Most apparent is the failure to separate civilian intelligence from policing, resulting in legislatures granting these agencies policing powers. A case in point is the Botswana Directorate of Intelligence and Security (DIS), established by an act of parliament in 2008: over four decades after the country achieved independence in 1966 through a general election. Botswana enjoys a reputation as a stable liberal democracy. However, a look under the hood of its intelligence arrangements provides a less flattering picture and points to the dangers of conflating policing with intelligence. The Botswana Democratic Party (BDP) dominates the country's electoral politics. The contradiction of a democracy where one party dominates for decades was a system that was encouraged by the British colonialists, as it provided them with a more stable and predictable post-colonial outcome. Consequently, the BDP has ruled Botswana since independence in what has been widely referred to as an arranged handover of power by the British (Mogalakwe 2013).

The country has suffered a proliferation of intelligence agencies, with limited oversight, coupled with a failure to delineate their powers and functions. In the colonial era, the British administration established intelligence capabilities to track what it considered to be threats to its interests in the colony, and these capabilities were retained in the police after independence through a national security-orientated Special Branch. Intelligence capabilities after that were developed on an ad hoc basis in the police and military (Gwatiwa 2015: 43–4). While efforts were made to distinguish the work of the post-independence Special Branch from the pre-independence one, this entity's continued focus on what it considered to be subversive groups meant that it failed to depart completely from its pre-independence role of monitoring domestic dissent (Tsholofelo 2014).

It was only when Ian Khama became president in 2008 that he established a separate civilian intelligence agency through an act of parliament, as previous presidents did not see the need for one. As a former military man himself, Khama has been accused of having militarized and personalized political power (Good 2010: 315–24). The establishment of the DIS occurred when Khama lost trust in the military, leading to him attempting to establish an alternative to it; this move had the unintended consequence of fuelling inter-agency rivalry for surveillance tools and budgets, and created the temptation for them to spy on one another's activities (Mmeso 2016). The establishment of the DIS was an advance on previous arrangements, though, in that it brought into being a civilian intelligence agency governed by law, and included some judicial and parliamentary oversight, but only after public controversies about executive overreach when the act was still a bill (Maundeni 2008: 135). But the lack of controls over its operations meant that it morphed into a regime security agency, as was feared at the time of its establishment (Mogalakwe 2013).

In establishing the DIS, Botswana adopted a generic and overbroad definition of threats to national security in its founding legislation, the Intelligence and Security Service Act of 2007. This definition includes conventional national security threats (such as terrorism) but also extends to any activity that is detrimental to the national interests of Botswana. Lawful advocacy is excluded, though, unless it relates to the listed national security threats, which nullifies this caveat somewhat. Echoing the trend in other southern African countries, the DIS falls under the president, and intelligence officers in this Directorate have the powers of arrest, including warrantless arrests if they are reasonably believed to be connected to an initial investigation where arrest powers have been authorized. These powers easily lend themselves to the DIS engaging in covert action, and not just intelligence collection and analysis, but action that could easily mutate into secret political policing (Maundeni 2008: 143). The president can also determine the duties and functions of the DIS that s/he considers to be in the national interest, which is a practically unfettered power (Balule and Otlhogile 2016). Oversight structures do exist in terms of the act, including a Tribunal headed by a serving or former judge or legal practitioner, to consider complaints about the activities of the DIS. However, the scope of the Tribunal is reduced significantly by the fact that it can exclude complaints that it deems to be detrimental to national security, which given the overbroad definition of threats to national security could include a great deal indeed. As things stand, Botswana's intelligence oversight structures have not been particularly robust, and the cloud over the DIS's establishment has meant that it lacks public confidence (Tsholofelo 2014: 4).

The president has absolute discretion to decide what constitutes a threat to national security. According to law professor Tachilisa Balule, these unfettered powers could turn the very institution that is meant to protect national security into a national security threat itself. He referred to a Forensics for Justice investigation (Forensics for Justice 2019: 10) containing information from whistle-blowers that the DIS was implicated in the 2019 national election results, and observed:

> There's always been a distrust amongst the general public of the DIS. And mainly because people feel that, instead of serving the public interest, in reality, it has been manipulated by the executive to serve the interests of the executive,

particularly the interests of the ruling party . . . [Now in my view] the president is given very wide, absolute powers to decide what would constitute the national interest, and there's a danger in that because when you give the president such very wide powers, the state can easily be confused with the interests of the individual or the ruling party . . . [That] becomes a worry because now you have an institution that is supposed to safeguard national security, but now if it's actually implicated in events that destabilize democracy, then it becomes a threat to national security.[8]

Khama's mistrust of the military, and the need to create an alternative entity, was not the only reason for the DIS's establishment. The demands of global intelligence liaison were also placing pressure on Botswana to establish a civilian intelligence agency, as agencies elsewhere did not feel comfortable with liaising with the police. They feared that their sources might be compromised if their intelligence led to prosecutions (Tsholofelo 2014: 5). Ironically, though, by granting DIS officers the powers of arrest, Parliament exposed the identity of its agents as, at times, arrests took place in the open. The DIS also did not have holding facilities, leading to people just disappearing for the duration of their arrest as they could not be traced to a particular police station. These features of the DIS's operations scared and alienated the populace.

Namibia, colour revolution and regime change protests

Even the country that has been most widely celebrated as a success story of the United Nations (UN) system, Namibia, has a civilian intelligence agency, the Namibia Central Intelligence Service (NCIS), that includes in its remit monitoring of domestic dissent, especially if they suspect that the dissent is influenced by foreign entities that may be hostile to Namibia. This is in spite of the fact that the NCIS does not have enforcement powers in terms of its founding statute. The NCIS replaced the National Intelligence Service (NIS), established by Namibia's then colonizers, the South African apartheid government. Namibia gained independence from South Africa in 1990, in a transition that was largely peaceful. However, over thirty years later, the wealth gap continues to plague the country, which remains one of the most unequal in the world (National Planning Commission of Namibia 2014: 4). Consequently, youth disaffection and protests have been increasingly widespread (Mare 2019: 22–4). Namibia does not face any significant conventional threats to national security; however, the NCIS remains concerned about the possibility of youth radicalization, particularly in view of the insurgency in the north of Mozambique. Concerns about youth radicalization may also be linked to fear on the part of the ruling South West African Peoples' Organization (SWAPO) – which has been in power since the country gained independence from South Africa – that their power base may be eroded as young people become more disaffected with its rule.[9]

Namibia operates with a very similar broad and unspecific statutory definition of national security to that of Botswana, suggesting that Botswana drew inspiration from Namibia for their definition. In this regard, the terms 'regime change' and 'colour revolution' have also made an appearance in official speeches, as a descriptor of growing protest movements in the country.[10] These terms refer to a diverse series of pro-democracy protests that swept the Eurasian region after the collapse of the Berlin Wall. The protests adopted particular colours or flowers to represent their struggles, such as the Orange revolution in Ukraine, the Rose revolution in Georgia and the Tulip revolution in Kyrgyzstan. Largely, these protest movements used non-violent strategies, focusing on peaceful regime change through democratic elections, rather than insurrection through forceful direct action. Some were true mass protests, while others were middle class-led, with significant involvement of students and NGOs. The initial wave of protests was largely successful in removing authoritarian regimes. Later protests were less successful, though, mainly because governments had learnt from one another about how to contain them. By the time the Arab Spring swept across the Middle East and North Africa, governments had fine-tuned a range of democracy-prevention strategies (Finkel and Brudny 2012: 1–14; Duncan 2017). The colour revolution evolved into a full-blown intelligence doctrine, or a statement of principles developed by Eastern European governments, and especially Russia, that guided intelligence actions. This doctrine adopted a nominally anti-imperialist stance, although in reality it was anything but emancipatory, and served to consolidate Russian sub-imperialism in Eurasia and beyond. The colour revolution doctrine maintained that the protests took place not because they were spontaneous responses to authoritarian rule, but because imperialist powers had supported them, aiming to bring regime change to countries benefitting the major imperialist powers to the affected countries. For these governments, colour revolutions amounted to subversion. Foreign-funded NGOs, especially those funded by the Eastern European investor and philanthropist George Soros, were the targets of particular suspicion as they were considered to be the sponsors of several protest movements.

The colour revolution doctrine proved useful as it allowed intelligence agencies in Eurasia, the Middle East and southern Africa to target lawful, non-violent protest movements on the basis that they were bent on regime change, even if the movements were not revolutionary in the true sense. While some protest movements received US funding, it could not be said that these protests as a whole were engineered by imperialism (Korosteleva 2012). Given the potentially high political costs of outright repression, governments preferred to engage in what Vitali Silitski (2010) has referred to as pre-emptive authoritarianism, where they adopted measures to counter protest movements before they occurred, and thus preventing the need for violent state repression. Intelligence agencies became central to these strategies, as they could operate in secret, using highly targeted counter-intelligence strategies to neutralize and impede protest movements, and particularly their leaders and financial backers. Thus they developed counter-strategies to the protests, focusing particularly on pre-empting them before they took place. These strategies included governments insulating themselves from the movements, marginalizing them, supporting rival movements or persuading them against continuing with their protests. If these prevention strategies failed, then they resorted to repression as a last resort, given the danger that repression could escalate rather than discourage protests (Finkel and Brudny 2012: 1–14).

The Arab Spring came as a huge shock to southern African governments, as the protest movements brought the power of protest home to their own region. They engaged in a process of authoritarian learning from Eurasian and North African governments, absorbing the lessons learnt from their prevention strategies. In typical sub-imperialist fashion, South Africa played a key role in popularizing the doctrine of the colour revolution on the continent, providing other southern African governments with the pretext to investigate NGOs, clamp down on protest movements and prevent fundamental challenges to entrenched interests, and possibly even capitalism itself if the protests escalated. Former state security minister David Mahlobo, who trained in Russia among other countries,[11] argued at a meeting of security officials of the BRICS countries that African countries were threatened by colour revolutions. Mahlobo explained:

> In Africa we have, as intelligence and security services, observed the importance of NGOs in Africa's development and poverty alleviation programmes. We however remain concerned that the nefarious activities of rogue NGOs contribute to Africa's persistent insecurity. We note that rogue NGOs are not only a threat to the national security of our respective states but they also threaten our collective security as a continent and have the potential to derail the African Union vision of a conflict-free Africa.

> It is for this reason that South Africa, as a member of both BRICS and Africa's multilaterals, stand firm against external interference or imposing one's will on others, oppose external forces in seeking regime change or colour revolution. We are, therefore, supportive of BRICS's initiatives geared towards opposing and countering external interference, even if it is indirectly carried out through rogue NGOs. In this regard, we concur with the need to strengthen cooperation on NGO management, including improving laws and regulations, upgrading the management level and improving the oversight mechanisms. (Mahlobo 2017: 2–3)

Mahlobo's statements were not mere words: they led to the SSA infiltrating the media and South African NGOs who were fighting against a deal with Russia to build nuclear power plants (the deal was subsequently declared unlawful), and NGOs that led a campaign to unseat former president Jacob Zuma (Mufamadi et al. 2018: 64–6). While it was shocking but not surprising that the SSA used the doctrine to protect Russian interests in South Africa, activities to frustrate a purported colour revolution were not confined to South Africa, though. In making these statements, Mahlobo was using BRICS as a conveyer belt to disseminate colour revolution doctrine beyond Eurasia, so it was hardly surprising that other southern African countries picked up on it when they were faced with youth protests.

The former liberation movements were also used as conveyer belts to popularize colour revolution rhetoric, through a grouping consisting of the ANC, ZANU-PF,

Frente de Libertação de Moçambique (FRELIMO), the Popular Movement for the Liberation of Angola (MPLA), SWAPO and the Chama Cha Mapinduzi (CCM) of Tanzania. The year before Mahlobo's statements, the secretaries general of these movements had concluded that the single biggest threat they faced in government was regime change as characterized by Russia and China. This form of change involved the 'increasingly widespread Western practice of overthrowing legitimate political authorities by provoking internal instability and conflicts against governments that are considered inconvenient or insubordinate to their interests, replacing them with pliant puppet regimes that then pander to their interests' (Secretaries General of Governing Former Liberation Movements of Southern Africa 2016: 3–4). In order to achieve regime change, Western governments supported local NGOs and opposition movements to mount colour revolutions against these liberation movements in government and commandeer the natural wealth of these countries. Their interests placed them on a collision course with parties such as ZANU-PF and other governments that are 'socialist-inclined, anti-imperialist and inconvenient' (Secretaries General of Governing Former Liberation Movements of Southern Africa 2016: 6), and which practised resource nationalism. Ignoring any legal injunctions in their own countries confining intelligence collection to designated state agencies, the secretaries general argued that the former liberation movements should set up mechanisms for the sharing of intelligence, and early warning centres to warn one another of regime change strategies (Fabricius 2017). Wrapped in this undeniably self-serving rhetoric is a kernel of truth, which is that the major imperialist powers do want pliant southern African states that do not threaten, and preferably facilitate, their strategic interests in the region. Funding agencies such as the United States Agency for International Development are well recognized for being foreign policy tools of the US government and vehicles for pursuing imperialism by other means. However, in practice, the former liberation movements took colour revolution rhetoric onto another level entirely, using it to paint opposition movements and journalists they feel threatened by as regime change agents, simply for being critical.

Namibia was one country that picked up on regime change and colour revolution doctrine, which began to make more appearances in official statements. By invoking the terms, the Namibian government implied that the youth protests were being stoked by a foreign-funded invisible hand (possibly a Western government), bent on interfering in Namibia's sovereignty. According to Frederico Links, Namibian journalist and governance researcher affiliated to the Institute for Public Policy Research:

> We have hints of [growing NCIS concern] over the last four years or so, where youth radicalization has been linked to social media use . . . [So there is a low level] attempt to create a national security threat through these ongoing messages or narrative that is being spread in the more rural parts [that] if SWAPO loses power, the country will degenerate into war, chaos and bloodshed. So, in order for peace and stability to prevail, SWAPO has to remain in power. There is this orchestrated ruling party-created narrative of there being a national security

threat if SWAPO loses power. [The whole situation] in northern Mozambique, the Islamic insurgency, is also being used increasingly, not just in Namibia, but across southern Africa, to create this regional, national security threat, and this has come up in speeches of ministers and so on. Talking about this sort of insurgency, and once again linking it to youth radicalization . . . [has become] a common narrative in speeches here . . . the implication being that growing opposition to the ruling party is being orchestrated beyond the borders of the country by forces who want to discredit liberation movements, southern African liberation movements, including SWAPO, and then orchestrate regime change, in order to take over the country. We've even [had it] in civil society. My networks have been accused of being part of the forces . . . trying to orchestrate regime change.[12]

The Namibian government almost certainly overplayed the possible spillover of the conflict in the northern Cabo Delgado province of Mozambique. Not only does Namibia not share a border with Mozambique, it is more than likely that the conflict will remain one that is specific to Mozambique. Given the localized nature of the conflict in Cabo Delgado, and its trigger point being natural gas in the area, the potential spillover of the insurgency into Namibia is not a strong possibility. If youths are recruited from Namibia and return to the country, though, then there could be a spillover from Mozambique.[13] According to a researcher on intelligence matters in Zimbabwe – a country that shares a border with Mozambique:

Northern Mozambique has always had particular dynamics. I think, historically the inability of the Mozambican state, if you will, particularly from the centre of power in Maputo, to project what Max Weber called the monopoly on the means of violence, explains that problem. They've had that problem for a long time historically with RENAMO [Resistencia Nacional Moçambicana, a political movement formed by the then-Rhodesian CIO to counter the state socialism of the ruling FRELIMO party]. So I think the difficulties in northern Mozambique are particular to that context. I don't see them escalating beyond the terrain of Mozambique itself. RENAMO certainly never did.[14]

In Namibia, the structural arrangements for ensuring accountability of intelligence gathering and analysis – including through interceptions – are inadequate. The NCIS is located in the office of the president, which puts the service directly under the control of the president (Lindeke et al. 2007: 136). While the NCIS's founding act does not offer a definition of national security per se, it does in relation to threats to national security, which is very much a cookie-cutter definition that could be found elsewhere and which does not relate to any specific threats that Namibia faces. In addition to the standard list of terrorism, espionage and sabotage, it also includes subversion: a very vague term indeed that could easily be abused to persecute political opponents. These dangers are mitigated somewhat by the fact that the definition does not extend to any lawful advocacy not performed in conjunction with any such activity. This formulation is curious, because it implies that if lawful advocacy was performed in conjunction with any such activity, such as subversion, even if it was lawful, then it could still fall within the definition of a national security threat.[15] Consequently, the NCIS operates with a very broad definition of threats to national security.

Namibia has a Parliamentary Committee on Foreign Affairs, Defence, and Security, but its effectiveness as an oversight body is unknown and there is no inspector general for intelligence providing administrative oversight to assist the committee. The committee lacks powers, in that the director general can decide not to hand over particularly sensitive information for a period of six months, and with the authorization of the president, which effectively makes the committee beholden to the executive in the performance of its oversight duties.[16] These lax controls predispose the NCIS towards becoming an instrument at the service of the ruling party, in spite of a provision in the NCIS Act committing the service to political neutrality and non-partisanship.

However, Namibia continues to reproduce relatively unaccountable surveillance not only because of post-independence dynamics but because of a legacy of apartheid repression that perversely it has failed to free itself from. A case in point is the governance arrangements around the NCIS's secret services account, carried over from the apartheid-era National Intelligence Act. The account was modelled on the South African secret services account, established by the apartheid regime to fund the activities of the notorious Bureau for State Security and other state crimes against the liberation movements. In line with the 1978 South African act that governed this account, the Namibian NCIS merely needs to show that the funded activities are in the national interest. No definition is provided of national interest, which gives the NCIS the latitude to stretch the term to include whatever they see fit to protect the country against what it perceives to be national security threats. It also allows the NCIS to carry over any surpluses from the previous financial year into the new financial year.[17] South Africa, too, retained these provisions in the post-apartheid period, and they were instrumental in allowing the SSA to starve other sections of the Agency to create surpluses for the next financial year. Spies in the SSA used these provisions to fund special operations against perceived opponents of then-President Zuma, who were accused of plotting a colour revolution as justification (Mufamadi et al. 2018). As these lax controls have turned covert operations into a lucrative business model, it would be surprising if the Namibian government or individuals in the intelligence establishment have not abused these provisions in similar ways. After all, the apartheid government designed these arrangements to facilitate abuse. It is therefore telling that the post-colonial Namibian government has retained them, and it problematizes the 'post' in post-colonial.

Programme for change? The politics of security sector reform

Southern Africa does not have a particularly strong record of accomplishment of effective intelligence and security reform. However, during moments in the post-colonial period, political spaces have opened up for changes that are more progressive, if not radical, to intelligence. Possibly the most significant blueprint for the transformation of security institutions in southern Africa is Security Sector Reform (SSR). Claire Short, secretary of International Development for the UK government, popularized the term from 1999 onwards. At the time, she argued that security sector failures were a result of state weakness and the failure of critical institutions; consequently, she believed, state building in the areas of intelligence and security needed to become central to addressing these weaknesses. Multilateral institutions such as the United Nations Development Programme (UNDP), the Organization for Economic Cooperation and Development (OECD), the World Bank and the EU then took up SSR. While the origin of human security is often traced back to the UNDP Human Development report of 1994, which Short subsequently seized on, it actually had much deeper roots back into the 1970s. However, once it was taken up by the UN system, it rapidly gained popularity.

SSR is a programme of reforms that purports to offer human security as an alternative doctrine to state security and focuses on reforms targeting civilian intelligence agencies, the police and the military. The human security doctrine contends that security is central to development, in that vulnerable social groups are likely to be worst affected if conditions of insecurity, such as war, prevail. Insecurity, crime and underdevelopment tend to be mutually reinforcing: yet, rarely are security issues considered to be part of national development strategies. SSR establishes a link between the security sector and good governance, in that if they were well managed, democratically controlled, and transparent, and if they incorporated public participation, then the state's monopoly on the use of violence could be put to socially beneficial uses (Mustafa 2015: 212–30). SSR's doctrine of human security, as opposed to regime security, advances a liberal world order, where the human, rather than the state, is the main referent of security. In other words, state security focuses on protecting the state from threats, whereas human security focuses on a wide range of threats facing individuals, and addresses the underlying drivers of these insecurities. Old forms of security that had the state as the referent were outdated once the Cold War ended, as the world faced new non-traditional security threats from poverty, disease and environmental degradation. The UN General Assembly captured human security as being about enjoying life characterized by 'freedom from fear and freedom from want' (United Nations General Assembly 2012).

The liberal, political humanitarianism underpinning human security emphasized individual development, whereby a security apparatus serviced rather than hindered people (Mustafa 2015: 212–30). More controversially, normative assumptions that liberal-democratic governance and free market capitalism could be used to raise standards of living, and, ultimately, realize human potential, also underpinned SSR (Christie 2010: 173). The programme's proponents also advanced human security as a soft-power alternative to the hard-power security agenda of the US, which has proved itself ready to resort to military interventions to achieve its foreign policy objectives. SSR proponents argued that programmes designed to address human security should be people-centred, multi-sectoral, comprehensive, context-specific and prevention-orientated. They should start with mapping and analysing human insecurities and their root cause, and develop action plans to tackle them. Insecurities may be economic, food-related, environment- or health-related, or related to personal, community or political insecurity (Office for the Coordination of Humanitarian Affairs 2009).

Since the early days of human security programmes, global thinking about how to operationalize the doctrine has evolved and become much more nuanced and detailed. The OECD guidelines on SSR for the intelligence services are a case in point. These guidelines stressed the need for a national policy framework on intelligence. Such a framework should set out the range of acceptable activities, and the kinds of resources needed, and provide a basis for the fair and uniform application of rules. It required that the powers and functions of an intelligence agency should be set out in a law that regulates intrusive powers such as surveillance. The guidelines argue that the oversight mechanisms should include parliamentary oversight, complemented by judges who approve intrusive powers, and supported by an ombudsman to handle complaints from the public. A minister should conduct executive oversight, overseen by a national security council of senior officials. The finance ministry should conduct financial oversight, with parliament having final approval powers. Government should not exploit secrecy to conceal abuse or corruption. While intelligence agencies need to accept political direction from decision-makers, they should offer politically impartial intelligence and be open to sources of analysis and policy inputs outside the intelligence community to prevent themselves from being caught in echo chambers of their own views (Organization for Economic Cooperation and Development 2007: 140–50).

Multilateral institutions working on both security and development set about changing the perceived gap between security and development through funded interventions in some of the more insecure and underdeveloped parts of the world, especially in Africa. While much of the SSR donor support flowed to the major conflict zones on the continent, few southern African countries experimented with elements of SSR. These programmes invariably incorporated the four basic objectives of SSR. These were the establishment of effective governance, oversight and accountability in the security system and the promotion of the rule of law; the improved delivery of security and justice services; the development of local leadership and ownership of the reform process and sustainability of justice and security service delivery (Organization for Economic Cooperation and Development 2007: 20–2).

SSR has attempted to respond to criticisms that it offered a blueprint approach towards security change, where donors pursued generalized reforms at the expense of bottom-up, democratically developed ideas based on local needs. What also damaged the credibility of some SSR efforts, especially in Africa, was the use of donor interventions to pursue bilateral security interests, thereby undermining community ownership (Detzner 2017: 116–42). Consequently, next-generation SSR programmes sought to ensure more local buy-in. By that stage, though, SSR and its underlying human security doctrine had become security orthodoxy, and the inherent disparities between donors and recipients limited the potential for genuine local control. Consequently, SSR still remained state-centric in nature, focused overwhelmingly on state building, and tied to the Weberian notion of the state having the legitimate monopoly on the use of violence. At times, governments and their donors reduced reform efforts to box-ticking exercises of changes to state institutions (Ansorg 2017: 129–44).

SSR has been criticized for becoming a mechanism of imperialist biopolitics to deepen neoliberal globalization (Camps-Febrer and Farres-Fernandez 2019: 3–10). Examining the application of SSR to the occupied Palestinian territories, Tahini Mustafa argued that SSR is not a benign model, but a highly intrusive means of population control of non-Western societies by Western societies, and one that strengthens rather than weakens authoritarian rule. This was because, in the Palestinian situation, SSR underwritten by EU support handed security responsibilities over to the Palestinian authority (PA). However, to all intents and purposes, the PA operated as proxy police for the Israeli state and its security concerns, including against resistance to the Israeli occupation. In other words, the Israeli state did not need to police the occupation as much, as the Palestinian authority did that on its behalf, using SSR as a justification to do so. While SSR did transform the police into a professional service, it failed to reform the political authority for policing (Mustafa 2015: 212–30).

These failures were hardly surprising, as the human security doctrine underpinning SSR was flawed conceptually, and ultimately become a conservative security agenda that assisted rather than challenged global inequalities. This it did by pathologizing weak states, based mainly in the South, in the process legitimizing interventions by Northern countries and multilateral institutions. Human security puts a large portion of the blame for insecurities in these countries on factors internal to those countries, and particularly weak state institutions, while making invisible the impact of global inequalities. In other words, SSR misdiagnosed the causes of poverty, inequality and instability, and remained blind to a particularly pernicious form of violence in global South countries, namely, structural violence (McCormack 2010; Turner et al. 2010). The management of global security has shifted from an East–West axis under the Cold War to a North–South axis, with the North trying to manage the perceived disorder and instability of the South to prevent a spillover to Northern countries, through migration, for instance. Yet at the same time, Northern security interventions have become less constrained by SSR 'best practice', evidenced by growing mass surveillance and the expanding military exports to authoritarian countries. In other words, the rules that are meant to apply to Southern countries do not necessarily apply to Northern countries.

Operationalizing and contesting SSR in southern Africa: The case of Zimbabwe

Apart from apartheid South Africa – which destabilized the entire region in its quest to maintain its existence – if there was any country in the region that needed an overhaul of its security services, it was Zimbabwe. Post-colonial Zimbabwe was a creature of a deeply problematic constitution cobbled together by the country's then colonizers and the main liberation movements in 1980, as it was hobbled by compromises with the UK government and the indigenous white minority. Fearing popular power, the representatives of colonial and white minority power favoured a political system that placed considerable authority in the presidency and the executive arm of government more generally: an enduring legacy in post-independence politics. This concentration of executive power acted as an anti-democratic brake both on the legislature and on the judiciary: a problem that was amplified by subsequent constitutional amendments (Dzinesa 2012: 2). While the Lancaster House constitution contained basic democratic rights and freedoms such as privacy and freedom of expression, these rights were circumscribed by caveats that the law should make reasonable provision in the interests of defence, public safety, public order, public morality, public health, to protect reputations and the like (Lancaster House Agreement 1979: 20–2). The constitution made provision for a police force and defence force falling under the control of the president, with no requirement for parliamentary oversight.

The rise of the opposition Movement for Democratic Change (MDC) in the 2000s provided the ruling ZANU-PF with a challenge to power unprecedented in the post-independence period. This moment of political ferment did not come out of the blue, though, as it was preceded by popular momentum to rewrite the 1980 constitution. By that stage, a mass movement had developed around the need to establish a Constituent Assembly to rewrite the undemocratically negotiated constitution. Popular demands for a Constitutional Assembly risk diverting popular movements into a legalistic mechanism where the grassroots are marginalized and experts dominate the struggle, depoliticizing demands in the process (Woods 2002). However, in Zimbabwe at the time, the demand to establish a Constitutional Assembly was necessary, given that there were few actually existing democratic institutions, and the conditions for the development of popular power did not really exist.

These mobilizations culminated in the establishment of the 1997 National Constitutional Assembly (NCA), a coalition of individuals, religious groups, trade unions, women's organizations, youth and human rights organizations, media institutions, political parties and members of parliament, that had elements of a genuine mass movement. The NCA drafted a constitution that it put forward as a genuine alternative to the 1980 constitution and its many subsequent amendments by the ZANU-PF government. This constitution proposed a less executive-driven government, with political power dispersed across a variety of institutions. Consequently, it proposed the establishment of a Security Services Commission consisting of the Chief Justice and ten other members appointed by the president on recommendation of the National Assembly after a public process. The Commission would oversee the Defence Force, the police, the prison service and the intelligence service, and ensure that they were impartial and operate lawfully, without prejudicing any political party (National Constitutional Assembly 2001: 69–70). While failing to provide guidance on the mandates of the security services, and while offering a rather technocratic and legalistic solution to the problem of outright executive (and more specifically ZANU-PF) control of these services, at least it provided a more democratic alternative to what existed at the time.

However, the MDC used the demands for a new Constitution to strengthen its negotiating arm, rather than them encouraging a genuine mass movement to realize a Constituent Assembly. When ZANU-PF and the MDC – which by that stage had split into two factions – entered into negotiations to conclude a global political agreement in 2008, the parties made a real effort to shift the country's national security policy towards one that was more democratically inclined. This reform process incorporated aspects of SSR and human security, although the process was not a mainstream SSR programme.[18] In fact, civil society active in this area made conscious efforts to distance the process from SSR, as ZANU-PF suspected that SSR was a Western agenda to interfere in the security sector, and consequently represented a reversion back to colonialism (Hove 2017: 425–45).

According to Jeremy Brickhill, who co-founded the ZPSP as a civil society initiative, activists engaged in these issues even avoided using the term SSR because it smacked of a donor-imposed agenda. Instead, they preferred to refer to security sector transformation. They also made an effort to turn this transformation into a locally-owned and locally-driven grassroots movement, rather than adopting an elitist approach of negotiations with ZANU-PF that cut out the grassroots. The fact that the ZPSP was established as a civil society initiative to provide technical assistance to those engaged in the transformation of the security sector, and the fact that its founders had liberation movement backgrounds and understood the security sector as former military and intelligence officers in the liberation struggle, assisted the organization's founders to establish its bona fides. They brought legitimacy and authenticity to the work in a sector that was highly sensitive to perceived outside interference.[19] At the same time, some elements within the bureaucratic layer of security services recognized the value of security sector transformation as they, too, hankered after a professionalized environment insulated from the political layer.[20] Brickhill explained their methodology:

> There was no external role in policy and no external funding was allowed to influence the policy and the programme instrumentation. We established on that basis, a steering committee that was modelled on the new Government of National Unity (GNU) structures to ensure consensus, and what that meant was our steering committee had the government and the ruling party and the opposition party all represented. That created the basis for the buy in, because if you sat on our steering committee, you could veto an activity. That's how ZANU-PF came into the programme, so that we wouldn't do anything they didn't want . . . Everything we did was transparent, above board and known by the intelligence service in advance. In particular, the fact that we had no foreign representation on the steering committee [was important]. So, we were saying, this is an entirely national dialogue that's taking place in a protected zone, so we can discuss these issues here . . . And on that basis, we created a mechanism to engage the state. Now, this was not without problems. We had very hostile reactions, including threats from certain circles. But we also had allies in the

system, and basically we set out to build allies and knowledge inside to create an entirely legitimate engagement process.[21]

Human security doctrine became a glue binding the competing actors to sit around the same table and agree to common principles during the establishment of the GNU and the constitutional reform process (Mendes 2015). Perhaps sensing that if it played the long game of political negotiations, it could placate its adversaries by offering them constitutional reforms that would never materialize in reality, ZANU-PF conceded some significant reforms. The Constitutional Assembly movement, combined with the slow, painful technical work on security sector transformation, led to positive changes in the 2013 constitution, including the establishment of a multiparty National Security Council responsible for the development of national security policies and strategies on a multiparty basis. Security sector transformation was actually written into the Zimbabwean constitution, making it a legally required priority (Nyakudya 2010). The constitution adopted a human security definition of national security and a rights-based approach to security. The security services were required to submit themselves to a civilian authority, in the form of parliamentary oversight, and to reflect the diversity of Zimbabwe in their composition. The constitution forbade the services from acting in a partisan manner and from violating rights. Perversely, ZANU-PF recognized some value in embracing human security, as it allowed the party to divert attention from hard security issues to issues relating to poverty and unemployment, claiming that those needed to be addressed first as they were more fundamental to insecurity in the country. According to political scientist Munyaradzi Nyakudya:

> Human security became the easy way out for the state. The concept speaks of security from a whole range of broad perspectives, hence deflecting attention from the contentious issue of state security. It was politically expedient for the ZANU-PF government to push for it [human security]. Many players, civic organizations and academics all eagerly embraced it. It is easy to see why. Socio-political and economic conditions in the country were characterized by struggling service delivery across many sectors. It became imperative also to address those issues. Of course, many realized that addressing human security while ignoring state security is like putting the cart before the horse . . . difficult choices.[22]

More troubling, though, was the provision in the 2013 constitution requiring intelligence services to be established in terms of a law, or a presidential or cabinet directive or order, which left the door ajar for the president to establish the CIO, not through a parliamentary process, but through a secretive founding document drafted by the presidency. Consequently, there is no public understanding of what the powers and functions of the CIO are. The constitution also required the government to set up a body to receive complaints about the intelligence services (Constitution of the Republic of Zimbabwe 2013: 100–9). This requirement is likely to result in a body with a much narrower remit than one that is actually required to perform administrative oversight. This is because such a body should have the ability to self-task and initiate its own investigations, and monitor compliance with legislative prescripts, in addition to receiving complaints from members of the public.

Despite these gains, the MDC was disadvantaged in the constitution-making process, as it lacked the hands-on expertise of security matters that ZANU-PF members had. An additional aggravating factor was the MDC split, further weakening its ability to participate fully. Full-scale repression against the MDC also weakened the links between the political leaders and the grassroots, making it difficult to mobilize around the constitution-making process. The MDC's links with civil society also declined, and as it lost contact with mass movements, it drifted more towards reformist politics. According to an interviewee:

> The MDC traditionally came out of . . . [churches], unions, the students' movement. There was this big thing called the National Constitutional Assembly, and it was a kind of a political party that came out of civil society groups, and for a long time it had links, strong, durable links with civil society. But, by at the time of the General Political Agreement negotiations, those links have somewhat broken down and there are a range of reasons for that. . . . There's a lot of capacity in civil society. So for instance, you have, you know, groups that work on peace, peace and security, so experts on that. Various experts on policing. Experts on a range of issues. [The MDC] . . . couldn't tap into those networks that have expertise in civil society because they had grown quite apart from civil society at that point.[23]

Consequently, the reforms that were realized in the constitution did not really take root in the state or broader society. The National Security Council became defunct after the Government of National Unity and the global political agreement that underpinned it collapsed in 2013 (Geneva Centre for Security Sector Governance 2019). In any event, legislators included a sunset clause in the founding act, ensuring that it would lapse after the global political agreement, which showed that ZANU-PF envisaged it as a temporary affair (President of the Republic of Zimbabwe 2009). During the short period of its existence, very few matters of substance went to the Council, resulting in what one interviewee called a 'fuzzy National Security Council that didn't really have any power'.[24] Consequently, in reality, security powers reverted to the president: a process that was completed once Mnangagwa deposed Mugabe in a military coup.

Nevertheless, the framework set in place by the 2013 constitution remains in place, which Zimbabweans could use as a shield against security sector abuses in future. Zimbabwe's constitutional movement, however imperfect, did make real and lasting changes. The National Security Council remains in some form, with a committee of the Council still functioning. There is also the possibility of a legislative mandate being developed for the CIO, ironically because it fell afoul of the Mnangagwa government, which has created political space for a long-standing problem to be addressed, namely, the fact that CIO is not established in terms of any law.[25] However, in the Mnangagwa era, Zimbabwe is beset by another problem, namely, that the military has become ascendant, eclipsing the CIO as the dominant surveillance institution, and leading to a creeping militarization of Zimbabwean society. Very little SSR has been focused on the interrelatedness of security services, as reform efforts have tended to focus on services in silos, and particularly the police and defence forces (Hutton 2009: 2). Consequently, when one security institution becomes too unreliable, then it is entirely possible for the president to shift power and resources to another institution: perhaps a lesson that Mnangagwa learnt from Khama.

Civilian intelligence agencies in southern Africa: Issues and alternatives

Some issues become apparent from this overview of intelligence agencies in Zimbabwe, Botswana and Namibia. These include the following:

- *The legacies of colonialism* – Agencies in the region emerged largely from the colonial police, but in practice, there are unsettling similarities between contemporary intelligence agencies and the policing Special Branches of old. Colonial policies and practices have not been eradicated completely. In fact, agencies continue practices of their colonial predecessors, especially domestic political policing to keep dissent in check, which is a characteristic of decaying or authoritarian societies (Maundeni 2008: 137). Anti-colonial rhetoric is used to demonize opposition groups as being puppets of the West, and the 'colour revolution' doctrine has proved useful in that regard. Imperialism has been used as a bogey to justify surveillance of NGOs and protest movements, with little evidence of a genuine commitment to anti-imperialism on the part of intelligence agencies, evident from their lack of transformation from the colonial period.
- *Enforcement powers, including policing powers* – Related to the above point, there is little evidence of clear separations between intelligence collection, analysis and enforcement. Powers that existed under colonialism, such as the powers of arrest being given to intelligence officers, persist to this day, which blurs the distinction between intelligence and policing. At their most extreme, intelligence agencies become the praetorian guard of the president, assisting sitting presidents to remain in power.
- *Presidential control* – Centralization under the presidency is a major feature of intelligence agencies in the region, including the three under discussion. The director general is generally appointed by the president and serves at the pleasure of the president. Consequently, there is little incentive to act at a relative distance from the government or the ruling party of the day. The absence of a separate minister for intelligence means that control of intelligence capabilities is not dispersed across government. Presidents in the

region have been known to stay in office for exceedingly long periods. The political parties they come from are typically the parties that took power at the time of independence, and they use the fact that they achieved liberation to stay in power. The region's peoples have a not unrealistic expectation of their leaders aspiring to remain in office until they die. Consequently, there is a growing disconnect between an increasing geriatric political leaderships and their younger populations. It is also not unusual for presidents to have an intelligence or military background (or both), as intelligence and security agencies present opportunities for social mobility, which also undermines attempts to professionalize these agencies (Paterman 1992: 571).

- *Factionalization* – When one intelligence or security agency falls out of favour with the sitting president or the ruling party, then power and resources may shift to another one. This leads to instability in these agencies, followed by patronage politics as the agencies fear marginalization if they fail to remain on the right side of power. There is also evidence of poor coordination and few attempts to structure and even require coordination. Overlapping mandates, powers and functions lead to a lack of cooperation and even conflict between these agencies.

- *Vague legislation with broad definitions* – Definitions of national security are vague definitions that are not tailored to the specifics of different countries. This lack of specificity allows the agencies to claim broad powers to protect national security without having to justify their existence, as clear threats are not identified and consequently they cannot be challenged as being overstated or even non-existent. These definitions typically include both threats and interests, and cover economic and political intelligence: definitions that offer few constraints on what or who can be targeted, including perceived domestic opponents. There is also a tendency to leave the mandates, strategies and operating principles of intelligence agencies as vague as possible. Laws are scanty and hardly ever reviewed, with too much detail relegated to often secret regulations or policies. There is very little in terms of written doctrine or strategy, leaving the public in the dark about what these capabilities are actually being used for.

- *Absence of democratization* – The democratization of the 1980s did not extend to intelligence agencies, and even passed these agencies by. To that extent, democratization has largely been a failed experiment. Where changes did occur, they did not necessarily lead to changes in intelligence architecture that became rooted in broader society, leading to stasis in the field. One-party democracies – to the extent that they can even be called democracies – have become the rule rather than the exception. The parties the colonialists favoured as their successors are the parties that continue to dominate the political landscape, and there is very little evidence of genuine political contests.

- *Construction of national security threats* – Apartheid was the last major threat the region faced and agencies of the frontline states were important to countering the regime's destabilization of the region. Yet, the current capabilities appear to be far in excess of what are needed to maintain regional stability. The relative absence of national security threats has led the region's agencies to construct threats to justify their existence. Where real threats do exist, such as the insurgency in the Cabo Delgado province of Mozambique, they are seized on to justify measures that bear little resemblance to the imminence of the threat. Few external threats has led to a greater focus on domestic stability, driven by the fear of Arab Spring-type uprisings and the potential for youth uprisings. Increasingly younger societies coupled with rising youth unemployment have placed youth in the crosshairs of these agencies. Social media and its potential for radicalization have become a focus area.

- *Accountability and oversight* – Agencies tend to be accountable to the executive and more specifically the president. Where oversight bodies have been established, they tend to be weak and ineffectual, and in some cases exist in name only. Excessive secrecy has also exacerbated these problems as there have been few attempts to bring transparency to the activities of these agencies. Some are more responsive than others to public disapproval and pressure, though. Nevertheless, serious questions exist about what the value-add of these agencies is for the public. Do they actually contribute to making societies safer and more secure? Little publicly available evidence is on display, leading to deep public mistrust of the agencies and what they're actually about.

These broad trends suggest that Pateman's assessment of intelligence agencies in Africa was not without merit. Furthermore, Svendsen's assertion that the UK preferred to encourage intelligence agencies in the former colonies to develop on their own trajectories without being dominated by their former colonizers is complicated by the fact that the colonialists established a path dependency for intelligence that post-colonial agencies have not departed from to this day. To that extent, the legacy of colonialism remains imprinted firmly on how these agencies operate. Path dependency occurred because the political elites that befitted the most from decolonization and the dismantling of apartheid, developed a vested interest in limiting these agencies to the functions they had developed during those periods, particularly domestic political policing or the policing of domestic dissent. As a result, post-colonial agencies have not transformed as much as expected.

In order to chart a way forward for intelligence agencies in southern Africa from an anti-capitalist perspective, it is necessary to ask: Would a post-capitalist, socialist society[26] need intelligence powers at all, and if so, what powers would these be and what would the future organs of state power look like? What would a genuinely anti-imperialist programme to get to this point look like? What could future organs of state power look like?

Southern Africa has a rich history to draw from of alternative, self-organized intelligence functions, formed during struggles against colonialism and apartheid. The major liberation movements established intelligence capabilities, which usually started out as defensive capabilities designed to protect the movements from threats. The better developed and formalized had several basic functions, such as counter-intelligence, covert action, analysis and strategic intelligence. Defensive counter-intelligence capabilities existed to protect the movements from infiltration and repression, while offensive counter-intelligence capabilities allowed the movements to infiltrate the structures of the oppressor and mount attacks on them. Strategic intelligence emerged once movements were able to rise above the day-to-day demands of the struggle and focus on longer-term goals. These capabilities allowed the movements that developed them to answer broader questions about the future and what it should look like, using intelligence that forewarned them about future threats and opportunities.

For instance, the ANC's intelligence structures in exile separated themselves out from the military wing, Umkhonto we Sizwe, or MK, and evolved to include strategic intelligence and counter-intelligence functions, a central evaluation unit and protection of important persons, or VIPs (Ellis 2012: 155–7). These capabilities were important to the movement's ability to chart a way forward over the long term, and determine strategic tasks and policy. Russia, Cuba and East Germany assisted with the development of these capabilities in the region's liberation movements, as these countries had a stake in seeing the collapse of colonial domination and apartheid around the world, given their stated commitment to proletarian internationalism. However, because of the legacies of these countries in supporting liberation movements, including through training, intelligence structures in the major movements tended to be uncritical of the Soviet system and its contradictions (Kasrils 1993: 84–91). Consequently, these structures imbibed a Soviet legacy of Stalinism, acting not only against external threats, but to maintain ideological purity. Some policed dissent within movements, leading to massive human rights abuses against suspected spies and even dissidents who had no connection whatsoever to oppressor governments. These structures manifested the classic tensions of movement-based security institutions, namely, the need for secrecy and power, which at times undermined democracy, accountability and political controls.

Nevertheless, even if the Eastern bloc countries could be disputed as examples of actually existing socialism at the time, the solidarity shown by these countries to liberation movements, and their exposure to societies that were organized very differently to Western capitalism, left a lasting legacy in these movements. Intelligence officers of ZAPU's armed wing, who were trained in the Soviet Union, were moved by the country's commitment to egalitarianism, anti-racism and anti-colonialism, and appreciative of the internationalism underpinning their hospitality. However, they were also quite clear about their own priorities as a liberation movement, maintained their focus on those through a continual process of negotiations with their hosts and shaped the content and uses of their training. Their own intelligence wing, the NSO, focused on state building in a future society while providing intelligence for covert operations and military strikes (Alexander and McGregor 2017: 49–66). Many of their operatives were trained by the Stasi, who inculcated in them the need to build relations with local communities in the course of struggle, and not alienate them with violent and abusive conduct. The NSO had five directorates falling under political control, and they developed capabilities in research and analysis for strategic intelligence purposes, counter-intelligence capabilities to detect threats to security of the movement and a security directorate to respond to physical threats. They also established an informal police service and trained local youth militias to boost this service. These structures prefigured what ZAPU envisaged future intelligence capabilities would look like in a liberated Zimbabwe. It was deeply embedded in democratizing security and intelligence functions. According to Jeremy Brickhill:

> So all of this was a process which today you'd call it SSR of ZAPU. And we had this experience of it with our own certain features, and the most notable one was this focus on citizen security governance by political authority, and citizen protection, what people might call human security, right? So this was deeply embedded in the thinking, the governance issue, establishing clear political control, but also there's the whole thing about the codes of conduct and humane treatment of prisoners and so on. Again, something the MK struggled with, you know? They continued torturing people right to the end.[27]

These intelligence capabilities that developed in struggle do point to the fact that they are needed as basic societal functions, protecting and advancing struggles against oppression and exploitation, including anti-capitalist struggles. In fact, an anti-capitalist perspective should fight against the tendency discussed in the previous chapter of governments claiming that the organs of state under their direction are the only legitimate sites of intelligence. Social movements can and do have need for these capabilities for tactical and strategic decision-making, and can and do practice intelligence. In fact, it would be impossible to realize political alternatives to capitalism without them. Furthermore, as the ZPSP experience has shown, it is entirely possible to prefigure future intelligence organs by developing a bottom-up security policy and strategy, encouraging people to engage in open conversations and debates about the threats that actually exist and what strategies are needed to counter these threats, and demystifying intelligence in the process.

However, there is the reality that governments are likely to repress movements with highly organized intelligence functions, on the basis that they and they alone own the monopoly on violence, and that extends to intelligence capabilities that allow them to maintain that monopoly. In fact, state intelligence agencies are likely to see attempts to develop these capabilities informally as a gift, as it shifts the struggle onto a security terrain where it most likely has the upper hand. These movements may actually attract state surveillance and even infiltration on the basis that they are conducting illegal spying activities and establishing a parallel state. These dilemmas are likely to be particularly acute for movements organizing in situations that fall short of outright repression, where the nominal trappings of democracy exist, such as multiparty elections. Largely, southern Africa is in this political conjuncture, having transitioned out of direct colonization and formal apartheid. In these situations, movements could focus on developing those functions in very careful ways: in the current conjuncture, movements really do need some defensive counter-intelligence capabilities and strategic intelligence capabilities. Beyond that, the focus may need to shift to changing, shrinking and defunding state intelligence, while keeping in mind the fact that governments will not relinquish these powers under capitalism. This is particularly so in southern African countries, which largely cannot afford to offer meaningful social programmes, so repression and surveillance are the only answers to keep domestic populations in check.

Movements could argue and struggle for reforms that are achievable (such as limiting executive powers), escalating the struggle into reforms they know are unlikely to be conceded by the current system but that may precipitate a political crisis. These could include calls to shut down intelligence agencies when abuses spark public outrage, which could evolve into organized campaigns. Within capitalism, movements will need to consider what kinds of intelligence capabilities they intend to struggle for as a stepping stone to a more complete transformation, if capitalism remains dominant in the foreseeable future. Therefore, movements would need a transitional programme of sorts to guide their actions, while keeping the bigger and longer-term objectives in mind. Struggles to shrink and defund intelligence agencies would need to focus on doctrinal issues, mandates, powers and functions and effectiveness. For instance, movements could demand that national security be defined, if it is not defined. Doing so would force governments to articulate a definition that can be debated and challenged, rather than allowing them to leave it vague deliberately so that they can frame all kinds of actions as national security threats. Challenges should be aimed at narrowing down the definition, rather than broadening it. Forcing governments to define national security will require them to demonstrate that the threats are to the citizenry as a whole rather than individuals, as the latter could be dealt with by agencies that don't have national security mandates. They would need to prove that the harms they are concerned with are material and clearly demonstrable and that they are so egregious and of national importance that they require intelligence intervention. The acts that would qualify as national security threats would need to be spelt out, and they would need to show that violent attacks on critical infrastructure are imminent. Such acts may include hostile acts by foreign actors designed to undermine a peoples' sovereignty such as sabotage and serious violence aimed at overthrowing a democratic dispensation, including terrorism.

While there is no universally accepted definition of terrorism, the most common elements of the definition include the use of violence or the threat of violence by non-state actors for ideological purposes, to compel other influential actors to follow a course of action or prevent them from continuing with a course of action. 'Terrorism' is a deeply contested, ideologically loaded term, having been used by political elites the world over to entrench their power by using extraordinary emergency measures and greater secrecy. Terrorism is also heavily laden with racist and classist assumptions, targeting Black people and working-class movements disproportionately, while terrorism perpetrated by white people may barely feature on spy agency radars. White right-wing extremism has been a growing problem globally, yet it cannot be said that it has received the same level of attention as terrorism conducted by Black and Muslim people. States who commit acts of terror are all too often not considered terrorist. In certain contexts, violence through armed struggle is the only ethical response to a particular social order: but violence of a terrorist nature cannot be condoned on this basis. To this extent, activists should have little difficulty in calling these acts by their name – in spite of how terrorism is manipulated politically – in order to distinguish them from more politically significant and ethically grounded forms of organization and action. Terrorism is a politically weak response to state violence, as it emphasizes spectacle at the expense of mass politics, which encourages apathy. In assuming that existing social change can be brought about through individual acts of violence, terrorism fails to identify the social force that is most likely to bring about meaningful change. It is with these views in mind that I use this term throughout the book.

Any definition of national security would need to be qualified with a caveat that excludes acts of dissent or protest, as well as genuine struggles for self-determination or national liberation, including those that use force: a caveat that governments will have extreme difficulty in agreeing to, as they will insist on maintaining a monopoly on the use of force. When national security is defined, movements could argue for it to be narrowed to strip out domestic political intelligence and intelligence that focuses on national interests rather than national threats. Economic intelligence needs to be limited to the most destabilizing economic threats, and state actions committed in the name of economic intelligence, such as espionage. Of course, movements are likely to face the argument that limiting economic intelligence in this way leaves a country vulnerable to foreign espionage when it cannot return the 'favour', which is why it is important to internationalize the demand to strip economic intelligence largely out of agencies' mandates.

On an institutional level, and most relevant to southern African countries, policing should not be conflated with national security intelligence. No intelligence agency should have enforcement powers, and offensive counter-intelligence functions should be located either in the police or in the military, to prevent agencies from suffering the conflicts of interest inherent in them acting on their own intelligence. Movements could argue for enforcement to be stripped out of the powers and functions of civilian intelligence agencies, especially the powers of arrest. Intelligence agencies should not be centralized as that increases the potential for abuse: foreign and domestic branches should operate separately, as should analysis and counter-intelligence. Neither should a civilian intelligence agency fall under the presidency: it concentrates too much power in the president. Even having a separate minister for intelligence would be preferable, as the minister is meant to perform executive oversight without becoming involved in operational matters.

In terms of parliamentary oversight, a dedicated multiparty parliamentary committee is needed, with the powers to enquire into operational matters. Such committees may not have these powers, which reduces their effectiveness as they are unable to probe into the actual workings of spy agencies. Parliamentary oversight is also important because it is more likely to be performed on a multiparty basis than executive oversight, which increases the potential for more debate about intelligence, especially if a left-wing party with a more critical stance towards security powers is represented. An independent inspector general for intelligence, which is functionally and structurally independent from the agencies they are overseeing, should support the work of the committee. However, this inspectorate would need genuine independence, which means that it would need to receive its budget directly from parliament, rather than operating as a spending centre of the very agency it is meant to oversee (as is the case in South Africa). The inspector general should also have full and direct access to all intelligence agency files: having this power makes it more difficult to hide information that may point to abuses. An inspector general should also have the ability to self-task; in other words, to determine what to investigate and on what basis.

Secrecy could be restricted only to those operational matters that need secrecy as a matter of absolute necessity, such as concealing the names of operatives and sources on legitimate operations. The left should have no difficulty in naming and shaming those operatives engaged in illegitimate operations, including against their movements. And as what an agency considers to be legitimate may not be the same as what left movements would consider legitimate, what qualifies as a legitimate operation? Answering this question is contingent on a range of factors, and would need to be answered in class terms. What operations would strengthen the working class, and what operations would weaken the class? Operations that target organized white-collar criminal networks that extract corrupt rents from the state, for instance, could be an example of the former: yet, these may very well be the kinds of national security threats that intelligence agencies may not act against. Infiltrations of trade unions to weaken their organizing capabilities could be an example of the latter. The agency and its inspector general should publicly release available reports annually on their activities, and the national intelligence estimates that they base strategic intelligence priorities on should be declassified on a regular basis, to allow public scrutiny of the quality of the intelligence. Intelligence agencies should be forced to justify their existence by demonstrating their success; this is particularly important in a regional context where traditional threats are limited, creating the temptation for agencies to manufacture threats under the guise of secrecy to justify their existence.

These agencies may argue that the public has no idea of the attacks that they have stopped or the threats that they have disrupted. After all, they are unable to boast about their effectiveness as secrecy prevents them from doing so. In terms of this view, dismissing these agencies as being all about abuse, and not being capable of serving the public good, is inappropriate. To the extent that this is the case, and to the extent where these agencies have served important public purposes, then they only have themselves to blame if their victories aren't recognized. For them, secrecy is a double-edged sword. It is difficult to see the purpose of secrecy when operations reach non-sensitive stages. In fact, they have more to gain from boasting about their achievements transparently than they have to lose, in that they build public confidence and trust in them, rather than instilling fear and suspicion. Typically, intelligence agencies are far too secretive for their own good, and far from enhancing their effectiveness and protecting legitimate operations, excessive secrecy may actually impede them. The 'trust us' argument that these agencies often resort to simply isn't good enough. Rather, the onus for justifying their existence and their budgets should rest firmly with the agencies, and not with sceptical publics who may question their existence.

This point also requires us to engage on the tricky question of intelligence professionalization. As uncomfortable as it may be for anti-capitalists, the professionalization of intelligence may also be important to support for tactical reasons, and not for any innate belief in its value. Professionalization is a product of modern societies, where in order to secure the consent of the governed, the nation-state had to establish professional, impersonal security institutions that claimed to act in the general interest, while, in reality, acting in specific class interests (D'Souza 2018: 29–30). In other words, claims of professionalization are what allow modern intelligence agencies to maintain legitimacy, despite continuing to act illegitimately. However, while being aware historically of the origins of intelligence professionalization and its political objectives, it is also possible and in some cases necessary to appeal to professionalism to drive a wedge between intelligence officers and the political class that control them. Undoubtedly, there are those who are in intelligence work for the right reasons, and it is important to recognize their existence and their efforts as they can act as internal bulwarks against abuse. This is especially so in southern African intelligence agencies informed by histories of anti-colonial and anti-apartheid struggles. These agencies are likely to include intelligence officers who come from struggle, who haven't been co-opted into the ruling political classes by their former colonizers and who are still informed by revolutionary values. The more that intelligence officers develop a professional identity as impartial protectors of the public interest, the more they are likely to oppose abuse and manipulation of the agencies from within. Given the culture of secrecy that usually cloaks these agencies, encouraging officers of principle to act as whistle-blowers is of the upmost importance, as so much of the recent revelations about intelligence abuses have been as a result of whistle-blower leaks. Related to this point is the need to champion trade union rights in intelligence agencies. These rights are often opposed on the basis that they may divide loyalties between the union and the agency; at the same time, alternative labour relations frameworks set in place in these agencies are unlikely to create an environment that is conducive to internal dissent. All these institutional reforms, and more, are likely to decentralize and shrink these agencies and reduce executive control over them.

The doctrinal issues are the most difficult, though, because they involve having to take a position on national security: whether to expand, reduce, legitimize or dispense with the term entirely. As discussed, in southern African countries that have undergone some security sector transformation, human security has become the go-to alternative concept for those seeking to move away from doctrines that are about harnessing the state for narrow national interests, such as governments, ruling parties or factions within ruling parties. In diverting the focus of security from regime security to citizen security, and the problems that undermine it, the doctrine has been important as a mobilizing concept for those seeking alternatives to regime security. In the case of Zimbabwe, human security led to lasting and meaningful reforms, at least on a structural level, if not on the level of actual state security practice. In fact, the agencies treated human security as an add-on to traditional security concerns, without actually changing their security practices.

However, as well meaning as it is, the human security doctrine is misguided and even dangerous as it expands rather than shrinks national security mandates. It has placed much-needed emphasis on the real conditions that make people unsafe and insecure; but at the same time, it has also created the conceptual framework for these issues to become taken up by the state as security concerns. In recognizing security as a right that is inherent to individuals, rather than the state, people find themselves looping back into the very state machinery that is responsible for citizen insecurity; this is because they still need to look to the state to provide them with security (Goldstein 2009). In the case of southern Africa, where intelligence agencies lack even basic democratic controls, this is a very bad idea indeed. Implicit in the human security doctrine is the assumption that national security is state-centric and human security people-centric, but given the Weberian underpinning of security powers, when it comes to real-world operationalization of the concept, it is impossible to move away from looking to the state to exercise security powers, with all its attendant problems. Inevitably, the state, and more specifically state security services, including intelligence agencies, will be invited into more areas of life to use special emergency powers to address these security threats, traditional or non-traditional. Problems that could have been dealt with using non-security measures, through politics, negotiation or diplomacy, for instance, could land up being dealt with through policing, intelligence or military interventions. These problems have been framed as security issues that are outside the realm of normal politics. In circumstances where the security organs of state are being invited into more and more social issues – from food to environmental and water security – security departments can expand their reach across the state, becoming uber-departments and, ultimately, state watchdogs of society. The danger is particularly apparent in how human security has been used to expand the remit of bulk SIGINT surveillance (to be discussed in more detail in Chapter 4).

Anti-capitalists should be arguing for the reduction of the footprints of these agencies, not their expansion. In other words, the answer is not to broaden security and to make it more progressive but to narrow it. It has even been argued that security should not be a key concept for emancipation at all; instead, it should be abandoned rather than seeking to humanize it, which requires a paradigm shift where the human in human security is de-securitized (Turner et al. 2010; Wæver 1995). This point could be (and has been) taken even further, where the very concept of security is rejected as being inherently authoritarian, reactionary and incompatible with any radical remaking of society. This is because it is impossible to rescue security from its long association with the state and its contemporary mode of governing that relies on violence to survive. Instead, the language of security should be left behind in favour of an alternative political language designed to achieve the material foundations of emancipation, and banish exploitation and alienation from society altogether (Neocleous and Rigakos 2011: 15–21; Goldstein 2009). However, scholars who have made these arguments have offered no real guidance as to what that alternative language could look like, which makes practical applications of these arguments difficult. As compelling as they are, these anti-security arguments also do not seem to recognize the existence or even the possibility of anti-systemic security practices, and ones that operate within discourses of liberation.

It would seem that the more problematic concept, though, and one that really needs to be broken free from, is national security, as it is too bound up with the protection of nation-states in narrow and insular ways. National security does not offer a sound basis to conceptualize the collective security that society so desperately wants and needs. However, conceptualizing an alternative that captures wider security concerns, but without lapsing into state-centric or nation-centric ideas, would need to engage with the complex question of what an ideal society or alternative social order should look like (Kirsch 2016: 5–7). I will return to this question in the conclusion to this book.

Chapter 3

LAWFUL INTERCEPTION AS IMPERIALISM

Introduction

In this chapter, I examine the spread of targeted communication surveillance throughout southern Africa, focusing particularly on those used for national security purposes (known as 'lawful interception'). Originating from the US Communications Assistance for Law Enforcement Act (CALEA) (1994), lawful interception, or the act of undertaking targeted surveillance, has become globalized as a worldwide standard for law enforcement and national security investigations. It involves governments enlisting the assistance of communication service providers in intercepting communication content and communication-related information, usually pursuant to a judge's warrant granting the relevant state agencies permission to do so. Governments call lawful interception as such, not because all of it is lawful, but because the law compels communication service providers to assist governments to intercept communications. Lawful interception has also been an important means of pursuing US imperialism in southern African countries. I will discuss how in more detail in this chapter.

Pro-privacy and human rights advocates have argued that targeted surveillance, including through lawful interception, is an antidote to mass surveillance, apparently because the former requires intelligence and law enforcement agencies to demonstrate a reasonable suspicion of wrongdoing in order to access communications data and content, while the latter does not (Privacy International 2016b; Cannataci 2017; Emmerson 2014). In other words, pro-privacy advocacy has often framed targeted surveillance as 'good surveillance' and mass surveillance as 'bad surveillance': a binary that has become almost normative in anti-surveillance work. However, with the exception of some work that has been undertaken on deep packet inspection and other surveillance tools that are inserted into communication networks (Fuchs 2013; van der Velden 2015), these scholars have had little to say about targeted surveillance and how it contributes to the reproduction of inequalities and the maintenance of unsustainable futures. If targeted surveillance is part of the problem too, then scholars really do need to unsettle these assumptions, as activists that are seeking to bring state surveillance under democratic control should not be replacing one set of social control mechanisms with another.

How exactly does the social justice content of state-targeted surveillance in southern Africa measure up? To what extent are governments using lawful interception for emancipatory or repressive ends? I will explore these questions in this chapter. I conclude by discussing whether anti-capitalists should concede any role for targeted interception, and, if so, under what conditions.

Origins and worldwide spread of lawful interception

Some southern African countries have implemented lawful interception systems along the lines of the US CALEA. In terms of CALEA, communication service providers are required to assist these agencies to undertake interceptions, by making sure that their networks are interceptible. This they must do by ensuring that they meet the interception capability requirements in their country's law. One of these requirements is that they must install digital switches (known as handover interfaces) meeting prescribed standards into their networks to hand intercepted data over to government interception centres, and ultimately to law enforcement and intelligence agencies (Landau 2010). In the wake of the September 11 attacks on the US, CALEA and the European Telecommunication Standards Institute (ETSI) standards became internationalized as the standards to use for ensuring interceptibility. The US domestic intelligence and security service, the FBI, played a key role in briefing police agencies around the world about the necessity of requiring tappability and adopting the industry standards.[1] The US government extended CALEA to cover Internet Service Providers and Voice over the Internet Protocol services like Skype. However, their attempts to extend the law to all online communication services have not gained sufficient traction for it to succeed, as industry bodies and civil society have resisted the mandatory building of backdoors into these services. Importantly, CALEA requires communication service providers to isolate communications only after intelligence agencies have presented them with a court order or other lawful authorization, which entrenched the already-existing principle of judicial authorization for intercepts in the US.

CALEA supplemented existing interception provisions in US law, which required that the person who has been the subject of the interception should be informed of the interception. Intelligence agencies were required to do so within a reasonable time, but not later than ninety days after the warrant had lapsed, or in the case of an unsuccessful application within ninety days after the application for a warrant was lodged. Warrants would be granted only if law enforcement showed that there was probable cause to believe that someone is committing, has committed or is about to commit a serious crime listed in the enabling act, and normal investigative methods had failed to, or were unlikely to, succeed in providing the necessary evidence (US Code 18 1948). Annual statistics are also published about the number of arrests and convictions resulting from intercepts, the length and number of intercepts, including renewals, the number of intercepts that could not be concluded successfully owing to encryption, the average costs for intercepts and the methods of surveillance (United States Courts 2018).

Conveniently, these laws have pushed much of the cost of rolling out interceptible equipment onto communication service providers; not only has this turned these companies into extensions of law enforcement, but they in turn transfer the costs to their customers. In other words, governments are claiming the right to spy on all communication users, and then making the users bear the financial burden of doing so, so it is small wonder that lawful interception has been so popular with governments around the world. Some countries, though, did not adopt the CALEA interception measures without controversy. In the US, Australia and Hong Kong, security experts pushed back against governments imposing a unilateral requirement on service providers to introduce interception capabilities. This was because these requirements created new vulnerabilities in networks that could be exploited not only by law enforcement agencies but by hackers too. In effect, they turned digital switches that were interceptible into single points of failure for digital security.[2] In any event, interceptibility becomes less important as encryption becomes more widespread, as even if the state intercepted communications, they are useless if they cannot be decrypted (Law Reform Commission of Hong Kong 1996: 127).

A case in point of how lawful interception could be abused happened in Greece from 2004, when the phones of the mayor of Athens and at least 100 other prominent individuals were hacked in the run-up to the city's hosting of the Olympic Games. The hacking continued into 2005. The hackers used the built-in wiretapping features of the digital switches to access their communications. They did so by exploiting the fact that interception management system software that enabled warrants to be logged was not operational, allowing them to install their own software to access a remote-controlled equipment sub-system, and, ultimately, the digital switches the sub-system controlled (Prevelakis and Spinellis 2007). Interviews conducted by *The Intercept* investigative journalism site pointed to the leaks being an NSA operation to spy on Olympic preparations, but that continued beyond the operations to help them spy on left-wing politicians (Bamford 2015). Susan Landau has shown how, in the same year, the NSA conducted tests on CALEA-compliant switches and found that all of the ones they tested had security flaws in them.[3] According to documents leaked by Snowden, by 2012, the NSA had devised various access methods to penetrate lawful interception systems in countries they deemed to be of interest, including Russia, Egypt and Mexico (National Security Agency 2012).

The diffusion of lawful interception in southern Africa: The context

Globally, the pressure for intelligence reform has gathered speed since the Snowden leaks. New standards for safeguards include the 'Necessary and Proportionate' Principles (2019), findings of the European Court of Human Rights, policy directives by the United States Presidency under the Obama administration (The White House 2014) and pronouncements of the United Nation Human Rights Council (European Union Agency for Fundamental Rights

2015: 93). Yet in many countries, technological capabilities are running far ahead of the law and policy, with the danger that governments will use these capabilities for anti-democratic purposes. With the possible exception of South Africa, there has been little evidence of any major commitment to surveillance reform, much less intelligence reform. While some government-initiated surveillance activities have been terrorism-related, domestic factors have driven much of it, and government efforts to establish surveillance architecture have become particularly pronounced during election periods or in response to mass protests. Like many other regions of the world, southern Africa experienced an upswing in protests after the 2008 global recession, although protests have been a feature of the regional landscape for longer than that. The most pronounced protests erupted in Eswatini, Mozambique, Zimbabwe and Malawi, and they brought new political actors onto the streets, resulting in new forms of organization. Many of these countries have underdeveloped working and middle classes, which is a problem as these classes are key to holding governments to account: the working class owing to their ability to use collective power to bring industries to a halt, and the middle class through their tax contributions to the fiscus, access to the media and ability to litigate. This attenuated class structure led to what Padraig Carmody has described as a 'class gulf between the politically connected elites and the impoverished masses' (Carmody 2016: 220), making exploitation that much easier, but also making these political systems vulnerable to social instability.

Rather than relying on overt forms of state violence only, many governments responded by increasing their surveillance capacities, targeting protest leaders and journalists and engaging in internet shutdowns to strangle the communication capacities of protest movements. The nature of the capabilities they acquired will be discussed in subsequent chapters. Communication service providers have also been complicit in internet shutdowns; there was scant evidence of these companies pushing back in defence of their users' rights, as was the case in the US in the wake of the Snowden revelations. At least thirty-eight African countries have mandatory Subscriber Identification Module (SIM) card registration, where governments require mobile phone users to provide proof of identity to enable them to remain connected to the network, and eleven of these experienced full or partial shutdowns in 2016. SIM card registration has been controversial globally for making it impossible for mobile communications users to communicate anonymously, and for not really achieving its stated purpose of reducing crime levels; some countries have even abandoned registration efforts because of its unclear outcomes (GSM Association 2016).

While governments' efforts to control social media are well documented – with dozens of internet shutdowns across the region during times of protest and political upheaval – their use of surveillance and intrusion software has received less attention. Yet, an investigation by the *Wall Street Journal* showed that by 2015, at least four African countries had developed cyber-offensive weapons or cyber-military units for computer espionage or attacks: South Africa, Ethiopia, Nigeria and Sudan. While South Africa has the capacity to manufacture its own cyber-warfare tools, the other countries relied on purchasing off-the-shelf tools from private firms, usually in the global North. They used their cyber-tools to gather information, including on domestic targets in the case of Nigeria and Ethiopia, with Ethiopia using them on foreign targets as well (Valentino-DeVries and Yadron 2015). Even where terrorism has been a problem, governments have skillfully seized on these problems to expand their surveillance capacities, stretching the definition of what constitutes a national security threat to include a range of other perceived threats, such as opposition politicians, activists and journalists.

In spite of the fact that governments could have chosen different and more sensible surveillance paths, lawful interception laws and practices have diffused throughout southern Africa. Some countries, such as Zambia and Namibia, incorporated lawful interception into general omnibus communication laws dealing with everything from interconnection to e-commerce. Botswana incorporated lawful interception into an intelligence law. Zimbabwe and South Africa, however, adopted stand-alone lawful interception laws. Governments developed these laws in country contexts where intelligence agencies were typically lacking in independent oversight structures. The fact that these capabilities were used by agencies that generally fall under the direct control of presidents reinforced a post-colonial tendency for surveillance to be used to protect the head of state.

Intelligence oversight practices across the region are uneven: Botswana, South Africa and Lesotho require judicial authorization for interception of communications, Zimbabwe has a system of executive authorization, while the DRC and Namibia pursue a dual approach of executive and judicial authorization (Hunter and Mare 2020). The general trend, though, is for the judiciary to defer to the executive on national security matters, which is not healthy as it reduces oversight in this important area of state power. The regulatory environment is even worse in a country like Namibia, where surveillance takes place without any clear legal basis: a problem that led the UN Human Rights Committee to call for reforms to their surveillance regimes to bring them into line with international human rights standards.

A more detailed discussion of how lawful interception became integrated into the laws of South Africa, Zimbabwe, Botswana, Zambia, Namibia, Angola and Mozambique follows. However, this diffusion was uneven and, at times, highly contested. These countries have been chosen because they took different paths to integrating CALEA standards: some simply mimicked the standards, some adopted the standards while avoiding the introduction of a stand-alone act, others bolted these standards onto existing national security measures and at least one country was stopped in its tracks by public opposition.

Lawful interception mimicry: South Africa and Zimbabwe

South Africa and Zimbabwe are examples of two countries that have come very close to mimicking the most problematic aspects of CALEA without incorporating some of the strengths of the US lawful interception system. Of the two, South Africa's adoption of lawful interception measures was the most closely aligned to the war on terror. Zimbabwe's, on the other hand, was driven more clearly by domestic factors, although it, too, was promulgated after the 2001 attacks.

South Africa domesticated the CALEA/ETSI standards in 2002 through the Regulation of Interception of Communications and Provision of Communication-Related Information Act (RICA), which was one of a basket of anti-terror laws passed at the time (Landau 2010; Duncan 2015). RICA required the network operators to make their networks interceptible, although legislators failed to adopt positive features of the US system (such as user notification and more transparent reporting). User notification recently became a major point of contention during a Constitutional Court challenge to RICA brought by the investigative journalism organization amaBhungane, eventually leading to the Court declaring RICA unconstitutional on five grounds, including the fact that it failed to provide for user notification (Constitutional Court of South Africa 2021).

During a consultation on RICA when it was still in draft form, network operators opposed the requirement for their networks to be made interceptible, arguing that it was an unreasonable demand on them as the Bill suggested that they develop capabilities to decrypt encrypted communications. They voiced concern that the backdoors the providers needed to install to make their networks interceptible could be exploited by private hostile actors for espionage purposes, and one operator (Telkom) argued that this requirement should only obtain to the extent that it was technically and economically feasible. They also expressed concerns about the quality of the equipment the government planned to deploy in interceptible networks, which may hamper technological developments. In fact, the network operators could be faced with an absurd situation where the latest technologies could not be introduced until they were interceptible. After considering these submissions, the Commission recommended that the draft law retain a requirement prohibiting the provision of communication networks that were not capable of being monitored, with the caveat that service providers were not under any obligation to decrypt encrypted communications (South African Law Commission 1999: 223–35). The government proceeded to draft a Bill on that basis, which was processed by Parliament during 2001, around the time of the terrorist attacks on the US. While the development of the Bill preceded these attacks, they added to the urgency of getting the Bill onto the statute books and into operation.

The RICA process falls under the political authority of the Department of Justice and Constitutional Development, which ensures the provision of justice services to South Africa. RICA requires the minister to appoint a retired judge to issue interception directions (or warrants) to state agencies once they have requested intercepts. As is appropriate for such an intrusive power, not all state agencies can use it, as there is a closed list of agencies allowed to apply for interception directions. The RICA judge's work is overseen by an investigatory and complaints receiving body, the Inspector General of Intelligence, which is nominally independent from the intelligence agencies, and the Parliamentary Joint

Standing Committee on Intelligence (JSCI). The Office for Interception Centres (OIC) undertakes the RICA intercepts, which for operational purposes falls under the department tasked with national security matters, the SSA. The OIC receives the intercepted information from communication service providers, pursuant to the RICA judge's direction.

The RICA process has been hugely controversial, to the point where in 2021, as mentioned, the amaBhungane Centre for Investigative Journalism successfully challenged the constitutionality of the law on five grounds. Among these were the fact that surveillance subjects are never notified that they have been under surveillance, the RICA judge lacks independence and there are no procedural safeguards for the management of data that is collected through RICA intercepts (Constitutional Court of South Africa 2021). However, the judgement failed to touch on the issue of the interceptibility of communication networks. This judgement demonstrated clearly that despite an extensive law review and public consultation, the legislature still came up with a law that mimicked the worst aspects of the US system of lawful interception while ignoring its best aspects.

Zimbabwe's Interception of Communications Act legislated a relatively standard lawful interception regime into being in 2007, to be used by state security and law enforcement agencies to protect the national security of the country. It was promulgated when the ZANU-PF government faced an unprecedented challenge to its grip on power by the MDC, and undoubtedly this challenge to its authority was top of mind when developing the Bill. However, the fact that it predated the 2013 constitution meant that some of its more progressive protections could not be incorporated into the act. Neither has it been amended to bring it in line with the constitution. The act appeared to follow a blueprint approach, where it borrowed liberally from acts elsewhere, including South Africa. However, the lawmakers borrowed selectively, emulating weaknesses while ignoring strengths of other acts. According to Misa Zimbabwe's Nompilo Simanje:

> In our interaction with the act, we have noticed that it does have a resemblance to the Tanzanian one. It has resemblance also even to the Malawian one, but there are also some, some differences that you will note in the legislation. But really, if you look at other countries within the region, your Tanzania, your Malawi, there was, there were so many provisions that really seems to have been, word for word resembling each other.[4]

In line with South Africa, the Zimbabwean law required all telecommunication networks to be capable of interception. Yet it left out the requirement for judicial authorization of interception directions, or warrants, which are issued not by a judge, but by the Minister of Transport and Communications or any other minister assigned directly by the president. Bizarrely, the minister may also issue directives to service providers that do not involve any interception and monitoring of communications, but there is no indication of what these directives are limited to, leaving this power open-ended. However, on the upside, the minister can only issue warrants in relation to serious crimes and a basket of crimes listed in the Criminal Procedure and Evidence Act, or the vaguely defined national security threats, or vaguer still, compelling national economic interests (President of the Republic of Zimbabwe 2007). Only senior officials of the country's security services and its revenue service may apply for warrants, and, like South Africa's law, this too is a closed basket of entities. These provisions provide important safeguards against overuse of lawful intercepts. In their applications, applicants are meant to provide information on whether other investigative measures have been exhausted, except in relation to serious crimes where this requirement does not apply. This provision is problematic because they are not required to show that they have, in fact, exhausted less intrusive investigative measures, nor to provide any information at all about other measures they have used to investigate serious crimes, which opens these investigations up to abuse, as state agencies could resort to interception applications too quickly. No parties to the interceptions can disclose information about the interceptions, which means that intelligence agencies do not inform communications users about interceptions of their communication, even if the investigations have reached a non-sensitive stage (President of the Republic of Zimbabwe 2007).

The Zimbabwean act's definition of national security – which includes matters relating to the existence, independence and safety of the state – is incredibly broad and state-centric. The fact that this definition includes an open list of matters provides ample space for abuse as additional issues can be added at the discretion of the government. The costs of rolling out interceptible equipment are borne by the communication service providers, with only a limited basket of costs eligible for subsidy by the government (Zimbabwe Lawyers for Human Rights 2006). The Monitoring of Interception of Communications Centre (MICC) undertakes the interceptions, although the act provides little information about the powers and functions of the MICC, the appointment of its director and staff, or procedures for storing data. The Posts and Telecommunications Regulatory Authority of Zimbabwe (POTRAZ), the country's communications regulator, handles the appointment procedures (President of the Republic of Zimbabwe 2007). Apart from the fact that POTRAZ is not independent (Anonymous 2020: 15), it is not appropriate for a regulator, which should be acting as the referee on communication matters, to become a player as well by taking decisions about the staffing of an entity that it should regulate.

The Zimbabwean government has already attempted to stretch the act to the limits of interpretation. In January 2018, it used the act to attempt to justify a total internet shutdown in Zimbabwe, following protests about the high cost of fuel. The minister of state responsible for national security in the president's office issued a directive, through the director general, to internet service providers to shut down the internet in the country. The High Court of Zimbabwe overturned the directive on the basis that it had been improperly issued, but an important point about the unconstitutionality of members of the executive was not ruled on (MISA Zimbabwe 2019). Apart from this incident, little is known about how the act is used; in fact, there is a complete information vacuum on these powers.

Diverse lawful interception paths: Zambia and Botswana

In an attempt to sneak provisions into their statute books, some countries have included lawful interception measures in other laws, rather than adopting the politically risky approaches used by South Africa and Zimbabwe. South Africa succeeded in passing the RICA law when it did only because it used the global emergency of the September 11 attacks in America, when the public had largely been struck dumb by the scale of those attacks. While Zimbabwe's government showed some sensitivity to public opposition, it eventually rammed its act through regardless of what the public thought, refusing to concede the important issue of judicial authorization.

One country that took a less risky route to domesticating lawful interception was Zambia, in that it wrote its lawful interception rules into a broad Electronic Transactions Act. Passed in 2009, it covers a range of issues, including domain name regulation and protection of critical databases. The Central Monitoring and Coordination Centre is the only facility allowed to intercept communications and falls under the control of the government ministry responsible for communications. A law enforcement officer should apply to a High Court judge for a warrant if there are reasonable grounds to believe that a crime has been committed, and needs the prior written consent of the Attorney General. Only a law enforcement officer may apply for a warrant, which includes a police officer, members of the Drug Enforcement or Anti-Corruption Commissions, an officer of the Zambia Security Intelligence Service or any other person appointed as such by the minister for the purposes of the act. This provision is so broad that it is open to abuse as it gives the minister wide discretion to appoint someone outside of this closed basket of law enforcement agencies. The act also contains an emergency provision where a judge can be informed of the interceptions after the fact. Commendably, the act states that privileged communications retain their privileged character for the purposes of interception (President of the Republic of Zambia 2009).

The Zambian act states that service providers must use communications systems that are capable of being intercepted, and must install hardware and software that enables interception by the police (President of the Republic of Zambia 2009). Extensive regulations issued in terms of the act were more explicit in domesticating CALEA/ETSI standard, as they state that the providers must use ETSI standards for their handover interfaces, TIIT (Transport of Intercepted Internet Protocol Traffic) or CALEA standards, if the ETSI standards are not applicable. Furthermore, communication-related information, or metadata, should be archived for a period of at least ninety days, which, as preservation orders go, is an admirably short duration: in contrast, South Africa's RICA requires communication service providers to archive metadata for between three and five years.

Like Zambia, Botswana did not try to promulgate a separate interception of communications law. Perhaps worse, though, it subsumed these powers into its deeply problematic national security regime, governed by the Intelligence and Security Services Act. Reflecting the largely domestic factors that drove it, the powers to apply for interception directions is restricted to the DIS only in the Intelligence and Security Services Act (Republic of Botswana 2007). This means that no other law enforcement or intelligence agency should have the powers to intercept communications, including the police and the anti-corruption investigatory body, the Directorate on Corruption and Economic Crime (Balule and Otlhogile 2016). It is unclear why this is the case, or whether it means that these agencies are conducting interceptions unlawfully. Presumably, this arrangement relates to the determination of the Ian Khama administration to centralize intelligence powers in DIS, as DIS fell under the direct control of the president. Giving other agencies the legal power to conduct interceptions would have defeated that objective. Furthermore, leaving interceptions conducted by other agencies without a clear legal basis also makes them legally and politically vulnerable if they do undertake interceptions, as they could become embroiled in controversy: a vulnerability that the presidency could also use to keep these agencies in check. Having a separate interception of communications law would place legislators under pressure to extend the powers to these other agencies, as there would be no logical reason not to. So leaving the situation as is – where only one agency enjoys these powers – is politically expedient. The promulgation of the act was not driven by global factors – and specifically the September 11 attacks – but by local factors, which could explain why Botswana deviated somewhat from the global norm and didn't promulgate a separate act.

Interception powers in Botswana are included in the search and seizure provisions in the Intelligence and Security Services Act. These provisions say that if information cannot be obtained by other means and is likely to be of considerable value to the DIS, then it can approach a senior magistrate or high court judge for an order in a secret hearing. While the fact that judges are involved in decision-making is an important check, the 'considerable value' threshold is far too low as it does not require them to show that there is a reasonable suspicion of a crime having been committed or a threat to national security. The fact that decisions can be taken both by magistrates and by high court judges is of concern as – given that decisions involve fundamental rights – decisions should be taken by high court judges only. A positive feature of the act, though, is that the power to apply for an interception warrant is granted to the director general, but he or she may authorize an officer or support staff member to do, which is a broad power of delegation that could lead to a lower-level DIS member taking such important decisions.

Even more significantly, and as noted in the previous chapter, the act provides practically unfettered powers to the president to decide what constitutes a national security threat, and this consideration does not have to confine itself to threats only but can extend to national security interests. An added problem is that the courts have shown that they will defer to the executive on national security matters, which means that review applications are almost certain to fail.[5] On the upside, however, the fact the Botswanan government promulgated the Intelligence and Security Act in response to local factors meant that Parliament was more susceptible to local pressure to change the act when it was a Bill. Civil society organizations achieved some successes when advocating for reforms, including the insertion of judicial decision-making for interceptions and parliamentary oversight of the DIS. Nevertheless, public consternation remains about the DIS, including the fact that there is no publicly available information about how, or even whether, communication interceptions contributes towards crime fighting or the protection of national security. The Botswanan government sees no need to maintain public confidence in the DIS, which may well be undertaking important and necessary work, but this work is kept from the view of the public. Excessive secrecy combined with poor public relations may well backfire on the DIS, especially if it needs to appeal to the public to justify its continued existence at some stage in the future.[6]

Contesting lawful interception imperialism: The case of Namibia

Namibia provides an interesting case of the official stasis that may emerge when public opposition paralyses attempts to push through deeply controversial lawful interception measures. The fact that opposition proved to be an obstacle to attempts to domesticate lawful interception was unsurprising; as the terrorism justification was simply not strong enough to convince the public that these measures were needed. Namibia guards its celebrated international status as a bastion of media freedom jealously, and it was highly sensitive to criticisms that these measures threatened media freedom,[7] although the threats to human rights extended beyond the media. Like the Zambian government, the Namibian government attempted to sneak these measures through in an omnibus Communications Act in 2009. Even before that, though, the NCIS had a legal mandate to conduct interceptions in terms of its founding statute. The NCIS Act includes provisions that empowered the NCIS to intercept communications and post, subject to a direction being granted to the director general by a judge (Republic of Namibia 1997).[8] The director general has to show that other investigative methods had failed or were likely to fail, and that the interception concerning an actual or potential threat to national security was necessary and could not be properly investigated without it. The fact that the most senior official in the NCIS is directly involved in the process provides a check on possible abuses of this power, as does the fact that interception of communications is an investigative method of last resort. However, the fact that the NCIS operates with such a broad definition of national security predisposes the powers to abuse.

What the NCIS Act does not do, though, is provide for lawful interception measures, which is why the Namibia government included a section on communications interception in the 2008 Communications Act. This section incorporates CALEA-type provisions, including the fact that communication service providers must offer services that are interceptible. This section augments but does not replace or repeal the provisions in the NCIS Act. The Communications Act covers many aspects of communication, including regulation of the sector and the establishment of a Communications Regulatory Authority for that purpose, and the management of the Namibian domain name. In addition to these provisions,

---

section six of the act provides for the establishment of interception centres, and requires service providers to make their networks interception-capable. The act also requires the personal details of users to be registered with the service providers and forbids anyone involved in interceptions from releasing information publicly. However, the relevant section has not been implemented yet, as regulations to give effect to the act had not been completed for over a decade, making it likely that the government was relying on the wholly inadequate NCIS Act.[9] Yet, the Namibian government has been importing interception equipment, for use presumably in terms of the NCIS Act (Links 2019). Whether the government is actually operating interception centres on an extra-legal basis is unknown, although there is a strong suspicion that this is the case, even within the UN Human Rights Committee, which has struggled to obtain confirmation or denial despite questioning the government on this matter (Privacy International 2016c).

The inclusion of interception provisions in the Communications Act took the Namibian public by surprise, as they were not expecting them. Consequently, what should have been a fairly routine act was met with massive controversy and opposition. It is possible that these provisions were snuck into the act precisely because the government knew that a stand-alone act would cause a public backlash. It is also likely that the regulations authorizing the establishment of interception centres were delayed for over a decade because their finalization would have reignited public opposition. The failure to operationalize section six because of the lack of regulations has also led to delays in the implementation of SIM card registration as well. According to Frederico Links, the legislature's failure to anticipate the ferocity of the public opposition put the government on the back foot, leading to them having to park their plans around the establishment of interception centres for an indefinite period. Links explained:

> Submissions were made when the Bill was already in Parliament, so they steamrolled it through. And so, there was this sort of sham process of having a public hearing that a lot of my associates attended and made submissions, and so on. None of the concerns were included, but what it did do was actually lead to that section not being operationalized, because I think then they realized, okay, so now people are looking at this when they probably thought they could sneak this through and nobody would notice, and they could operationalize the whole thing and that would be that. But after that, the law was passed in 2009 and the act itself was operationalized in 2011. And, more than a decade later, part six is still not operationalized, even though they regularly say, you know, at conferences and the like and workshops that they are close to finalizing the regulations that will finally operationalize this section of the law. But, I think they realize now that it's still unconstitutional, so then creating regulations doesn't suddenly make this [problem] go away.[10]

Although Links was of the view that the Namibian government was not operating in good faith, when they promulgated Communications Act and then postponed the implementation of section six, it is clear that they were susceptible to public pressure. At the same time, they were unwilling to concede constitutional problems with the act, and, as a result, they found themselves in a deadlock that they found difficult to break.

'The madness of power':[11] Mozambique and Angola

Mozambique and Angola were both Portuguese colonies, and Portugal was not willing to give them up without a fight: hence, armed struggle was the only viable path to liberation, and this reality has continued to shape these countries to this day. Gaining independence did not stop conflict; rather, the conflict took on an internal character, although fomented by external elements, including apartheid South Africa, who destabilized the region to try and achieve a more pliant constellation of states. These conflicts combined with structural adjustment programmes and congealed into environments that were ripe for conflict (Omari and Macaringue 2007: 46–7).

The International Monetary Fund (IMF) has portrayed Mozambique as a poster child for democratization, liberalization and successful economic growth after a late decolonization process and devastating civil war, having achieved Gross Domestic Product (GDP) growth of up to 9 per cent per annum at one stage. Yet, this narrative hides huge inequalities and internal conflicts, showing that the democratization process has been highly exclusionary (Lalá 2007: 108–22). The sixteen-year civil war between the FRELIMO government and apartheid South Africa-backed RENAMO continues to shape the country's politics and security practices. FRELIMO embraced socialist policies and was orientated to the Eastern bloc, especially Russia, as they supported the movement during its struggle for liberation and claimed to be a socialist government at the time of independence. The FRELIMO government instituted one-party rule at the time, but in 1990, a new constitution created the legal basis for multipartyism. During this time, FRELIMO has made peace with international capitalism, to the point of presiding over an economic recolonization of the country through massive external aid and structural adjustment (Lalá 2007: 108–22). The UN was heavily involved in the Mozambique peace process, and the US, the World Bank and the IMF were involved in post-conflict economic reconstruction.

Since assuming office, FRELIMO has become dominated by powerful political elites, and this elite orientation of the party has undermined its massive achievements in the post-independence period, such as the mass literacy programme that achieved near-universal literacy. Despite the transition to multipartyism, FRELIMO has remained the dominant party and has all but abandoned its progressive legacy of socialism and anti-colonial nationalism. However, FRELIMO took a deliberate political decision to orientate itself towards a particular interpretation of socialism, namely the Stalinism of the Soviet Union,[12] where the state bureaucracy acted independently of, and often contrary to, workers' interests. FRELIMO retained Stalinism's authoritarian legacy, and once the Soviet Union collapsed, it could not envisage political and economic alternatives outside neoliberalism (Saul 2005: 94–106). The democratic culture that took root after the introduction of multipartyism from the 1990s onwards was superficial. The country's rich natural resources have been both a blessing and a curse for the country, as they have come to be a focus of ongoing conflicts, most recently in the northern Cabo Delgado province. The country experiences ongoing problems with systemic crime and corruption, coupled with weak policing: a legacy of civil war felt in the prevalence of organized crime. FRELIMO also made use of communal villages and facilitator groups as informal vehicles for human intelligence surveillance, where loyalists reported people to the party at the communal level if they were acting contrary to the party's values and speaking out against it.[13]

While there was security sector reform in post-war Mozambique, it was heavily donor-driven, with limited local involvement. These problems produced a fragile transformation with insufficient local ownership. Reflecting the country's credentials as one that had fought for, and won, independence from an oppressive colonizer, the 1990 constitution was strongly internationalist and grounded in regional solidarity. It provided a reasonable, although vague, framework for national security, stating that the defence and security services need to take an oath to the constitution and the people, and remain non-partisan. But, at the same time, it also needed them to be obedient to the president as the commander in chief. The constitution also established the National Defence and Security Council as a consultative organ of state, which required that defence and security activities should be set out in law. However, the authoritarian orientation of the government, and the superficial nature of security sector reform, emerged more strongly in 1991 when the government made its approach to national security clearer, which it reduced unapologetically to state security. According to the 1991 law that was meant to give effect to the constitution, state security was defined so broadly that it extended to defamation of the president, ministers, Supreme Court judges and even general secretaries of political parties to be a crime, punishable by one to two years of imprisonment. Consequently, the authorities could intercept communications of people merely if they criticized such figures. The civilian intelligence agency, the State Information and Security Service (SISE), received a legal foundation in 1997, in the form of the Defence and Security Act (1997), which addressed the legal vacuum in how the intelligence and security services were governed. By that stage, citizens were enjoying a modicum of personal security as the civil war had ceased, as had apartheid, its war of destabilization and its support for RENAMO as its proxy.

The Defence and Security Act claimed to be anchored in the resistance of Mozambiquans to foreign domination, and the need for national unity that preoccupied FRELIMO in the aftermath of Portuguese colonialism and civil war. The act is based on principles that do not sit easily with one another, and at times conflict with one another. On the other hand, it nods towards human security by recognizing that all sectors in the state and society should be involved in the defence of the country's security, and demands non-partisanship of defence and security institutions. Reflecting its liberation roots, the act also requires security institutions to play a strong regional and internationalist role to promote peace and stability. On the other, it requires a special duty of obedience to the president as the commander in chief, in addition to allegiance to the constitution and the law, and requires the security institutions to defend the internal and external security of the state. Rather than developing a generalist act, though, its drafters did show sensitivity to the specifics of Mozambique's security situation, referring particularly to the need to counter drug trafficking and other forms of organized crime. In an attempt to roll back the long-standing militarization of Mozambiquan society, it also made clear that the military was responsible for external security and the police services for internal security. While SISE is provided for in the law, unfortunately it is referred to narrowly as an institution of state security. It has a mandate to collect, research, produce, analyse and evaluate information useful to the security of the state (a very broad mandate indeed), prevent acts that threaten the constitution or the functioning of the organs of power of the state, and combat espionage, sabotage and terrorism. The act also requires a mechanism to be set up that coordinates the intelligence functions of SISE, the police and the military (Lei da Política de Defesa e Segurança 1997).

There is no specific interception of communications law in Mozambique. Rather, there are provisions scattered around in other laws and decrees relating to the usage of telecommunications networks. For instance, decree no. 33 of 2001 states that network providers must cooperate with the authorities regarding the legal interception of communications. Interceptions should be through the communications regulatory authority's credentialed members, although the procedures and processes are not spelt out. Article 68 of the Telecommunications law of 2004, which was essentially a liberalization of telecommunications law, also enabled interception of communications. Parliament amended the act in 2016 to include a provision stating that telecommunications operators are obliged to have an operational and efficient system of interception of communications, for the purpose of criminal investigation, noting that such interceptions must be made, upon the issue of a judge's authorization. Like its neighbours, Mozambique requires mobile phone users to register their SIM cards. Furthermore, the new Criminal Procedure Code opens space for the carrying out of interceptions and recordings of telephone communications or other electronic means of communication of suspects, as evidence of crimes. However, there is also scope for telecommunications service providers to pass on communications 'that have criminal content or that threaten the security of the state' to the state without a judicial warrant. In fact, it is normal practice for SISE to operate without judicial warrants on the basis of national security. According to Ernesto Nhlanhle from the Mozambique chapter of the Media Institute for Southern Africa (MISA):

> They do that in the name of the security state . . . they are like our security state service. So, they don't need to make a request from the judge because they are dealing with state security. But the problem is this definition of state security, there is a lack of a definition of state security. Then, also existing today is a culture of suspicion, and also a lack of professionalization . . . The last attack on

Cabo Delgado [late in March 2021], the security service had marked the attack, the potential of the attack, but then they failed to communicate with the local authority to protect people. Sometimes, it is like they do their work, but the level of professionalism is lacking. Sometimes, you will find someone in this kind of service, not using the power they have or hold to serve the public. There is also the culture of protecting the president as an institution being confused with protecting the president as a person. Sometimes they will spend their time surveilling people for private issues, more than for the state. They will use those institutions, not exactly for state security because of a lack of professionalization.[14]

In other words, the FRELIMO government has not encouraged the professionalization of the security services, with the result that they lack the ability to respond adequately to national security threats even when they exist and require urgent intervention. Political power has become personalized, particularly in the president, which has led to intelligence protecting the person of the president rather than the presidency as an institution, and even less the public interest.

Like Mozambique, Angola had to wage a war of independence against Portugal, which was brought to an end only by the popular revolution in Portugal itself in 1974, and which was followed by a conflict between the major nationalist movements. As it did in Mozambique, apartheid South Africa also waged a war of destabilization in Angola, supporting a proxy movement, the Union for the Total Independence of Angola (UNITA), to counter the main liberation movement and by then governing party, MPLA. But it has been its rich natural resources that have propelled post-independence Angola onto the global stage, especially its abundant oil supplies and its diamonds, with the US and China among its major customers. This abundance of natural resources, and their unequal appropriation by local and global elites, has led to a country with both extreme wealth and extreme poverty. Angola rode the wave of the commodities boom in the early 2000s, but when the boom subsided and oil prices dropped, the country entered a prolonged recession that increased social tensions. Growing political consciousness is developing among the youth, and increasingly the MPLA is losing support, threatening the arrangements in Angola that has kept the country's wealth dominated by a small number of politically connected families (Serrano 2017). The exposure of businessperson Isabel Dos Santos, daughter of the then president, as a corrupt person who acquired massive wealth by manipulating her family's political connections in the MPLA has added fuel to the resentment.

Protests have become a commonplace feature of the Angolan landscape, and the government has responded with intolerance, bringing the full might of the law to bear on peaceful protestors, squashing the most basic democratic rights and freedoms. Possibly the most notorious case in this regard, touched on in the introduction, involved seventeen activists who were arrested for organizing a reading group that discussed two books advocating for non-violent protest. Electronic surveillance videos by the Angolan secret service featured heavily in the prosecutor's evidence in the trial (Serrano 2015; Verde 2021). Prolonged war and the tenuous nature of peace, coupled with Angola's highly unequal society and growing social protests, made the state deeply committed to expanding its surveillance powers and capabilities. Military intelligence has been at the forefront of clamping down on domestic dissenters, including celebrated journalist Rafael Marques, well known for his campaigning journalism against corruption, who in 2014 discovered intrusion software on his laptop.

In spite of Angola's protracted civil war and highly truncated transition to a multiparty democracy of sorts, the country's framework for interception of communications has some strong points. Initially, an old rule from Portugal's 1929 penal code requiring judicial authorization for official interference in correspondence was not included in Angola's legal framework. However, once the civil war between Angola's main political movements came to an end and limited democratization was introduced, this situation changed. The National Security Act of 2002 was a mixed bag of progressive and regressive powers. On the upside, the act set out in writing the powers and functions of the organs of state responsible for national security. It required judicial authorization for interception of communications on national security matters, and even then, only a senior judicial officer could grant authorizations within seventy-two hours of the application having been received and for no longer than forty-five days. However, these warrants could be extended for equal periods, and there was no limit on the number of extensions.

On the downside, national security was defined broadly as state activity designed to ensure public order, security and tranquillity and to ensure the functioning of democratic institutions, the regular exercise of the fundamental rights, freedoms and guarantees of citizens and respect for democratic legality.[15] Importantly, the act required the organs of national security to be non-partisan, yet unfortunately it also offered immunity for those who collaborated with the intelligence agency, a provision that could well be abused. It also required organs of state security to be subject to political oversight, and administrative and judicial proceedings. The act also made provision for data processing centres to undertake interceptions, but their powers and functions were not spelt out clearly, with the technical specifications left for regulations. Another safeguard was that use of the data collected by the data centres was prohibited for purposes other than the democratic rule of law or the prevention of crime, and officials and those who use the data must be authorized by a senior official. Unauthorized use of intercepted material was also prohibited.[16] The president is responsible for directing and coordinating national security policy and is empowered to take steps necessary to protect national security, including employing the capacities of the entities established in terms of the act. This power implies that the president has the legal authority to become involved in operational matters. Unlike the intelligence agencies in countries like Zimbabwe and Botswana, the civil or military officials and agents of the Angolan Intelligence Service do not have policing powers, such as the powers of arrest. In fact, they are expressly forbidden from detaining any individual or instituting criminal proceedings.

The 2010 constitution required a new legal framework and stronger protections for privacy that covered communications as a whole and that required judicial authorization for surveillance. This was an advance on previous protections, to the extent that they existed. Angola's code of criminal procedure also provided that interception must only be undertaken with the permission of a judge, and is restricted to major crimes. It must be noted, though, that the government had a stake in promoting general paranoia about communications being under surveillance, even if this is not the case, as it leads to self-censorship (Verde 2021). When the new president, João Lourenço took over office from dos Santos in 2017, after thirty-eight years of rule, there were real hopes in the country that his administration would be open more democratic space. However, if the 2020 Cellular Identification and Location and Electronic Surveillance Act is anything to go by, it appears that the new administration is going to disappoint Angolans. The Lourenço administration stepped back from judicial authorization for surveillance powers – in spite of what the constitution says – and provided a broad range of means of electronic surveillance.

In any event, the fact that the law has, at least until recently, required judicial authorization has not stopped the organs of state from conducting operations completely outside the law and without any such authorization. As to why these flagrant violations took place, legal researcher, academic and writer Rui Verde explained that the government's interpretation of Marxism led to it seeing the law as being part of the superstructure of society. Therefore, it was willing to overlook the law if it felt the need to, as it did not form part of the real basis, or base, of society. This cavalier approach towards the need for judicial authorization meant that the security services could take urgent action against what it perceived to be Arab Spring-type protests in Angola, which included extra-legal surveillance. Verde explained:

> The trial of the seventeen activists was seen as a kind of pre-emptive strike from the government to decapitate the possibilities of an Arab Spring. They are very much afraid because there are a lot of shanty towns around Luanda, and if those people took a chance and went downtown, then there could be a revolution, because they are very poor. And nowadays, the press is controlled directly by the government. So, when people protest, and there are a lot of activities, they use social media. So, yes, the conditions for our Arab Spring are more or less there.[17]

Considering alternatives to lawful interception

It should be apparent from this discussion that interception laws did not follow a linear path in spreading across southern Africa: in fact, there was considerable diversity in the approaches taken. Ironically, despite their problems, lawful interception measures were often an advance on what existed. Either there were no laws at all regulating interceptions, or governments failed to regulate these powers properly: so, the diffusion of lawful interception regimes was not entirely negative for the region. On the one extreme, countries such as South Africa, Namibia and Zambia were happy to disperse oversight power somewhat between the executive, legislature and judiciary. Zimbabwe took a different route, in that it maintained strict executive control over the process: to that extent, it was something of an anomaly in the region as it eschewed judicial decision-making entirely. For its own domestic reasons, Botswana securitized interception, reserving this power for the civilian intelligence agency. Despite having some progressive elements, Angola and Mozambique share a problem of governments simply ignoring controls that do exist. Most countries have overbroad definitions of national security, alienating the very publics that their governments claim to want to protect.

Despite the diversity of approaches, what these countries absorbed without question was state compulsion of communication service providers to provide interceptible communication networks: to that extent, there was government consensus that this requirement was necessary. However, they absorbed this invasive power from the US without absorbing the more progressive elements of its lawful interception system. South Africa set the ball rolling on what it was willing to accept and reject from the US template, and then in an example of what Silitski (2010) calls authoritarian learning, government across the region appropriated these powers selectively. With the very limited exception of South Africa, they shared a culture of excessive secrecy around how they used these powers. Publicly available information about the contributions of these powers to crime fighting or protecting national security was non-existent. This information vacuum has been self-defeating, as it has mystified these powers of lawful interception and prevented public buy-in. In fact, public resistance or the possibility of public pushback influenced how governments adopted such powers. In some countries, governments feared pushing through full-fledged lawful interception regimes, and quietly inserted them into other more benign laws. Governments in countries that had emerged from recent civil wars demonstrated that they were more likely to engage in unlawful interception than countries that had not.

Lawful interception has become a worldwide standard for law enforcement and national security investigations. This bias towards lawful interception risks normalizing this form of surveillance, placing it beyond the scope of legitimate debate. This bracketing out of targeted surveillance can occur in spite of a great deal of documented evidence that, like mass surveillance, it too is used by the state to reproduce inequalities by targeting Muslims, Black people and working-class movements, and contributing to the criminalization of these social groups (Gürses et al. 2016: 576–90). In fact, like untargeted mass surveillance, targeted lawful interception regimes can be, and often are, structured to reproduce inequalities and the rule of capital more broadly: something that becomes more evident when examining southern Africa's lawful interception systems.

Undoubtedly, meaningful reforms of lawful interception measures are possible, and the left can pursue these even within capitalism as doing so will undoubtedly strengthen the working class. In fact, activists should support any reform efforts that expand rather than reduce democracy, as doing so opens up political space for more radical political work. Doing so will separate out their support for reforms from more liberal demands, which will be focused on improving democratic controls, but within capitalism. Anti-capitalists, on the other hand, will recognize the reforms as a means to an end – namely the achievement of a post-capitalist, socialist society – rather than an end in themselves. The Constitutional Court victory in South Africa is likely to put pressure on legislators in the region as the country's law has been widely seen as a model. Possibly the most important reform needed across the region is user notification, where intelligence agencies notify surveillance subjects that they have been under surveillance once investigations reach a non-sensitive stage. This will allow people who were put under surveillance for improper reasons to challenge decisions to spy on them. Making sure that judges take decisions about who should be placed under surveillance and who shouldn't would be an advance on executive decision-making, as the judiciary is more likely to take decisions independently of the bureaucratic executive layer. However, this is by no means a given, as the judiciary may be controlled by the executive. Even in a country with a severe repression problem like Zimbabwe, the judiciary can and does surprise with judgements that open democratic spaces. This is not to say that activists should look to the judiciary to win radical redistributive demands: but winning these demands requires space to organize, and the defensive battles that activists need to fight to defend democratic rights and freedoms can and should include strategic litigation.

There also needs to be much greater transparency in reporting on interceptions that have occurred, and not just bald statistics. Most important is information about the number of interceptions that result in arrests and convictions. In other words, in improving lawful interception in the short to medium term, there is much to emulate from both the South African judgement and the US system. If countries have shopped selectively in international law, selecting the worst practices while ignoring the best practices – and this is largely the case in southern Africa – then activists aiming for reforms should politicize these problems, as it provides them with powerful material for public education on the issues.

While the powers to intercept communications on a targeted basis have developed under capitalism, there is little doubt that a post-capitalist society would need them too, including a socialist society. While crime will most likely decrease greatly, as such a society would have addressed many of the conditions that drive criminality, no doubt it will not disappear entirely. However, if targeted interceptions should remain, then how should a society structure these powers to eliminate the risks (including the political risks) of building vulnerabilities into the network? Could a different path be chosen to the one offered by CALEA? In view of the fact that lawful interception has provided eavesdropping capabilities, not just to law enforcement and intelligence agencies, but to everybody, a group of academics and cybersecurity experts has proposed an alternative to mandated vulnerabilities. This approach involves the legalized hacking of suspects' devices, using already-existing vulnerabilities in software and platforms, rather than creating new ones. Hacking involves interference with a system to make it act in ways that the manufacturer or user did not intend or foresee. Cellphones and laptops can be hacked, but so too can devices such as autonomous cars and electricity meters containing sensors and linked to the IoT (Duncan 2019a). Hacking may be undertaken using a variety of vulnerabilities. Suspects may not have updated software, for instance. The agencies could use man-in-the-middle attacks to intercept communications as they travel from originator to recipient, and gain access to devices that way. Modern communications are sufficiently insecure for there not to be a shortage of vulnerabilities. The agencies can use vulnerabilities that happen in day-to-day development on a targeted basis, and tailored to specific operating system or devices. Where vulnerabilities do not exist – for instance when criminals use end-to-end encryption – then lawful interception methods will not be able to analyse the intercepted communications anyway, which requires other methods to be used (such as hacking). This approach may have perverse consequences, such as creating an incentive for the state not to report vulnerabilities, although exploiting a vulnerability and reporting it are not necessarily mutually exclusive, as the agencies can report after exploiting them (Bellovin et al. 2014).

The alternative option of lawful hacking will be more intrusive for a few interception targets, but overwhelmingly it will be less intrusive for whole populations. Nevertheless, it is likely to be opposed by the likes of the FBI and the NSA because they have developed a stake in insecure communications because they can exploit the insecurities. In fact, as cybersecurity policy expert Susan Landau has argued, the US has promoted insecure communications at home and abroad, while failing to promote public cybersecurity measures outside of narrowly focused state-centric measures to secure government communications and critical infrastructure. For Landau, because governments claim the right to intercept communications, this does not necessitate building interception capabilities into networks, as this creates cybersecurity threats for all users in the process of pursuing law enforcement and national security investigations into a few users (Landau 2010: 233–53). Yet, lawful interception laws and equipment have spread throughout the world, as telecommunications companies would have to cease selling digital switches to major markets such as the US and Europe if they did not build interception capabilities into them.[18]

Trusting our devices: Mitigating the dangers of lawful hacking

Substituting lawful interception with lawful hacking carries the risk of substituting one surveillance problem with another. Hacking can affect privacy and freedom of expression even more severely than lawful interception, as it can access encrypted communications if they are still on the hacked device. Government hacking is even more poorly regulated than lawful interception in many countries. Hackers can access communications that are incidental to an actual investigation, and even suck out the entire contents of a device. This danger leaves people working in sensitive professions such as journalism exposed, particularly to government hacking, as governments are able to procure extremely high weapons-grade hacking tools. Even more worryingly, spy agencies can use hacking as a weapon of disinformation, where they alter hacked information and release it publicly to embarrass or even incriminate someone. Such has been the case in Mexico, where the government has hacked the emails of opposition politicians and journalists regularly and with impunity. They altered hacked communications slightly to embarrass their targets (Privacy International 2017: 3–7).

Hacking is becoming increasingly popular with intelligence agencies, who feel that criminals are using encryption increasingly to conceal their activities. Hacking allows them to access the criminal's device and access the communications at source. They have become concerned that since the Snowden revelations encryption is becoming democratized and more of a feature of everyday communications. This is leading to more communications 'going dark', where intelligence agencies cannot access them (Martin 2015). However, as has become evident in the US, the intelligence agencies there have vastly overstated the 'going dark' problem, as encryption actually thwarts very few lawful intercepts (Electronic Privacy Information Centre 2015). Hacking is certainly preferable to forcing communication service providers to hand over encryption keys – which in any event is not possible if communications are encrypted end-to-end – or creating a key escrow system, where a government-created agency stores the encryption keys.

However, hacking can also compromise the security of the internet, which affects innocents and criminals alike, as the entire device that is hacked is exposed. Legalized hacking can also create perverse incentives for governments to stockpile vulnerabilities in the internet that they are aware of, known as zero-day vulnerabilities; instead, they should be reporting or patching these vulnerabilities as they come to learn of them. Another problem is that very few countries have publicly avowed their uses of hacking, exploiting legal loopholes to use these powers. However, a growing number of countries are adopting laws to regulate hacking that address the unique threats to privacy posed by this form of surveillance (Gutheil et al. 2017: 30–6).

These unique risks require key safeguards to be put in place if lawful hacking is to become a practical alternative to lawful interception. Hacking should be regulated by laws that prevent intelligence agencies from altering, deleting or adding data to the targeted device. They should be compelled to keep audit trails, so that access to the intercepted data can be tracked. Surveillance subjects should be notified of the surveillance on the investigation. A judge knowledgeable enough to weigh up competing interests should approve warrants. Warrants should include sufficient information for the judge to weigh up the risks, but if they do not have sufficient technical knowledge, then security experts could support these judges. There should be no place in the system for bulk hacking; the application for the warrant should be targeted, and relate only to the device of the criminal suspect. Once the agencies have obtained the relevant information, then they should delete non-essential data.

The law should forbid intelligence agencies from stockpiling zero-day vulnerabilities to ensure that they contribute to a freer and more secure internet. Governments may experience problems with hacking the device of a user who has a new or updated operating system; but at the same time they will be contributing to crime by not disclosing vulnerabilities as soon as they find them. This does not mean that they cannot exploit vulnerabilities as they find them and report them, as they remain to be exploited until a patch is created (Bellovin et al. 2014). Only public agencies strictly regulated by law should hack; this requirement will preclude private security organizations from doing so, as invariably they will be more difficult to hold to account. There is no reason why these controls cannot be won, even within a capitalist society.

While powerful interests have prevented countries from exploring alternatives to lawful interception – which in its current form is an enabler of imperialism – any alternative must be assessed for its own risks. Such is the case with lawful hacking by state intelligence agencies, which destroys our ability to trust our devices. Hacking can be a public good, too. Ethical hackers have exposed some of the most egregious surveillance abuses in the modern world. Ethical hacking also challenges hardware and software developers to design robust systems. Developing a system that targets legitimate criminal suspects rather than risking the security of whole populations is undoubtedly a worthwhile challenge for anti-capitalists and broader society to rise to.

Chapter 4

MASS SURVEILLANCE AND NATIONAL SECURITY IMPERIALISM

Introduction

The Snowden revelations focused mainly on bulk surveillance abuses in the global North. In this chapter, I examine southern Africa and bulk surveillance practices here. I examine southern Africa as a target for SIGINT surveillance by the major surveillance powers, and the ways in which signals intelligence reproduces and reinforces imperialism. In the same way that imperialist countries divided the globe up among themselves, so it has been with bulk communication surveillance too. Snowden's disclosures revealed the worldwide reach of the NSA and the Five Eyes alliance. However, state surveillance by the major surveillance powers is not a free-for-all. Different actors have entered into intelligence-sharing agreements with one another, leading to each of them being tasked with undertaking surveillance on particular regions of the globe, based on the legacy of regions being the dominions of certain colonial powers. The UK's GCHQ was tasked with the surveillance of Africa.

I also examine the mass surveillance practices that southern African countries use, and to what end. I conclude by looking at whether there should be any place in an anti-capitalist vision of society for mass surveillance for national security purposes, and how movements in the region could potentially take up the struggle against it more effectively.

SIGINT surveillance as an intelligence practice

SIGINT involves the surveillance of electronic signals for intelligence purposes and has matured into a full-blown intelligence discipline in recent years. In fact, SIGINT has become increasingly important to modern intelligence work as it offers a fast and flexible source of intelligence on security threats. The fact that SIGINT does not rely on HUMINT assets or sources – who may provide second-hand reports or whose identities may be uncovered – increases its attractiveness for intelligence agencies (Wells 2016). A sub-discipline of SIGINT, COMINT involves using big data analytics to develop intelligence from communication signals. SIGINT has become increasingly important to modern intelligence work as it offers a fast and flexible source of intelligence on security threats (Gill and Pythion 2012: 92–8). Bulk surveillance for SIGINT purposes involves the collection and analysis of massive amounts of information obtained from electronic signals, including communication and internet traffic, on an untargeted basis for intelligence gathering purposes. There does not have to be a reasonable suspicion of criminality to trigger this form of surveillance, which is why it may also be called suspicionless surveillance. Intelligence agencies use SIGINT mainly for strategic purposes, to enable policymakers to anticipate long-term trends in the national security environment. Electronic signals, including communication networks, provide the spies with easy sources of intelligence, especially outside their countries.

However, precisely because it is so wide-ranging, SIGINT is controversial as it allows intelligence agencies to scoop up huge quantities of data on an untargeted basis, irrespective of whether the agencies have a reasonable suspicion of criminality. Its vast reach has compromised communication rights such as privacy, freedom of expression and freedom of association in the name of protecting security (Hintz et al. 2019). Governments usually use SIGINT surveillance for bulk collection of foreign signals only: in fact, one of the main reasons why the Snowden revelations were so controversial was because they showed that the NSA used its SIGINT capabilities to spy on Americans on US soil. SIGINT agencies can collect intelligence by tapping into over-the-air or cable-borne signals as they enter or pass through a country.

The operational basis for using untargeted SIGINT surveillance is that intelligence agencies typically lack investigatory powers outside their own borders, which means that they need to use the few methods they have to obtain intelligence. Agencies also use SIGINT to detect national security threats they may not be aware of and that they could not come to know of using other means, such as a military build-up on the border or a plan to attack the country from outside its borders. This is why SIGINT is used for strategic intelligence purposes: it allows the agencies to anticipate threats as they emerge, and this forewarning allows them to develop responses to prevent these threats from being realized. One of the major problems with foreign intelligence collection, though, is that it may only give them fragments of information. Consequently, agencies use SIGINT to collect as much bulk data as they have the capabilities to collect, so that they can connect the fragments and build up as complete a picture as possible. GCHQ has claimed that because the internet uses packet switching, they need to collect as much internet traffic as possible to reassemble communications. In the words of the UK's intelligence complaints body, the Investigatory Powers Tribunal, GCHQ has a 'need for [access to] the haystack in order to find the needle'. The Independent Reviewer of Terrorism Legislation, David Anderson, also concluded that GCHQ had a clear operational case for these powers (Duncan 2019b; Wickremasinghe 2019: 15; Anderson 2016: 122). However, although they may wish to, there is little evidence that even the most powerful SIGINT agencies have the capabilities to operate on a collect-it-all basis.

The Five Eyes alliance: Monopolization and concentration of surveillance powers

The Snowden revelations revealed that the Five Eyes alliance is the most significant and invasive SIGINT network in the world today, giving it a global reach that allows it to all but monopolize global surveillance. This monopoly power makes it practically impossible for other countries or even regional blocs to compete. SIGINT surveillance practices tend to follow global patterns of production and consumption more generally, and it is not coincidental that the major economic imperialist and sub-imperialist powers have become the major surveillance powers.

The Five Eyes alliance began its life as an agreement between the US and the UK in the wake of the Second World War and was governed initially by the UKUSA agreement, signed in 1946. Tasked with collaborating on collection, analysis and sharing of SIGINT, the UKUSA agreement eventually incorporated the other English-speaking nations and former dominions of New Zealand/ Aotearoa, Canada and Australia as collaborating dominions. According to the 1946 UKUSA agreement, the US and UK agencies were tasked with collaborating on collection, analysis and sharing of COMINT communication traffic, acquisition of documents and equipment, cryptanalysis, decryption and translation and acquisition of information about communication organizations' practices, procedures and equipment, and sharing of communication intelligence (British-US Communication Intelligence Agreement 1946). The dominions in the global South were South African, then-southern Rhodesia (now Zimbabwe), then-Ceylon (now Sri Lanka) and India. Owing to their histories as former colonies of the UK, the communications of African countries that were members of the Commonwealth did not fall within the definition of foreign communication; consequently, at least on paper, their communications were not supposed to be intercepted in terms of the agreement. The scope of the agreement was astonishingly broad, covering intelligence of a political, military or economic value, and it enjoined the parties not to limit the scope of the agreement (British-US Communication Intelligence Agreement 1946). Significantly, the agreement did not limit the activities of the partners to serious crime-related or terrorism-related matters.

In addition to the Five Eyes countries, there are an additional four European countries involved in a Nine Eyes cooperation agreement. A Fourteen Eyes cooperation agreement involves even more European countries, and a much looser cooperation of Forty-One Eyes has collaborated on intelligence about Afghanistan. Several African countries struck up third-party agreements with the NSA, though, to assist the agency in signals intelligence gathering, and these include countries in the North and East of Africa such as Algeria, Ethiopia and Tunisia. Not all of those countries that have struck up agreements have been named, so it is impossible to have a full picture of cooperating African countries (Madsen 2014). Partnering with these countries in these ways makes it less likely that they will partner with other countries or alliances that may be hostile to the Five Eyes alliance. Effectively, these partnerships took these countries out of the global SIGINT-sharing 'market', reinforcing the cartel-like character of the Five Eyes.

There is some value in understanding the Five Eyes as a field in the Bourdieuian sense, where relatively autonomous actors cooperate on national security matters. At the same time, they may also engage in struggles over priorities, where different members form alliances-within-alliances based on prior histories of cooperation and the need to control the 'rules of the game' for its more junior partners (Kniep 2016). However, doing so may miss questions of how power is structured in the alliance. The Snowden revelations point to an alliance that is unequal, with the NSA at its helm, with even its more important collaborator, GCHQ, being a subordinate partner.

The UKUSA agreement tasked the UK government with keeping the parties to the agreement informed about any arrangements or proposed arrangements with the intelligence agencies in the dominions, suggesting that these agencies were not expected to exercise any independence from the British signals intelligence board (British-US Communication Intelligence Agreement 1946). The agreement was later amended in 1955 to make clear that all members of the Commonwealth were not considered to be third parties, yet of those members, only Canada, Australia and New Zealand/Aotearoa would be considered collaborating partners of the UK–USA partnership. In spite of the fact that the US could be considered a 'first among equals' in the alliance, more junior intelligence partners such as Australia have benefitted from the alliance through, for instance, the joint establishment of interception facilities and access to US intelligence that it would otherwise never have access to. However, Australia has done so at the expense of its autonomy on intelligence matters (O'Neil 2017). New Zealand/Aotearoa found itself in an even weaker position, where SIGINT priorities were set outside the country and where interception stations are, to all intents and purposes, neocolonial pockets controlled by the major partners (Hager 1996: 237–50).

Global territorial divisions and surveillance imperialism

Members of the Five Eyes alliance have also carved up surveillance activities into regional responsibilities. During the 1960s to 1970s, the Five Eyes countries established Echelon to intercept communications traffic on a massive scale. GCHQ became the coordinating centre for Europe up to the Ural Mountains, as well as Africa, the Soviet Union (west of the Ural Mountains) and the western part of Asia. The NSA covered the rest of the Soviet Union and most of the Americas (North and South) and the northern part of the Pacific Ocean, while Australia coordinated the electronic monitoring of the South Pacific and South East Asia. Interception sites were set up in various localities around the world, including on Ascension Island, off the coast of West Africa, and St. Helena. More recently, an NSA programme called X-Keyscore – which searched and analysed global internet traffic using search terms (or 'fingerprints') – was shared with other countries' spy agencies, especially those in the Five Eyes alliance. The Snowden disclosures revealed that X-Keyscore was located in over 150 sites and 700 servers around the world. In Africa, the programmes had locations in Zambia and Sudan (National Security Agency 2008: 6; Oxford 2013).

Historically, its colonial interests and its need to keep anti-colonial liberation movements in the region under surveillance sparked GCHQ surveillance of Africa. It also had an interest in countries where there was insurgency during the apartheid period, such as Angola.[1] GCHQ also used a South African naval listening post in the past, as well as diplomatic missions in the frontline states during the struggle against apartheid, to track the activities of the South African liberation movements and their regional allies. On balance, GCHQ's interventions supported apartheid and disadvantaged the frontline states as the British feared that Soviet and Cuban interventions would become stronger if the movements gained in strength. The Five Eyes alliance even placed Nelson Mandela, former president of the ANC and of South Africa, under surveillance.

There is little evidence in the Snowden disclosures of the entire southern African region being of interest to the Five Eyes countries in the post-apartheid period, however, as their main focus appeared to be in countries that could provide them with intelligence on the activities of China and Russia. This is in spite of the fact that in August 2010, the Foreign Intelligence Signals Court granted the NSA legal authority to spy on 192 of the 196 countries in the world, including African countries (Foreign Intelligence Surveillance Court 2010). The NSA's attention has focused more on North and East Africa, especially Egypt, Kenya, Somalia and Libya. Furthermore, the Five Eyes countries could conduct listening operations from outside the continent, to the extent necessary. According to investigative journalist Duncan Campbell, who has investigated the Five Eyes SIGINT operations over several decades:

The interest they have in southern Africa is determined by geography. So there are geostrategic issues. From the point of view of the English-speaking alliance, as you come into the 1950s, you have a huge colonial interest in southern Africa. Where British power goes, spies go. So each country within the British sphere would have liaison officers. It was very territorial; seeing the colonies as dominions, so MI5 [the UK's domestic intelligence agency] claimed it had the right to exercise sovereignty. Cable & Wireless intertwined with GCHQ all along, and the work was done by them. BT did everything that was required of it. In the dominions, they were very focused on putting down the natives, but that doesn't require strategic intelligence. In the 1960s to 1970s, there was more focus on dealing with other principal adversaries, such as the Soviet Union, China and the Middle East. South Africa is largely isolated, as there is no communications path that could traverse the ionosphere over southern Africa. The main interest in southern Africa was in countries where there was insurgency, such as Angola. The normal thing is to get listening stations in place, but [in the case of southern Africa], they did it outside Africa in St. Helena and Ascension where they could comfortably pick up signals.[2]

Campbell's observations underscored the fact that Five Eyes alliance had a very specific time-bound interest in the region, which related initially to their colonial interests, and then later to the struggles against the South African apartheid regime, what various liberation movements were up to and whether these movements constituted threats to their interests in the region.

Certainly, from the Snowden documents, the SIGINT infrastructure in Africa appeared to be concentrated on North Africa. According to one document leaked by Snowden, as of 2010, the Five Eyes had eighty Special Collection Sites throughout the world, including the following staffed locations in Africa: Abuja, Addis Ababa, Nairobi, Kinshasa and Lusaka. Two more sites, in Monrovia and Luanda, were dormant, and an active survey for a new site was being conducted in Bamako. There was also an unmanned remote site in Lagos. Tellingly, most of these sites were located in the East and the Horn of Africa, and reflected the Five Eyes concerns about these countries being used as terrorism launchpads. X-Keyscore had only one collection point in southern Africa, in Zambia, GCHQ's well-established listening post in the region.

However, it is instructive to look at the recent circumstances in which the Five Eyes alliance has taken an interest in southern African countries. By 2007, the Five Eyes alliance expressed some concern about the internal security risk in Zimbabwe and the Great Lakes region, with evidence of specific interest in the Zimbabwean elections (National Security Agency 2007). More interest was shown in relation to specific events, where Five Eye partners wanted to establish the negotiating positions of specific African leaders on economic matters. In the case of South Africa, for instance, according to the Snowden documents, GCHQ had spied on South African officials to establish their negotiating positions in relation to the G20 summit in 2009. Furthermore, oil-producing countries such as Angola and Nigeria were of interest to GCHQ, as were countries where rebel movements were active. GCHQ's interests extended to business people in Nigeria, the DRC and Angola (Piel and Tilouine 2016). GCHQ also spied on the employees of South African multinational mobile phone company MTN, especially roaming managers who travelled extensively to negotiate roaming agreements with other countries.

GCHQ's interest in these countries was not coincidental. Much of the world's reserves of coltan – a metal essential to the information economy – as well as copper, are to be found in the DRC and have been significant contributors to the country's internal instability (Carmody 2016: 166–73). The UK has also become increasingly reliant on oil imports from the Organization of Petroleum Exporting Countries (OPEC) countries, including Angola and Nigeria (Office for National Statistics 2016). Apart from its historical interest in Zimbabwe, by 2017, the UK was importing diamonds from the country (Observatory of Economic Complexity 2017). These interests are not surprising, as the UK has embraced an expansive definition of national security to include possibly the most contentious intelligence focus area, namely economic security: that is, the security of its economic interests abroad. This is in spite of the fact that economic intelligence has proved to be of dubious value to the protection of national security (Hager 1996: 241–43), and as discussed in Chapter 1, including it in any definition of national security risks shifting intelligence activities from focusing on threats to interests. The South African and Nigerian surveillance also contradicted the assurance in the original UKUSA agreement that Commonwealth countries would be protected from foreign SIGINT surveillance, and rendered hollow the UK's original idea of establishing the Commonwealth as a political community of free and equal partners. At the end of the day, when its economic interests came into play, it was willing to violate its own agreement and treat the countries' governments as any other foreign surveillance targets.

Internet Protocol network bulk surveillance: The case of South Africa

South Africa is the only country in the region that has acknowledged publicly that it has Internet Protocol (IP) bulk surveillance capabilities, undertaken by the National Communication Centre (NCC), which falls under the control of the SSA. While RICA established the Office for Interception Centres (OIC), which undertakes lawful interception, the NCC has no founding statute. As a result, mass surveillance is desperately under-regulated, which has been a subject of considerable controversy in South Africa, and was found by the Constitutional Court to be an unconstitutional practice because no law regulated its powers and functions (Ministerial Review Commission on Intelligence 2008; Duncan 2018; Constitutional Court of South Africa 2021: 65–71).

According to the SSA, bulk surveillance is an internationally accepted method of monitoring transnational signals to screen them for certain key phrases, and to ensure that the country is protected from transnational threats from individuals or organizations outside South Africa's borders. For the SSA, bulk surveillance is an automated process, with no real human intervention; machines select the internet traffic for further analysis, and not humans, and the agency discards the rest without anyone having looked at it. The SSA has also argued that it wants to retain only that data that is of interest to them, as it would be too expensive to store too much.[3] It has also set out its understanding of what constitutes foreign signals intelligence, which 'includes any information that emanates from outside the borders of the Republic (in this case, South Africa) and passes through or ends in the Republic'.[4] Conceivably, this definition could include the communications of locals as well, as some of their internet traffic is likely to be routed through foreign-based servers (particularly in the US) and could qualify as a foreign signal if a South African is pulling data from a foreign server.

The SSA also gave examples of the kinds of areas it would consider using bulk surveillance for: these included food security, water security and illicit financial flows. These issues related directly to the SSA's understanding of its national security mandate as encompassing human security. In fact, so serious were the writers of the constitution about changing the state security mindset prevalent under apartheid that they incorporated the definition of human security as freedom from fear and want into South Africa's final constitution in 1996. The constitution defines national security as 'the resolve of South Africans, as individuals and as a nation, to live as equals, to live in peace and harmony, to be free from fear and want and to seek a better life'.[5] In an interview, Moe Shaik, who was involved in the drafting of the constitution, gave insight into some of the debates about this definition in the Constitutional Assembly. Shaik is a former ANC intelligence operative and former head of the South African Secret Service, the foreign intelligence branch that preceded the SSA:

> We did have a huge debate about socio-economic challenges with HIV/Aids representing a kind of intelligence threat. I was a proponent of addressing socio-economic challenges and the intelligence services need to give policy-makers a very informed view of many of the socio-economic practices, not that they were going to act on it, but they were going to be able to advise on it. Now, that argument ran into serious challenge, that it is the mandate of the health department, or the labour department with respect to unemployment, and I argued that that was a misunderstanding of the intelligence service's capabilities. They have research capabilities and essentially they counter confirmation bias of existing departments, and bias is a huge thing in departments, when you are engaged in that department . . . my argument is that all departments have a confirmation bias. They do not know what they do not know and what they do know, they will seek to interpret in a particular way and it's the task of the intelligence service to bring the other view onto the table. Difficult as it may be, hard as it may be, but we could only benefit from a lot of discussion, rather than a lack of it.[6]

Shaik's comments point to one of the most serious challenges in operationalizing human security, namely, that mandates are likely to overlap with other government departments, as they may feel threatened by an intelligence agency concerning itself with issues that fall within their remits. At the same time, an agency's involvement could bring a viewpoint to issues that emphasized their national security implications: a viewpoint that may not necessarily arise if government departments dealt with these issues on their own.

Water security is a case in point. In a water-scarce region, the dangers of prolonged drought are real. A human security perspective would require the government department responsible for water to work with the intelligence agency to strategize around the possible national security implications of severe drought, such as the prospect for social instability. However, inevitably, it will do so by bringing its extraordinary emergency powers to bear on the issue. In fact, far from opening up discussions on water security, its involvement is likely to close them down given the excessive secrecy around SSA activities. Data collected by the NCC to track water security in the region would not be up for debate, even in government, as they almost certainly would classify the information. Furthermore, given the nationalistic tenor of the SSA's mandate to protect South Africa's sovereignty from external threats, it could well pursue solutions that are in South Africa's interests rather than the region's.

The NCC was set up with extremely powerful surveillance capabilities and assisted a number of countries in sub-Saharan Africa to ward off serious national security threats. In spite of the NCC not being regulated by RICA, when Shaik was there, the SSA had in place stringent internal controls over how the NCC operated. According to Shaik:

No international operation could go ahead without the approval of the Director General [of the SSA, or DG]. The culture at the time, 2009 to 2011, was that the DG was very insistent that everything must follow legal requirements and that everything must be followed by the book within delegated authority. I know there were intense discussions with OIC and NCC to enforce a more regulated environment for signals intelligence capabilities but then our lines were cut short. We were working primarily with the NCC, but the OIC also fell within the ambit of the budget allocation of SSA, and as a result, the OIC also came under the direct supervision of the DG. It was the OIC process that coordinated directed interception on behalf of the SSA. The NCC refers to the broader capabilities [of the SSA] and the law at least to my understanding was vague as to whether it covered the NCC. So if you were doing a cross-border grab for instance, then that didn't require a direction, so the NCC in itself would provide its data and make a determination over if it was a domestic matter, it would go to domestic intelligence, if it was a foreign matter it would go to foreign intelligence, and the analysts would then say, we want directed interception here. We would say, we were concerned about this issue, and they would then guide the NCC on what kind of intelligence should happen, working primarily with the NCC.[7]

In referring to the kinds of cross-border national security issues that could potentially be tracked through foreign SIGINT surveillance, Shaik gave an example of the cross-border drug trade. Some drugs go by several names, but once these names are known, they could be used as selectors and foreign communications could be scanned for these words, and the Financial Intelligence Centre could provide information about money flows, where needed. If calls were intercepted that involved South Africans, then they should be referred to the RICA judge for a warrant.[8] Shaik's comments showed that the SSA's bulk SIGINT capabilities had important uses, and, despite the lack of an enabling law, attempts were made internally to regulate how these capabilities were used to prevent abuse.

However, signs emerged that these controls lapsed as Zuma's presidency continued. Shaik and the director of the domestic branch of the SSA were forced to resign by the minister after they raised concerns about the national security implications of Zuma's close relationship with an Indian family of businessmen resident in South Africa, the Guptas. Furthermore, it remained for the NSA to raise alarm bells about the pending sale of an important platinum mine to the Guptas. The NSA's intervention suggested that the NCC's powerful surveillance capabilities had been neutralized by a ministry that had become an enabler, rather than investigator, of state capture by corrupt elements (Myburgh 2017: 87–94; Pauw 2017: 41–59; Kasrils 2017: 85–97; Swilling et al. 2017). The fact that the NCC fell outside the RICA process meant that not even those inadequate checks and balances that applied to domestic intercepts could be brought to bear on this failure.

The diversity of mass surveillance practices in southern Africa

Bulk IP surveillance is extremely expensive and demands complex analytical capabilities; otherwise, it would be impossible to make sense of the masses of data intercepted during bulk interception. Very few countries around the world have publicly avowed the use of these powers, although information about these capabilities has often come into the public domain through investigative journalism. The Zimbabwean government was interested in acquiring these capabilities but lacked the resources to acquire them (Anonymous 2020: 18). This has meant that the region is unable to compete with the Five Eyes countries in the global SIGINT arms race, turning its countries into potential (and at times actual) objects of surveillance without themselves having the capacity to become global surveillance actors. However, this does not mean that Zimbabwe does not practice mass surveillance per se: in fact, regional governments use a huge diversity of untargeted mass surveillance practices. In other words, they have had to adapt to the realities of what they can afford and what they have the analytical capabilities to exploit. Referring to the Zimbabwean government's surveillance practices, Nompilo Simanje argued:

> Well, I think mass surveillance is happening. The first example that I could give you is that during the 2018 elections, so many people were receiving messages from the ruling party, being encouraged to vote for the president, and these messages knew the name of the person and would go directly to their phone, meaning they also knew your phone number and your voting station and your identity number. So, what that indicates is that the government has the capacity to access information that relates to thousands of individuals. That's mass surveillance because those specific people who received those messages had not been advised prior that that information was going to be given to that specific political party. So, as much as mass surveillance has been done, it has been done through different channels . . . [And the president] said the government, through the use of ICT data, did have the capacity to check the location of individuals and acquire communication details. That clearly indicates a capacity to institute mass surveillance. SIM card registration is a channel for mass surveillance, because everyone is obligated to register their SIM card, whenever they purchase a SIM card. All that information is collected and people don't have an indication of where that information is.[9]

Simanje's comments make it clear that it would be a mistake to reduce mass surveillance to IP network surveillance, simply because the Snowden revelations have focused public attention on it. Countries that cannot afford this form of surveillance can find (and in the case of Zimbabwe have found) creative workarounds to bypass the affordability problem, and still practice mass surveillance. Mandatory SIM card registration is a form of mass surveillance, as it involves the indiscriminate collection and storage of personal details when a SIM card is registered in an individual's name, and mobile phone users who opt out of the registration process do so on pain of being disconnected from the network. The effect of SIM card registration is that users cannot communicate anonymously without the potential for being tracked. However, SIM card registration is notoriously ineffective as a crime-fighting tool, as criminals are more likely to use creative workarounds to prevent themselves from being tracked (such as buying pre-registered SIM cards that are sold illegally). Consequently, some countries have not pursued SIM card registration, or, when they have, have abandoned it (Duncan 2018: 95–6; Swart 2016).

Governments in all southern African countries have introduced SIM card registration, with the exception of Namibia. Doing so would mean implementing the disputed chapter six of the Communications Act (see Chapter 3 for more details). The government has really wanted to institute this measure, and in 2017, the NCIS argued for SIM card registration to assist them in countering extremism and radicalization on social media (Links 2021). In Mozambique, after a series of street protests, the government instituted SIM card registration. The communications regulatory authority, Autoridade Reguladora das Comunicações (INCM), sold the practice to the public as a means of protecting innocent mobile phone users. Stating that this practice had started in Europe, the regulator argued that the then existing system opened itself up to crime or as a means to insult other users as the authorities could not trace mobile phone activity to specific individuals. INCM also argued that they could use SIM card registration to offer value-added services as they had verified the identities of users. While acknowledging that criminals could still forge documents used to register SIM cards, they decided nevertheless to proceed with registration as not doing so could destabilize the country economically and politically (INCM 2017: 10). However, there appear to have been more complex reasons motivating SIM card registration, as the government announced its intention to compel users to register shortly after mass protests in Mozambique, where protestors used Short Messaging Service (SMS) as an organizing tool (Nhanale 2021: 6–7). While the majority of countries around the world require some form of SIM card registration, many of the countries with significant terrorism problems do not. Of the Five Eyes countries, only Australia requires SIM card registration (Yongo and Theodorou 2020: 7–16), suggesting that the alliance has recognized that this practice has limited utility in the fight against terrorism.

In fact, a prevalent surveillance practice throughout southern Africa involves the exploitation of metadata, including location data. Governments resort to the exploitation of metadata because most countries give lower privacy protections to metadata than to communication content (Hunter and Mare 2020: 6). An extreme case in point is Malawi, which has practically no controls on surveillance, yet possesses capabilities to conduct some of the most invasive surveillance in the region. While Malawi's constitution protects the right to privacy, there is no law explicitly governing interception of communications. While existing laws touch on interceptions, they do not provide anything close to an adequate framework for its regulation (Hunter and Mare 2020: 27–30). Yet, this lack of controls has not stopped the Malawi Communications Regulatory Authority from procuring what is widely referred to in the country as a 'spy machine', or a Consolidated ICT Regulatory Management System. Reportedly, this system is capable of intercepting communication traffic, mobile phone data such as call data records and equipment identity data. Acquired to monitor communication licencees' compliance with their licencing obligations, as well as to assist in the collection of taxes, there is nothing stopping the regulator – which lacks independence from the government – from using this system for purposes far beyond these stated objectives. The fact that the procurement of this system coincided with mandatory SIM card registration also added to public discomfort about its true objectives. This discomfort escalated into a legal challenge, but the court found in favour of the Malawi regulator (Gondwe 2020).

Another mass surveillance instrument that is becoming increasingly popular with southern African governments, and that is capable of capturing massive amounts of location data, is the International Mobile Subscriber Identity-catcher (IMSI) catcher. These devices mimic a cellphone tower, emitting a strong signal that draws mobile phone connections to it, enabling it to capture data from these devices. Potentially, thousands of mobile phones can connect to an IMSI catcher at the same time. Basic models can capture a phone's IMSI and International Mobile Equipment Identity (IMEI) numbers, while sophisticated models can intercept communication content and even change content, and identify suspicious activities using voice recognition (Duncan 2018: 135–6). Typically, governments keep the technological capabilities of their intelligence agencies secret so as not to reveal their defences. However, UK export control records showed that Namibia has procured IMSI catchers (see Chapter 5), although it is not clear which state agency procured them. As IMSI catchers are generally classified as dual-use goods, or goods with military and civilian uses, they are subjected to export controls and usually sold only to governments to prevent their abuse by non-state actors (see Chapter 5). Given how powerful they can be as mass surveillance devices, governments usually reserve them for use in intelligence or law enforcement operations. However, according to information provided to Frederico Links by sources in the intelligence services, very few people in Namibia actually had access to the IMSI catchers, as they were under the direct control of the president. According to his information, the IMSI catchers were used, not for national security purposes, but to fight factional battles in the ruling SWAPO by keeping opposing factions under surveillance.[10]

Governments do not even need to acquire sophisticated surveillance technologies to engage in mass surveillance: by using a creative mix of HUMINT and SIGINT, they can achieve a large footprint, allowing them to shift from an untargeted to a targeted approach once they know who their people of interest are. A case in point is the DRC, where the government engaged in mass surveillance of social media networks by infiltrating them. When elections took place in the

DRC in 2019, there were high hopes that the repression that characterized the dying days of Joseph Kabila's presidency would abate. Protest movements had sprung up to oppose his bid for a third term, and the government responded with hostility, killing and injuring scores of protestors. The government also instituted an internet shutdown in 2018 in a bid to stop protestors organizing over social media: a self-defeating measure as it prevented them from continuing online surveillance. However, once Felix Tshisekedi took power, the new government continued with repressive practices, including surveillance of protest movements. Intelligence services strengthened their presence on social media in an attempt to establish who the protest leaders were. According to one intelligence officer from the national intelligence agency, ANR, who spoke to journalist Prince Murhula on conditions of anonymity, thousands of them were involved in infiltrating social networks and spying on activists. The officer said: 'Personally, I joined around a hundred groups on social networks. Sometimes I pass myself off as a journalist, a civil society activist or a pressure group. So it's easy to know where a certain action should be taken, who are the leaders, where and how to stop them' (Murhula 2020).

Governments may also want their citizens to think that they have more surveillance capabilities than they do, in fact, have. A case in point is Angola. In the wake of the killing of opposition leader Jonas Savimbi by the Angolan Armed Forces in 2002, which has been widely reported as having resulted from digital surveillance, the government circulated messages that their surveillance capabilities were powerful enough to track the country's most feared enemies, and encouraged a myth of an all-seeing state. As Rui Verde commented:

> The birth of the myth was the death of Savimbi, the leader of UNITA. They put everywhere that he was under surveillance, and you heard the most extraordinary stories . . . and it created the myths of our powerful capacities of the government to survey everything. Savimbi was in the bush, [and] even in the bush they [managed to] target him and kill him. I think this is the birth of the idea, and it spread.[11]

The future of bulk SIGINT surveillance: Reform options

In spite of the abuses of SIGINT surveillance revealed by Snowden, intelligence agencies continue to use these bulk powers and some are even expanding them. However, civil society has won some reforms, and more countries are being pushed to legislate for these powers. These legal changes are forcing governments to be more transparent about this form of surveillance, the powers they are willing to give to their intelligence agencies and the circumstances in which they can use them. There is a general global acceptance of a set of legal principles developed by the European Court of Human Rights for lawful strategic surveillance. Known as the Weber principles, they require intelligence agencies to seek warrants for strategic surveillance, where the warrants contain basic information. This information includes the nature of the offences that gave rise to the application and the categories of people likely to have their communications intercepted. The warrant should also place limits on the duration of interception and spell out the procedures to be used for examining, using and storing information. It includes the precautions to be taken when communicating intercepted information to third parties, and the circumstances in which information may be erased or records destroyed (European Court of Human Rights 2006). There can be little doubt that these principles provide a sound basis for authorization, providing that the decision-maker is a judge rather than an executive authority.

Intelligence agencies may argue that the very nature of bulk surveillance makes it incompatible with judicial authorization associated more generally with targeted surveillance. However, legal jurisprudence emerging in Europe and the UK appears to have accepted that bulk surveillance is here to stay, leading to the debate focusing not on removing these powers but reforming them to make them less susceptible to abuse (Wetzling and Vieth 2018: 10). After an initial spurt of judicial activism seeking to have bulk surveillance outlawed completely, a creeping judicial deference to governments on national security powers has become apparent. This shift has become especially apparent in the wake of the terrorist attacks linked to Al Qaeda and the Islamic State in Europe since 2015, which have reinforced judicial reluctance to second-guess governments on what it will take to defend national security. A case in point was the European Court of Human Rights ruling in 2018, which stated that given the many unknown threats to national security, bulk surveillance should fall within a government's margin of appreciation in choosing how best to achieve the legitimate aim of protecting national security (European Court of Human Rights 2018: 130). In making this finding, the court endorsed the security establishment's arguments and rejected an argument made by a group of ten NGOs that surveillance must be authorized only if there is individualized, reasonable suspicion of a crime having been committed.

If anti-surveillance activists take the continued existence of these powers for granted, then the most that they could aspire to is to subject their SIGINT agencies to narrowly tailored authorization procedures. These procedures could require governments to show that they are resorting to bulk powers only when more targeted approaches will not yield the intended results. SIGINT agencies could be required to apply for bulk warrants, for instance, relating to the classes of individuals or activities they intend to place under surveillance, and each stage of the surveillance process – such as collection, storage and analysis – could trigger the need for a new warrant. The warrants could be narrowly tailored to include information about the fibre-optic cables to be intercepted and the geographical areas to be targeted, as well as the private actors (if any) assisting with the interception. Warrants could also include the selectors or search terms the agencies intend to use to search internet traffic, and if they do not know all of these in advance, then they could inform the judge of the additional selectors after the fact. To prevent indiscriminate overuse, SIGINT agencies could also be restricted to particular quotas when using particularly invasive surveillance tools, Selectors that relate to an individual should trigger a duty on the part of the intelligence agency to inform the individual once the investigation reaches a non-sensitive stage (Wetzling and Veith 2018: 91–8).

Governments would also need to place limits on the circumstances under which their SIGINT agencies use bulk surveillance. For instance, governments could forbid their agencies from using these powers to achieve economic advantages over other countries or their businesses, and prevent them from using SIGINT to discriminate against individuals or social groups. Public outrage about the Snowden revelations forced some changes in the US system, and led to then president Barack Obama to pass a US presidential policy directive on SIGINT that forbade the NSA from using SIGINT to suppress dissent, or disadvantage any person based on ethnicity, race, gender, sexual orientation or religion (The White House 2014).

Some countries, including the US and Sweden, do not leave SIGINT authorizations to the general court system, which generally operates in the open. Instead, they have set up special signals intelligence courts that consider applications to authorize SIGINT operations. However, these courts have their own drawbacks, as they operate largely in secret and – despite claims to being independent – are susceptible to capture by the very SIGINT agencies they preside over. An additional problem with these courts is that they rely on the flawed assumption that foreign communications should enjoy fewer privacy protections than local communications: an assumption that was roundly criticized in a German constitutional court judgement of international significance (Constitutional Court of Germany 2020). In fact, the Dutch system would be far more appropriate in that regard, in that it grants the same privacy protections to national and foreign communications (Wetzling and Veith 2018: 23).

However, even if governments institute these reforms, SIGINT agencies will be tempted to look for loopholes to circumvent them. One of these loopholes may involve intelligence sharing. While countries can and do share intelligence seemingly for sound reasons – such as to pool intelligence to solve transnational crimes or prevent global terrorism – the circumstances in which they do so are often shrouded in secrecy. In the case of the Five Eyes alliance, intelligence sharing can even go as far as allowing direct access to communication networks, sharing raw data and allowing access to databases. Countries can also engage in jurisdiction shopping, where one country could approach another country to collect intelligence for them on their own nationals to circumvent stringent domestic controls (Born et al. 2015: 33–40). The Snowden documents revealed how both NSA and GCHQ used their close relationship to task the other with SIGINT collection to bypass existing domestic controls. The Canadian SIGINT agency engaged in similar behaviour until it was prevented from doing so through a court judgement (Hopkins and Borger 2013; Farries and King 2018: 8–9).

In order to close these jurisdictional loopholes, as a rule, countries would need to reduce intelligence-sharing agreements to writing, release them publicly and debate them in parliament. Oversight bodies should subject these agreements and their implementation to scrutiny, and SIGINT agencies should not craft agreements that prevent oversight bodies from reviewing intelligence collected on the basis that third parties should not be allowed to access the intelligence shared. Furthermore, governments should not allow their SIGINT agencies to enter into agreements with countries that do not have minimum protections, such as prior judicial authorization for interceptions, independent controls and special protections for privileged information such as journalistic sources or lawyers' communications. No inbound intelligence that does not meet these standards should be accepted (Farries and King 2018; Born et al. 2015: 33–40).

The impossibility of SIGINT reforms, and anti-capitalist responses

While IP-based surveillance may be a technological capability that few countries in the southern Africa possess, anti-capitalists still need to grapple with how to view this capability and what to do with it. This is because the Snowden leaks made it clear that its uses have extended far beyond the high-minded objectives of protecting countries against terrorism and other national security threats, and into the grubbier realm of advancing national interests. In other words, IP-based surveillance has become a tool of imperialism and neocolonialism as well as nationalist populism. Snowden revealed several spying operations that amounted to espionage, where the British government and its Five Eyes partners used SIGINT surveillance to spy on African leaders and businesspeople, to give them competitive advantage in trade negotiations and business dealings, and consequently in the race for Africa's resources.

There can be little doubt that IP-based bulk surveillance is useful to intelligence agencies, and that they may well use these powers for legitimate national security operations. However, governments should not confer powers on intelligence agencies simply because they are useful. Arguably, agencies may find torture useful as an investigative method, for instance, but there are no circumstances in which torture should be condoned. Activists should not resign themselves to the 'reality' of the spy agencies having these powers, in much the same way that activists do not resign themselves to imperialism. As Snowden has argued: 'Mass surveillance is not about public safety, it is not about terrorism, it is about power. It is about economic espionage, it is about diplomatic manipulation, and it is about social influence, it is about understanding the actions of everyone in the world, no matter who they are and no matter how innocent their lives.'[12] Furthermore, the foreign policy errors of the Five Eyes countries in the wake of the September 11 attacks have contributed massively to the terrorism problem, destabilized the entire Middle East with disastrous consequences for global security and alienated entire populations from the imperialist powers. The fact that the invasion of Iraq was justified on the pretext of false intelligence (Taylor 2013) has also further delegitimized the intelligence agencies of these countries. It has also exposed the fact that the security problems in the Five Eyes countries are ultimately a creation of militarized and securitized foreign policy, and have earned them more enemies than they had already.

There are dangers in arguing that southern African countries such as South Africa, that do practice bulk IP surveillance, should lead by example and refrain from using these powers. Doing so would place the region at a competitive disadvantage in relation to the Five Eyes alliance. After all, these countries do not operate in a global intelligence environment of their own making, and they would be placed at a further disadvantage were they to cease using bulk surveillance, or aspire to acquire these powers to level the global playing field. It would mean that the Five Eyes alliance could continue to spy on these countries while they could not do so in return. One alternative could be for the BRICS group of countries to collaborate to set up an alternative Five Eyes to defend the global South from unchecked Five Eyes surveillance. This option is not far-fetched, as more southern African countries look to China and Russia on intelligence and surveillance matters. In fact, at one stage, the BRICS group aspired to establish an alternative internet infrastructure to the Five Eyes alliance. In response to the Snowden revelations, and spurred on by the fact that BRICS countries were major targets of NSA surveillance, Brazil and South Africa spearheaded the idea of building an undersea fibre-optic communications cable that would circumvent the US. The idea never came to fruition, partly because of the challenges of funding the project and partly because of political differences between the more democratically inclined BRICS countries and those that favoured a more state-led development path (Lee 2016). Not only are the BRICS countries constrained by fragile economic circumstances in the wake of the 2007–8 financial crisis, they are less politically united than the Five Eyes countries, making cooperation very difficult. In fact, other geopolitical constellations may overtake BRICS in the near future (Katz 2015: 76–7).

Given that the South African Constitutional Court has declared the operations of the NCC unconstitutional, it would be a good time to pause and reflect. Global South countries should not engage in this arms race at all. The more surveillance blocs are established, the more balkanized and weaponized the internet becomes. This outcome is almost inevitable in view of the authoritarian nationalist nature of most of the BRICS countries. Given emerging evidence of how southern African countries have used bulk surveillance powers already – as technologies to place whole domestic populations under surveillance to enforce domestic stability – it is not in the true interests of the broader mass of southern Africans to consider this option. It is not a principled argument, either. There should be no place in democratic societies of any stripe for untargeted bulk surveillance.

After all, it is important to bear the origins of SIGINT in mind. This form of surveillance evolved from a military environment, and intelligence agencies use it not just for defensive purposes but also for offensive purposes: the Snowden disclosures on southern Africa exposed this reality. Furthermore, the technologies that SIGINT agencies use are often weapons-grade and dual-use. Their deployment on the internet is eroding the internet's foundation as a free and open space and turning it into a weapon of cyber-warfare. If countries concede the legitimacy of this form of spying, then they also force other countries into an arms race where they seek these capabilities in order to keep up with the countries that have them. The only viable position to take is to champion disarmaments, including on the internet, The alternative will be too destabilizing, and inevitably to the advantage of the major surveillance powers and to the detriment of global South countries that will find it impossible to compete in the cyber-arms race. Anti-capitalists have long recognized that, ultimately, disarmament rather than greater weaponization will make the world a safer and more stable place.

As has been argued in this chapter, any anti-surveillance activist work around bulk surveillance needs to take the diversity of mass surveillance practices into account, and develop strategies that are relevant to a region like southern Africa. One particularly controversial surveillance measure that is not present in the US system though – and in fact that has been rejected in several global North countries – is SIM card registration. This practice is overwhelmingly a global South one: activists could politicize this fact. Anti-capitalists should oppose SIM card registration, as it is a form of mass surveillance with limited utility in crime fighting. After all, overwhelmingly the process targets innocents rather than criminals, as criminals are likely to find creative workarounds to the registration system. So unreliable has the registration process become in South Africa, for instance, that the South African Police Service (SAPS) have admitted openly that they cannot rely on the system to identify criminals (Duncan 2018: 95–6; Swart 2016). Boycotting SIM card registration could be a powerful political mobilizing tool, but only if there is a critical mass of people behind the campaigns: otherwise, being cut off from the network for failing to register a SIM card will be a politically symbolic, but ultimately self-defeating, act. Other forms of bulk surveillance widely in practice in the global South, such as mandatory data retention for long periods, should be opposed, as they too target innocent and criminal suspects alike. Instead, targeted preservation orders could ensure that communication service providers store only that data where someone is reasonably suspected of having committed a crime.

It is extremely tricky, and potentially dangerous, for activists to engage governments or intelligence agencies on the operational effectiveness of bulk surveillance, given the huge information asymmetries between them. Doing so shifts the argument onto a terrain where the agencies have the upper hand. Nevertheless, it is important for activists not to take the operational arguments at face value. Even former NSA intelligence official William Binney has disputed the effectiveness of these powers, pointing out that what the agencies may tout as bulk surveillance successes – thwarting planned terrorism attacks, for instance – are in fact successes achieved through a more targeted approach, where the agencies already knew who the people of interest were (Goodwin 2016). In fact, an overreliance on bulk surveillance may prevent intelligence agencies from uncovering criminal activities, as criminals may choose to 'go dark' and not use communication networks to plan their attacks, to prevent detection. Yet, given the huge industry that has grown up around bulk surveillance, and the powerful interests at work in ensuring that intelligence agencies rely increasingly on SIGINT surveillance, it may be difficult for them to concede that these powers are overhyped. I will discuss the growth of the surveillance industry and the relevance of this expansion for southern Africa in the next chapter.

Chapter 5

THE GLOBAL TRADE IN SPYWARE

Introduction

Southern African countries face a major surveillance problem, and one of the main contributors to this problem is the global surveillance industry. The UK, Europe, the US, China and Israel have exported some of the most invasive surveillance equipment in existence to southern Africa. Yet, they have shown little interest in the fate of this equipment, the uses to which it is being put and any oversight of its uses. According to Privacy International's Surveillance Industry Index (Privacy International 2016b), these countries have sold surveillance equipment to South Africa, Namibia, Zambia, Eswatini, Seychelles, Mauritius, Mozambique, Democratic Republic of the Congo, Botswana and Angola. It is more than likely that southern African countries have obtained other surveillance equipment, too, but there has been no systematic attempt to document sales to the region, including from countries that do not appear prominently in the Surveillance Industry Index, such as China.

In this chapter, I examine how the global trade in surveillance technologies reproduces and reinforces neocolonial and imperialist relationships cemented during southern Africa's past. When analysing the worldwide expansion of surveillance practices and industries, it becomes apparent that they follow a well-recognized economic geography, reproducing and reinforcing patterns of global power established during earlier periods of imperial conquest and colonization. I will look at how the surveillance industry has grown massively and consolidated over the past two decades, and converged with the armaments industry. This consolidation and convergence has created the industrial basis for the mass production of dual-use surveillance technologies, and their export to southern Africa with hardly any proper controls on how these tools are used. I will examine the diffusion of the most popular surveillance tools in the region, and the major importers and exporters. I will look at the uneven development of surveillance capabilities globally as a feature of surveillance imperialism, and the role of the BRICS alliance of countries. Most southern African countries have become net importers of surveillance technologies, with only South Africa enjoying an industrial base to manufacture and export these technologies. I will examine what can be done about the global trade in spyware, and how tactics and strategies used by anti-war and disarmament movements could be applied to activist work in this area.

Drivers of the global trade in spyware

In order to understand why governments and other surveillance actors have pursued expansive surveillance 'solutions' to criminal and national security threats, boosting the global trade in surveillance technologies or spyware, it is important to understand the factors driving these decisions. The push factors are self-evident. Smarting from some of the most recent significant intelligence failures of recent history, agencies such as MI5, GCHQ and the NSA have sought ways of improving their intelligence gathering and analysis capabilities. Investing in more technically sophisticated forms of surveillance, such as SIGINT and more specifically COMINT, is deeply attractive, as it reduces the need to rely on costly, risky HUMINT. Agencies also think that technologically enabled analysis will introduce an element of objectivity to intelligence work, as they can reduce the more subjective human factor.

However, less well understood are the pull factors driving the take-up of communication surveillance. Over the decades, an entire surveillance industry has grown up with a stake in creating markets for their equipment. In the 1970s, the number of communication surveillance companies started to grow, reaching an all-time peak in 2000, in response to the growth in the number of surveillance laws demanding private sector collaboration in surveillance. The passing of CALEA in the US and the development of the ETSI standards, and the spreading of these standards throughout the world (see Chapter 3), created a huge market for lawful interception equipment and explained the proliferation of companies just before the September 11 attacks. Declining military budgets also forced the arms industry to look elsewhere for markets, and the civilian security sector provided it with a potentially huge market. Producers of surveillance equipment also recognized the power of consulting for governments, in the process creating revolving doors between industry and government that were replete with conflicts of interest: a case in point being former NSA director Mike McConnell, who later became Vice-Chairman of Snowden's former employer, Booz Allen Hamilton (Bellamy Foster and McChesney 2014). These factors created conditions for the development of an industrial base for surveillance, allowing for its rapid expansion.

Curiously enough, though, after the September 11 attacks, the number of surveillance companies declined (Privacy International 2016b: 18). This decline is evident from Privacy International's work, which draws not only on Wikileaks revelations about surveillance companies but on a list of dual-use technologies developed by countries subscribing to a multilateral agreement to promote greater transparency and accountability in international sales of arms (known as the Wassenaar Arrangement on Export Controls for Conventional Arms and Dual-Use Goods and Technologies). Countries that sign onto the agreement should apply these controls domestically. The Wassenaar Arrangement is a voluntary reporting mechanism for tracking the export of conventional arms and dual-use technologies, to prevent destabilizing accumulations. Most major arms exporting countries are signatories. Participating states in the Wassenaar Arrangement should apply export controls to all arms listed on control lists, which are updated on a regular basis. South Africa is the only participating African state, having joined in 2006 (Department of International Relations and Cooperation n.d.). Governments should implement these control lists through national legislation, preventing them from using surveillance equipment for repressive purposes. In the wake of the Snowden revelations, participating states updated the control lists to include IP-based mass surveillance equipment and intrusion software (or hacking tools), which means that they have to report on their exports. A full 86 per cent of Western surveillance companies are located in countries that subscribe to the Wassenaar Arrangement, which makes this agreement important in the fight to control the spread of surveillance technologies. However, according to Amnesty International, the surveillance industry has continued to grow despite the tightening of export controls, and evidence of abuses of its equipment continues to mount (Amnesty International 2019: 5).

There are different kinds of communication surveillance systems, which could be grouped into the following categories: mobile telecommunications interception equipment (or IMSI catchers), intrusion or hacking software, IP network surveillance systems, data retention systems, lawful interception systems, monitoring centres and digital forensic systems (Bromley 2016). Categories Four and Five of the list of controlled goods in terms of the Wassenaar Arrangement cover computers and telecommunications. In 2013, shortly after the initial release of the Snowden documents, participating countries updated the Arrangement with important amendments. These incorporated IP-based surveillance systems and intrusion software into the lists. The Arrangement does not apply necessarily to the surveillance technologies as such, but to the products designed to facilitate their use or enable the infection of devices by intrusion software (Anderson 2015). The Arrangement has been updated to require the control of other surveillance equipment such as IMSI catchers (Omanovic 2015). However, the Wassenaar Arrangement does not cover surveillance technologies such as monitoring centres, lawful interception systems, data retention systems or digital forensics. Consequently, they are under-represented in government reports about surveillance imports and exports.

The US and the UK have become the major providers of surveillance equipment, followed by France, Germany and Israel, and most of these are top defence exporters as well. Between 2008 and 2014, software and technology, or Category Four and Five items, accounted for approximately 5 per cent of the total value of the UK's dual-use exports, vastly overshadowing the value of dual-use goods (Directorate General for External Policies Policy Department 2015: 25). Four per cent of companies that featured in the Surveillance Industry Index are also major arms producers, including BAE Systems (UK), Boeing (US) and Elbit Systems (Israel). Between 2008 and 2014, the majority of controlled exports from the UK were category 5 goods, accounting for some 66 per cent of control entries, with a steady increase until 2012, a massive spike in 2013, followed by a decline in 2015. This decline did not necessarily signal a reduction in sales of surveillance equipment, though: on the contrary, the decline was a sign of the industry's consolidation. Increasingly, large multinational conventional arms manufacturers ramped up their production of surveillance equipment as markets for their more conventional armaments shrank. Since the Second World War, the world has experienced an unprecedented period of peace. Consequently, governments have cut back military spending, and these realities have forced arms manufacturers to seek new markets to restore profitability (Perlo-Freeman et al. 2016). While the US ramped up its military spending in the wake of the September 11 attacks, its withdrawal from 'theatres of war' like Iraq impacted negatively on arms manufacturers, as did the reduction in military spending of other governments in the wake of the 2007–8 global recession (Weigley 2013). Governments remain the biggest customers for arms, though, and they have a stake in keeping their own defence industries alive as they can make significant contributions to gross domestic product (Beckett 2015).

In attempting to adapt to this changing global situation, some of the major arms manufacturers increased their involvement in the lucrative and ever-expanding surveillance and cybersecurity markets (Boulanin 2013). A case in point is BAE Systems, which has expanded the intelligence and cybersecurity aspects of its business from the late 2000s onwards, acquiring existing businesses in this area. The company intensified this focus as it experienced declining revenues owing to the falling demand for conventional armaments (Durham 2015: 74). Arms manufacturer Lockheed Martin expanded its activities to include providing intelligence gathering and analysis capacities to the CIA and other US government agencies, and even to commercial retail giant Walmart to spy on critics of its corporate practices (Durham 2015: 52). Another French company, Thales, traditionally a conventional arms manufacturer, also branched out into the communications surveillance business, but it was less agile than other companies in creating much-needed local partnerships. These partnerships were necessary for companies to develop tailored local security solutions for country-specific needs, instead of expecting them to purchase off-the-shelf technology. Arms companies saw the partnership approach as being essential for survival in 'developing country' contexts in the face of cutbacks to armaments spending by Western governments (Hoyos 2013).

Like the arms industry, the surveillance industry has become more concentrated. While there has been a proliferation of surveillance technology companies, a few have come to dominate the market. Some have emerged from arms manufacturers as they branched out into dual-use goods and software, others emerged as branches or subsidiaries of telecommunications companies, and some were start-ups. Some of the most prominent with known footprints in southern Africa are as follows:

- BAE Systems is a British arms manufacturer that has branched out into producing dual-use technologies, including surveillance equipment, from the late 2000s onwards. It is one of the world's largest manufacturers. Most of its sales go to the UK, the US and Saudi Arabia (Campaign Against Arms Trade 2020). The company intensified its focus on these sectors as it experienced declining revenues owing to the falling demand for conventional arms (Durham 2015: 74).

- Elaman is a German provider of security equipment, which focuses on providing marketing and consulting services for clients with surveillance needs. It also formed a partnership with the surveillance equipment producer Gamma Group to offer security services, and opened up offices in a number of countries (Elaman n.d.).

- The Gamma Group is a multinational company specializing in the provision of surveillance hardware, software and training. Its most famous (or notorious) product was the Finfisher suite of surveillance products, but Finfisher has been spun off into a separate company called Finfisher GmbH, a German branch of the Gamma Group. Finfisher is intrusion software that enables its users to perform deep packet inspection of data traffic, allowing penetration of all layers of internet traffic right through to the deepest layer of all, namely, the content of data packets as they are transmitted across the internet. While deep packet inspection provides invaluable tools for network service providers to analyse how the internet is being used and to counter spam, viruses and other online ills, it can also be used to place surveillances software on a person's computer or mobile phone to track their activities and even take control of their devices (Fuchs 2013). Worryingly, Finfisher has been sold to authoritarian governments such as Ethiopia, Egypt and Uganda, and has been used for political surveillance purposes.

- The Hacking Team is headquartered in Italy. This company provides what they call 'offensive technology' to law enforcement and intelligence agencies. As people who wish to maintain the privacy of their communications increasingly use encryption, more intelligence agencies are using offensive equipment interference, and this company specializes in providing equipment for these purposes. Their products allow their clients to monitor and manipulate target computers remotely by activating cameras and microphones, as well as by logging keystrokes, extracting passwords and other measures (Hacking Team n.d.). In a stroke of irony, the company itself was hacked, resulting in massive amounts of sensitive internal information being dumped on the internet. This hack revealed that repressive governments were among its major clients, leading to the Italian government revoking the company's global export licence (Omanovic n.d.). Hacking Team software has been detected in several African countries, but mainly in North Africa where they appear to have more market penetration than their competitor, Finfisher.

- The French company Amesys has been around for many years, but has come into its own with the burgeoning market in surveillance equipment, and is a subsidiary of the much older computer company Groupe Bull. The company became controversial when investigative journalists revealed that the company had provided Muammar Gaddafi's Libyan government with surveillance equipment to spy on political dissidents in the wake of the Arab Spring (the wave of protests that spread across the Middle East and North Africa from 2010 onwards) (Sonne and Coker 2011). A German supplier of surveillance equipment, Trovicor (formerly a branch of Siemens, which unbundled its lawful interception activities into this company), has also been exposed for having provided equipment to several countries in North Africa and the Middle East (Timm 2012).

- American company Blue Coat provides a variety of surveillance technologies to manage network threats and encrypted traffic, including by decrypting it (Blue Coat n.d.). Authoritarian governments have used their equipment, including in Syria. These revelations prompted media freedom organization Reporteurs sans Frontiers to label Blue Coat, Trovicor, Amesys, Hacking Team and Gamma 'enemies of the internet' for allowing their products to be used in repressive contexts (Reporteurs sans Frontiers 2012).

- Verint Systems provides a multitude of security and intelligence products and services, including data mining software for law enforcement and intelligence purposes. It is a multinational company headquartered in the US, although many of its employees are located in its cyber-intelligence unit in Israel (Verint n.d.).

- NSO Group is an Israeli technology group established by former military college graduates, and owned by its management team and founders after a buy-out from a US company, Francisco Partners (NSO Group 2019). The group sells surveillance equipment to intelligence and law enforcement agencies. They claim to sell only to government agencies investigating terrorism and other serious crimes (NSO Group n.d.). They market a highly controversial intrusion software product, Pegasus, which allows the operator to hack a user's device and take control of it without detection. Citizenlab has detected Pegasus in forty-five countries, and has been linked to a range of human rights abuses (Al Jazeera 2020). In southern Africa, they have identified the presence of Pegasus in South Africa and Zambia (Marczak et al. 2018).

- The Chinese company ZTE Corporation is based in Shenzen and is a leading provider of telecommunications equipment and software. ZTE produces phone and internet monitoring equipment and monitoring centres that provide one-stop-shop monitoring solutions to countries. The company is reported to have sold a monitoring centre to the Mozambiquan military (de Fundo 2016).

Some countries are responding to the demand for surveillance capabilities by becoming producers and exporters of niche products, especially countries that have not dominated the arms industry historically, but whose production capacities could expand if they found markets for their products. Israel and, to a lesser extent, South Africa have emerged as competitors for the 'developing country' market share, whose surveillance capabilities are typically less well regulated than those of 'developed country' markets. Security experts in mid-sized military powers like Israel are attempting to position themselves by monetizing skills gained in warfare against opponents of their continued occupation of Palestinian land (Kane 2016). In fact, Israel has the highest number of surveillance companies per capita as its own military-industrial complex has become an incubator for surveillance start-ups. The country's lack of controls over the transfer of security knowledge from the public to private sectors makes the commercialization of military knowledge possible (Kane 2016).

BRICS as a facilitator of surveillance

Given the dominance of the Five Eyes alliance, underpinned by the aggressive expansion of supporting surveillance industries, it was inevitable that influential countries outside the alliance would explore alternatives to a US-dominated communication system. Yet, there is little reason to believe that the alternatives that have emerged, or were attempted, are politically progressive. Where progressive proposals have emerged, they have not necessarily found favour with the most globally powerful alternative actors, namely, China and Russia, even if these proposals emerged from within the BRICS network. For instance, when Brazil and Germany proposed the establishment of a United Nations Special Rapporteur on Privacy in the wake of the Snowden revelations – given that citizens of both countries found themselves caught in the Five Eyes dragnet – South Africa failed to support this proposal. South Africa, China and Russia also supported a substantial dilution of a UN resolution on the protection and promotion of human rights on the internet. In the past, South Africa has avoided supporting resolutions promoted by the former colonial powers, even if a question of principle is at stake. Former South African ambassador Dumisani Kumalo captured this sentiment thus in 2009: 'We didn't do things the way the British and the Americans wanted us to do them, and if you don't do it like the big ones, the French and the Americans and the British, the way they want to do them, then you are a cheeky African. Well, I am happy being a cheeky African' (VOA News 2009; Davis 2015). In fact, by 2017, South Africa displayed one of the lowest voting coincidences with the US at the UN (US Department of State 2018). Rather than playing an anti-imperialist role, increasingly South Africa is playing a sub-imperialist role on surveillance, mouthing anti-imperialist rhetoric while itself engaging in and benefitting from the very imperialist surveillance practices it has criticized the North for. It is a small wonder that South Africa has aligned itself the most consistently with those other BRICS countries that are most likely to display sub-imperial tendencies, namely, China and Russia.

It is not surprising that the BRICS countries failed to take a principled anti-surveillance stand against mass surveillance in the wake of the Snowden disclosures: they, too, stood to cash in on the burgeoning industry. Little is known of surveillance companies outside the US and Europe like China and Russia, but what has become clear is that BRICS countries are becoming increasingly important producers and exporters of surveillance doctrine and technologies. Furthermore, mid-sized countries that have not dominated the arms industry, but whose production capacities could expand if they found markets for their products, have their eyes trained firmly on 'developing country' markets. While South Africa's surveillance industry is not as well developed as Israel's, like Israel, it too is vying for this same market. Possibly the most prominent (and controversial) South African company that has established itself as a player in this market is Vastech, which received government start-up funding. While claiming to provide surveillance products to legitimate law enforcement and intelligence agencies,[1] and only those that are not subject to UN sanctions (as so many of the surveillance manufacturers claim to do), their powerful surveillance equipment was sold to Libya and was reportedly used to monitor activists opposing the government of then-president Muammar Gaddafi (Groenewald 2011: 2).

Claudio Katz has argued that China's ascent to the status of global superpower is unlikely to lead to inter-imperialist rivalry, because China is aware of its still-subordinate role in the global political economy. Consequently, the world's second-largest economy is unwilling to confront the US. In other words, China is content with playing the role of regional police officer in Africa, providing local elites with the technological capabilities to stabilize politics and repress protests. When China has developed military and surveillance capabilities, it has done so to protect its borders and police its own and neighbouring populations. According to Katz, 'China inundates the planet with capital and products, but not with armies or covert operatives. It maintains a defensive attitude in the face of periodic harassment by US administrations, building up its surveillance and defensive capabilities' (Katz 2015: 74). Russia, on the other hand, maintains a more belligerent military/security apparatus, which is not under the control of US imperialism (Katz 2015: 80). However, the reality in southern Africa tells a somewhat different story.

Southern Africa has also proved to be very open for business when it comes to technologies that could be used for data exploitation and surveillance purposes, with China acting as an increasingly important provider, to the point of eclipsing the Five Eyes countries and Europe. Smart cities present BRICS communications companies with massive markets for their wares. These cities use digital technologies to promote urban development and meet urbanization challenges such as providing efficient transportation and traffic control, as well as other services that could benefit from the deployment of smart technologies connected to the internet. Smart cities have become controversial for commodifying digital spaces, exploiting citizens' data without their consent, reinforcing spatial inequalities and undermining their right to protect their data. Urban residents in smart cities are vulnerable to digital exploitation by a small group of private companies, as well as government and private sector surveillance. To the extent that these dangers exist, then residents have a right to claim what Joe Shaw and Mark Graham, drawing on Henri Lefebvre, have termed an informational right to the city. In claiming this right, they can disagree with how smart city infrastructure is being rolled out and controlled, especially by big multinational companies such as Google, and assert the right to re-appropriate and self-manage information that is generated in the smart city for the benefit of residents (Shaw and Graham 2017).

Governments and private companies involved in smart city delivery have an unfortunate tendency of promoting smart cities in technologically determinist ways: in other words, in their justifications they assume that digital technologies will automatically create social progress. Yet, all too often, smart city service providers enclose cities and appropriate their infrastructure and services for commercial exploitation. This these providers do by claiming the right to own the data that they generate, while not allowing the people who generate the data to access the data. Rather, residents should be sufficiently empowered to prevent companies from profiting from their participation in various platforms. They should also be in a position to demand transparency around what happens to their data and access to their own data so that they can use it in collectively managed projects for the common good, and insist on security for their data to prevent it from being hacked, or used for uncontrolled surveillance. Residents should also know how the data generated in the city is creating value and who the ultimate beneficiaries of that value are. Residents should claim the right to shape the city as an inclusive city that benefits them in terms of its design principles. Cities must be required to audit the various ways in which they generate data, and how these data sets can be used to promote a generalized right to the city. Asserting self-control over the circumstances in which residents' data is used can turn them from smart subjects into smart citizens. Public information intermediaries can incorporate local knowledge into the smart city, and package that local knowledge for the benefit of the city as a whole, in the process creating a more fulfilling and less alienating urban environment (Sadoway and Shekhar 2014).

In the age of the IoT, where everyday equipment emits data whether residents like it or not, they should also have the right to demand the rollout of technologies – such as in relation to electronic tolling or electricity provision – that incorporate privacy by design principles, and not just accept the most privacy insensitive technologies. Residents also need the right to opt in or opt out of data intensive initiatives, and demand the right to know about the logics applied to their data if it is processed using Artificial Intelligence (AI). Harnessing the benefits of AI in the smart city environment will most likely be possible only once its creators and users recognize it as a public or community utility, and the data that it processes is recognized as a commons rather than as a form of capital. An example of an experiment in reconceptualizing the smart city along public lines is Barcelona. The city council has used the struggle for Catalonian self-determination to reimagine what a smart city could look like. They have encouraged residents to take control of their data and, to this end, have experimented using AI to improve air quality through a non-market cooperative project (Calzada and Almirall 2019)

However, these basic democratic rights and freedoms are a pipe dream for residents of more and more southern African cities, where governments are turning to smart city initiatives as ways of retooling failing infrastructure and attracting foreign investment. Companies like the Chinese Huawei are making these initiatives easier to roll out by offering municipalities 'smart cities in a box', providing them with a complete set of solutions to set up and run smart cities. Southern Africa is particularly attractive for the company as the lack of data protection rules allows it to exploit data relatively unhindered. According to Edwin Diender, Vice-President, Government and Public Utility Sector, Huawei Enterprise Business Group: 'Europe is almost over-regulated, making it very difficult to proceed swiftly, compared to South Africa. In fact, if Amsterdam and Johannesburg were to compete in implementing a particular smart solution, I believe Johannesburg could easily win the race' (Van Dijk n.d.). Johannesburg and Cape Town have signalled their intentions to become smart cities, in spite of the fact that the country's data protection law, the Protection of Personal Information Act, and the privacy/information regulator it establishes, is only starting to come into force. In other words, the rollout of smart technologies is running far ahead of policy, which means that there has been little to prevent Huawei from cashing on in the practically unregulated market for peoples' data.

China has also become a major exporter of 'smart' CCTV cameras loaded with facial recognition technology, typically rolled out as part of smart city initiatives, used domestically for authoritarian purposes, to publicly identify, name and shame jaywalkers. As facial recognition and other smart technologies such as Automatic Number Plate Recognition become more prevalent on our streets, commuters will be less and less able to move around anonymously. These technologies can be (and have been) used to track and identify people leading protests, for instance. However, China has struggled to optimize its penetration of African markets, as facial recognition software is not calibrated to recognize African faces, heightening the potential for misrecognition of African people caught on 'smart' CCTV cameras. The solution of at least one Chinese company has been to enter into a partnership with the Zimbabwean government to provide a mass facial recognition programme, and in the process to allow it to train racial biases out of its algorithms (Hawkins 2018). As Nompilo Simanje argued in relation to Zimbabwe:

The surveillance tools and equipment has always been coming from China. You know through Cloudwalk technologies, through Huawei, through ZTE, and China as a country has a very bad precedent for authoritarian rule, for surveillance. There are so many elements of a repressive nature associated with China as a country. From a broader, global perspective, I think one of the key aspects for me is that we should always ensure that any surveillance tools or equipment, before they are exported to any country, that country has robust policies and laws for the protection of privacy and data. I think that is key, because currently in Zimbabwe, we don't have a data protection framework. Of course, it was proposed through a Cyber Bill, but there's still lots of work to be done. Every country that receives surveillance equipment, it should be a legal obligation that such country should have a robust framework for data protection and protection of privacy. What that also means is that even the exporting country should also be obligated to fully inquire and ensure that such mechanisms are in place.[2]

Surveillance exporting countries know that countries such as Zimbabwe lack vigorous data protection frameworks. Consequently, southern Africa has become a region to cash in on, mimicking the extractive practices of historical colonialism where commercial companies facilitated by governments appropriate data for commercial and political purposes (Milan and Treré 2019; Couldry and Meijas 2019: 337). These practices qualify as data colonialism, where data exchange between the region and increasingly powerful surveillance powers like China is inherently unequal, and involves governments and commercial companies surveilling and exploiting the data of marginalized groups (Mann and Daly 2019), who in the case of southern Africa are overwhelmingly Black.

Not all citizens of the region take smart cities and their surveillance potential for granted, though. Some push back. A case in point is Mauritius, where the smart city concept has been adapted as a safe city project to use digital technologies and intelligent systems to enhance public safety, in addition to providing services. The government claims that the project is needed to protect national security and public security, and incorporates several technology-driven systems to enhance intelligence gathering and enable more proactive policing. The Mauritian government commenced with the project in 2017, which involves the installation of thousands of CCTV cameras with 'smart' capabilities. In other words, these cameras incorporate features allowing them to collect and transmit huge quantities of data for further analysis by computers. The camera feeds are fed to a centralized command and control centre based in Ebene, the country's first cyber city established following the conclusion of a partnership with India. The centre analyses the feed for a range of law enforcement and traffic management functions (Republic of Mauritius 2020: 26–32).

According to Prime Minister Pravind Jugnauth, in the two years of its existence the CCTV system had detected numerous crimes that required police intervention, such as larceny, drug dealing and possession, assault, murder, and others. The government also planned to introduce facial recognition capabilities to these cameras; however, as in many parts of the world, the technological plans were running ahead of legislative controls to prevent abuses. Citizen concerns about the unchecked surveillance potential became so strong that members of parliament questioned the president in parliament about the effectiveness of data protection safeguards. Mauritius has a Data Protection Act: however, the government exempted the Safe City Project from the act, presumably on national security grounds. The president insisted that police processing of data is governed by an internal code of practice, which led to its release being demanded in the parliamentary debate (Republic of Mauritius 2020: 26–32).

Mauritius had a relatively low level of public consciousness about surveillance; however, when the government announced plans to introduce a smart ID card in 2013, public opposition to the scheme grew. Citizens feared misuse of their personal data for government mass surveillance (see Chapter 7). The struggle led to a partial decommissioning of the smart ID card system, but it also left a more enduring legacy in that public consciousness grew massively about the dangers of surveillance. Workers began to object to everyday forms of surveillance, such as cameras on their work buses and providing fingerprints at workplaces (Duncan 2018: 65). The partially victorious struggle against smart ID cards laid the ground for the struggle against smart and safe cities, as the former had turned surveillance into a mass issue. According to Rajni Lallah, an activist with the Mauritian socialist organization Lalit du Klas, unknown individuals took direct action against smart CCTV cameras and decommissioned them. This occurred after public debates about their effectiveness in actually bringing down crime, and these actions were a culmination of a growing consciousness about the true purposes of surveillance. Lallah explained:

> The amount of consciousness about electronic databases, about electronic surveillance, has grown from almost nil in the country, to a greater level of awareness about this, to an extent where now there's a big debate about safe city cameras. There are 4,000 of them in Mauritius on the streets everywhere. There have been questions in parliament about where the biometric photographs would be used to identify people, and the answers have not been very clear. It seems like it could be in the pipelines, or later. And there is a question about what the safe city cameras are supposed to be for, and this has become very much a debate . . . The good news is that, as time goes by, many of these cameras stopped working, and are not replaced. Sometimes it's a deliberate form of decommissioning. There have been many reports where people actually decommissioned them.[3]

Surveillance imports and exports in southern Africa

Leo Panitch has argued that the most salient conflicts in the world today are class conflicts within countries, rather than interstate conflict, with the most serious interstate conflicts having receded after the Second World War (Panitch 2015: 67). The US came to dominate world affairs, with other countries largely becoming facilitators of their expansion along neoliberal lines. Very few, if any, countries were willing to enter into direct military conflict with the US. Instead, the BRICS countries have shown themselves to be more than willing to administer US-style neoliberal policies forcefully within their own countries, thereby acting as regional policemen for a form of global capitalism that reinforces rather than challenges US hegemony (Bond 2015). Independence lifted those with petty bourgeois aspirations up into a full bourgeoisie, using national populism which eventually reverted to authoritarian nationalism as the pretext to realize and maintain their class aspirations (Mandaza 1986: 51). At the same time, class formation in southern Africa has followed a complicated path, with many countries in the region continuing to have underdeveloped working classes, with a large rural peasantry, despite the fact that former liberation movements–turned–governing parties such as FRELIMO attempted to proletarianize through rapid modernization and industrialization, but with authoritarian, vanguardist tendencies (Saul 2005: 39). These geopolitical realities increased the potential for these countries to use surveillance against their own people rather than foreign threats. As discussed in Chapter 2, Africa experienced a massive wave of anti-austerity protests in the wake of the 2007–8 global financial crisis. In fact, the crisis affected the continent particularly severely, as many countries export basic goods and import processed products, in addition to having their natural resources exploited, which made them susceptible to economic shocks as commodities markets shrank (Katz 2015: 85). New actors took to the streets with diverse and, at times, contradictory and incoherent demands. There was also a broader range of actors than was the case in anti-austerity protests elsewhere. These uncertainties created a demand for surveillance tools to enable ruling elites to map the actors and identify emerging leaders. However, mass surveillance did not appear to be the surveillance strategy of choice in many countries in the region, as they suspected who their targets of interest were. Consequently, there is evidence of a major uptick in procurements of surveillance tools enabling targeted equipment interference (or hacking).

If China and Russia do develop ambitions to become full imperialist powers, then more confrontational inter-imperialist relationships may emerge, and Africa may well become an important theatre of conflict as the scramble for the continent's resources intensifies. In line with their ambitions to provide geopolitical alternatives to Western (especially US) hegemony, and not content to export surveillance technologies only, China and Russia have become very active in exporting intelligence doctrine and surveillance technologies. While China appears to focus more on exporting surveillance technologies, Russia has focused more narrowly on using the state to protect its business interests abroad (Pozo 2015: 206–27). As discussed in Chapter 2, when faced with mounting social protests, former liberation movements in government adopted wholesale the intelligence doctrine of the 'colour revolution', associated most closely with Russia. In Zimbabwe, China also sponsored the establishment of an intelligence academy (Nehanda Radio 2011). This support suggests that China's interests extend far beyond exporting surveillance goods, and into influencing intelligence doctrine by controlling the training of future generations of intelligence officers. If this is the case, then it appears that China is not restricting itself to a diplomatic, 'soft power' approach towards relations with Zimbabwe, but setting the basis for a shift to 'hard power', where it confronts US hegemony more directly.

It is difficult to assess the value of imports of military-grade spyware to sub-Saharan Africa: a calculation that may be impossible to arrive at, as budgets are spread across military, law enforcement and civilian intelligence agencies. Nevertheless, the region is not exactly the most lucrative region of the world for the defence industry; in fact, overall it has the lowest military expenditure of all world regions (Stockholm International Peace Research Institute 2019a) A drill-down into the defence budgets of southern African countries reveals some intriguing anomalies. By 2018, and inexplicably for a country with high levels of peace and freedom and its small population of approximately 2.6 million people, Namibia had the highest military expenditure per GDP in southern Africa, at 3.3 per cent. Another country with relative peace and stability and an even smaller population, Botswana, has the second highest, at 2.8 per cent of GDP (Stockholm International Peace Research Institute 2019a).

The largest provider of military assistance in the world is the US, and Israel and Egypt are its biggest recipients. Priority countries in southern Africa are the DRC (most US assistance is channelled into peacekeeping), followed by Angola (non-proliferation, counterterrorism and de-mining), South Africa (narcotics and law enforcement, cooperative threat reduction and non-proliferation, anti-terrorism and de-mining) and Mozambique (non-proliferation, counterterrorism and de-mining).[4] The US sells fewer arms to southern African than to any other region of the world, with a mere 0.27 per cent of its sales going to the region, as compared to its biggest exporting region, the Middle East and North Africa, which accounts for 57.29 per cent of its sales.[5] It has made the largest number of sales to South Africa, followed by Angola, with most being direct commercial sales. This means that these markets are still relatively untapped, and the huge budgets per GDP of countries like Botswana and Namibia could become very attractive in an increasingly competitive market.

The export control reforms in the wake of the Snowden revelations have thrown up some information about military-grade exports from Europe and the US to southern Africa. Most of the information relates to sales of IMSI catchers, with only one entry for IP monitoring equipment and none for intrusion software. Privacy International's Surveillance Industry Index lists four approved sales to South Africa. These were a highly sophisticated IMSI catcher, capable of voice recognition, provided by Verint under mysterious circumstances that at the time of writing remained the subject of a criminal prosecution (Sole and Evans 2016); an IMSI catcher from an undisclosed company in Switzerland in 2015; another IMSI catcher from an undisclosed supplier in the UK and a sale of IP surveillance equipment by the Danish subsidiary of BAE Systems (manufacturers of the highly invasive Evident system). The Campaign Against Arms Trade lists the approval of three IMSI catchers by the UK to South Africa, three to Namibia between 2015 and 2016, and three to Botswana in 2016, although the companies involved are not known. Mozambique bought a monitoring centre from ZTE. Finfisher has been detected on servers in South Africa and Angola, and Blue Coat products have been detected in South Africa, Zambia and Mauritius.

Yet, as discussed in previous chapters, no real regulatory frameworks exist for these highly invasive forms of surveillance. However, these lacunae did not stop these sales from being approved, raising serious questions about the extent of due diligence practised by governments when they sell surveillance equipment to other governments. For instance, the US has sold IMSI catchers to Namibia despite the controversies in Namibia about whether or not interceptions are taking place extra-judicially – a controversy that has even reached the attention of the UN Human Rights Committee. However, he available information about their uses (discussed in Chapter 4) suggests misuse of this equipment in internal factional battles in the ruling SWAPO. No country in southern Africa has committed their law enforcement and intelligence agencies to using IMSI catchers pursuant to a warrant, but governments continue to sell IMSI catchers to the region. Even more worryingly, countries that are not signatories to the Wassenaar Arrangement, such as Israel and China, on all available accounts appear to be very active in exporting surveillance equipment, and Angola is a case in point. According to Rui Verde,

> Nowadays it appears that most of the technology, and even the craft [of surveillance] comes from Israel, from some retired officials from Israel. Apparently, what happens when they retire from Mossad [the Israeli intelligence agency responsible for foreign intelligence collection], they create private companies, and they sell their hardware to African countries. Apparently it happens a lot in the RDC [Democratic Republic of the Congo], and a lot even in Angola. For instance, the last surveillance of Rafael Marques, that was a very big operation, was made with Israeli technology.[6]

It would appear that governments' commercial interests in selling surveillance technologies have made them blind, deaf and dumb to the abuses in the region, and the lack of controls make abuse a near certainty.

(Under)regulating the global trade in spyware

Increasingly, the Wassenaar Arrangement is encouraging governments to take the human rights and fundamental freedoms of the recipient countries into account before exporting to them, and not just focus on not exporting to countries subjected to sanctions (Wassenaar Arrangement 2019). They are urging countries to look at whether these technologies violate privacy or enable repressive measures such as persecution, unwarranted arrests, torture or execution (Bromley 2017). The Arab Spring saw the widespread misuse of surveillance technologies, and those events combined with the abuses disclosed by Snowden have increased the pressure on exporting countries to take these concerns seriously.

As discussed in the previous section, spyware continues to be sold to southern African countries, and exported by South Africa to other countries, with little evidence of concern for how it is used, and with little regard to the inadequate safeguards to prevent abuses in the region. So why is the surveillance industry booming if it is being subjected to unprecedented export controls? One of the problems is that the Wassenaar Arrangement is voluntary. It does not have the status of a legally binding treaty, which means that countries can choose whether and how to codify the agreement into domestic law. There are no sanctions for violations of the Arrangement. As former UN Special Rapporteur on the Promotion and Protection of the Right to Freedom of Opinion and Expression David Kaye has pointed out, while the Arrangement is useful as it brings more transparency to the global arms trade, it does not require countries to consider the human rights implications of their exports as the system is voluntary. These realities led Kaye to conclude that '[It] is insufficient to say that a comprehensive system for control and use of targeted surveillance technologies is broken. It hardly exists' (Kaye 2019: 14).

So serious is the potential for abuses that in 2020, Kaye called for 'an immediate moratorium on the global sale and transfer of the tools of the private surveillance industry until rigorous human rights safeguards are put in place to regulate such practices and guarantee that governments and non-state actors use the tools in legitimate ways' (Kaye 2019: 14–15). Yet, too many countries are still focusing on controlling the sales of conventional arms. This focus is understandable, as conventional arms have a visible cost in the form of injuries and deaths, and are politically sensitive. However, if used inappropriately, governments can use surveillance tools to engage in invisible, or less visible, forms of violence that are very difficult to challenge. Global efforts to develop such international standards have intensified since the Snowden revelations, but the reality is that the global trade in surveillance tools has run far ahead of regulatory efforts to control it.

The commercial temptation to export surveillance tools to less well-regulated countries is huge, and all arms-producing countries have a responsibility to address these problems. One of the ways of doing so is to codify the Wassenaar Arrangement into law, so that it becomes enforceable. The only southern African signatory, South Africa, has national legislation that codifies the Wassenaar Arrangement into law, namely, the National Conventional Arms Control Act of 2002 (President of the Republic of South Africa 2002). This act established the National Conventional Arms Control Committee (NCACC), which must regulate the trade in conventional arms (which in the definition includes dual-use goods). The act requires all arms traders to register with the NCACC and obtain a permit. The permit system is used for very sound public interest purposes, including ensuring that arms traders do not threaten the security of South Africa, contribute to crime or terrorism or internal repression in the countries they are exporting to, or escalate military conflict. However, the act has not kept up with the most recent revisions to the Wassenaar Arrangement's control lists to incorporate internet-based surveillance tools. The last time the list of controlled items to which the act applies was updated was in 2012, and was related to the 2010 control list. In a submission to the United Nations Special Rapporteur on the Promotion and Protection of the Right to Freedom of Opinion and Expression, Alt.advisory and the Right2Know Campaign argued that the NCACC Act and regulations were outdated. This meant that the act does not provide an effective control in respect of the trade in surveillance equipment (Alt.advisory and Right2Know Campaign 2019). The organizations also argued that the government, state actors and private companies should be required to ensure that they are not facilitating human rights infringements either domestically or abroad, and should be held accountable for any infractions.

Activists have a massive task to reign in the surveillance industry and hold it to account. Where controls do exist, such as in the EU, they have proved to be inadequate, leading to the vast majority of export licences being granted (Amnesty International 2019: 5). Advocacy organizations specializing in privacy and data protection have adopted different strategies to address this 'law lag'. For instance, Privacy International has adopted a twofold strategy: stop the transfer of unlawful surveillance and promote the transfer of adequate privacy protections. So, if spyware is used for unlawful purposes such as spying on journalists or political activists, then they intend to stop transfers from taking place to these countries by placing pressure on exporting governments to stop the sales and naming and shaming the companies concerned. They further insist that any transfers only take place once recipient countries put in place adequate legal frameworks that respect international human rights (Privacy International 2019). Amnesty International has argued for export controls to cover existing and emerging technologies. These controls should prevent the export of surveillance tools where there is a substantial risk of human rights violations, including where legal frameworks do not exist to prevent abuses. Controls should protect information security research and offer sufficient transparency for the public to be able to track imports and exports, they argued further (Amnesty International 2019: 6–7).

In view of the extent of the abuses that are possible with surveillance technologies, it is not enough for exporting countries to be guided by whether there are UN Security Council sanctions against particular countries in deciding whether to grant or revoke export permits. That bar is far too low to prevent abuses of surveillance tools. It is also not enough not to export to repressive countries only, as even the so-called major democracies have used surveillance tools to violate human rights. Rather, at a bare minimum, countries could have an export control regime that requires minimum safeguards to be in place before they will sell surveillance tools to other countries, and Kaye goes into some detail on these safeguards in his report. These safeguards include ensuring that there is an adequate legal framework in the importing country. The laws governing surveillance in those countries should be clear and accessible, and restrict surveillance to serious crimes.

An adequate legal framework could include the fact that independently appointed judges should approve surveillance, with limits on the duration and scope of the surveillance. As there are particular risks associated with each technology, the most invasive should be regulated more stringently. Hacking could involve a much more stringent level of authorization and oversight. Surveillance targets could be notified of the surveillance once investigations reach a non-sensitive stage. Reporting on surveillance could be transparent and regular. Surveillance should be targeted; in other words, countries should not be exporting bulk surveillance monitoring centres to any country, period. Countries could demonstrate that they have a particularly high burden of proof before journalists or lawyers are put under surveillance. Surveillance technology manufacturers could also develop minimum standards of behaviour, failing which their licences should be revoked. These standards include customer policies affirming a commitment to human rights, due diligence processes for privacy and freedom of expression, and regular public disclosures of audits of the uses of its products. There could also be catch-all controls that allow for the inclusion of non-listed dual-use items that might be used for cyber-surveillance purposes. If countries cannot show that they have a proper legal framework in place to prevent serious human rights abuses, then exports to these countries should be banned (Bromley 2018: 21). In the meantime, and as Kaye has argued, governments should impose a moratorium on any exports of surveillance tools until these safeguards are in place.

However, while these reforms may curb abuses, governments are unlikely to accede to them, as they reduce the discretion of the state to undertake widespread surveillance. This is because such radical transparency measures are likely to expose the true scope of surveillance, which may well be well beyond the stated purposes of fighting crime and actual threats to national security. Consequently, these reforms should not be pursued as ends in themselves but as stepping stones to a more thoroughgoing dismantling of the surveillance state. They can be used to raise the broader political questions of the relationships of surveillance to capitalism, and the impossibility of rolling it back without rolling capitalism back too.

Anti-capitalist responses to the global trade in surveillance

Anti-capitalists and socialists have a rich history of campaigning against war and the arms industry that makes wars possible, although most of this experience is limited to conventional arms rather than dual-use technologies. However, key stances of these movements that position them as being anti-war and anti-imperialist would need to be updated for an environment where class antagonisms stop short of declarations of outright war. The major surveillance powers do not need war to suppress other countries: surveillance provides them with the invisible tools to remain ahead of the diplomatic and trade games, rendering the need to resolve tensions through open conflict less necessary. As argued in previous chapters, anti-imperialism remains a salient stance, given the way in which surveillance is used to perpetuate global relationships forged under classical imperialism. But, what anti-surveillance activists can learn from earlier generations of anti-war activists is the need to focus campaigns on disarmament, and not just on arms control (including of dual-use technologies), and to demonstrate how these campaigns are relevant to the broader crises of capitalism.

Major arms manufacturers such as the US and the UK are unwilling to depart from their countries' growth paths, which are built on militarism, financialization and automation. In fact, they have been willing to resort to military actions if their global supremacy is threatened, irrespective of how unsustainable these measures are. Yet, at the same time, many countries have severe shortages of scientists and engineers. Capitalism in its 'Fourth Industrial Revolution' iteration is seeing companies automating more functions, leading to a massive destruction of jobs. At the same time, the world is experiencing an unprecedented ecological crisis. Any response to the global trade in surveillance must take account of these crises, and focus on the fact that despite these crises, capitalism still skews production towards market demands rather than broader social needs. It is in this context that a key historical demand of the anti-war movement – namely transforming the arms industry into socially responsible, useful and necessary work – becomes relevant.

One of the most inspiring legacies of the labour movement was a plan developed by a group of workers in the British company, Lucas Aerospace, who were facing imminent retrenchment in the 1970s. The company produced technical products for the civilian market, as well as weapons for the defence industry. The workers used this threat to their livelihoods to re-envision their work and their contributions to society more generally as highly skilled engineers. The workers lamented what they referred to as the 'dehumanization of science and technology', not because of the misbehaviour of scientists and technologists, but because society misused their skills (Lucas Aerospace Combine Shop Steward Committee n.d.). They also expressed concern about the de-skilling of their jobs, as the increasingly popular principles of scientific management atomized them into separate production units, overseen by managers who left little room for discretion, much less creative problem solving. As more workers felt oppressed by their working environment, they lost interest and disengaged from the world of work. They also recognized that the shift from human intelligence to machine intelligence was exacerbating the problem. They argued that society has the capacity, in fact the duty, to shape the trajectory of technological developments, and governments should not allow people to be lulled into believing that these developments occurred autonomously of society. According to the workers:

> There is something seriously wrong about a society which can produce a level of technology to design and build [the] Concorde, but cannot provide enough simple urban heating systems to protect the old age pensioners who are dying each year from hypothermia ... [Further] it is clear that there is now deep rooted cynicism amongst wide sections of the public about the idea, carefully nurtured by the media, that advanced science and technology will solve all our material problems. (Lucas Aerospace Combine Shop Steward Committee n.d: 7–8)

The workers began a shopfloor-led discussion and plan to transform their work from military/industrial production into socially useful work. However, they recognized the dangers of planning for their shopfloor only, as the hostile environment would most likely impinge on them and scupper their plans. Consequently, they felt it necessary to link their plans to a wider industrial strategy that promoted economic diversification of areas dependent on arms manufacturers. The workers were decades ahead of their time, and perhaps even foresaw the current ecological crisis by arguing for the need for a just transition from arms manufacturing into socially useful work, especially renewable energy. In other words, they argued for the need to move from destructive to constructive work (Mason 2020).

The Lucas workers assessed their existing product range and workplace skills and drafted an alternative corporate plan, called the Lucas Plan. They did so by collecting ideas from the shopfloor (many workers were highly skilled engineers), and came up with 150 alternative products (Smith 2014). These products included scaling back on military submarine production and focusing on producing submersible vehicles for marine agriculture, as well as braking systems linked to velocity-sensing devices to address the inadequacies in braking systems in widespread use in public transportation. They even grappled with alternative energy storage solutions, recognizing that batteries that were being built at the time placed limits on any ambitions to transition to green energy. They proposed using lessons learnt in building batteries for defence ground support to offer hybrid alternatives to conventional battery production, which could be used in combined rail/road vehicles.

Although the Lucas Aerospace workers never implemented the plan, it has continued to inspire activists to this day. For instance, the UK-based Campaign Against Arms Trade (CAAT) has used the plan as a touchstone to develop detailed proposals for shifting defence manufacturing to socially useful work addressing the global climate crisis. According to CAAT, it is entirely feasible to shift employment in large-scale arms manufacturing to the renewable energy sector, and would go some way to freeing up scarce skills in the science, technology, maths and engineering fields. Focusing specifically on offshore wind energy, they have argued that the UK government could contribute to global security by demilitarizing its foreign policy and promoting sustainable, low-carbon and planet-saving energy sources (Campaign Against Arms Trade 2014). These proposals could well have application beyond the UK, including to southern Africa, where South Africa dominates the local defence industry, although Namibia, Tanzania and Zimbabwe have some industrial capacity to produce arms.

The most significant arms manufacturer in the region, the South African company Denel, is beset with financial problems. While some problems relate to the parastatal becoming embroiled in corruption, some are more deep-rooted and include unprofitable sales and loss-making contracts, and rising costs coupled with declining revenues (Denel 2019). Their turnaround strategy included plans to strengthen corporate governance, reduce internal costs, unbundle non-core functions and focus on core functions, explore diversification into related areas, find new markets for its niche products and possibly take on a private equity partner (Martin 2019). However, its reported diversification plans appeared to be limited to security, cyber-technology and advanced software solutions, and providing more services to the police, suggesting that it was also considering the markets for dual-use technologies and spyware (Campbell 2019). However, job losses remained imminent as the parastatal dispensed with what it had identified as non-core parts of the business (Phakati 2020). Controversially, Denel's business activity has shifted towards partnerships and contracts with undemocratic and internally repressive Gulf and the Middle Eastern states, including the United Arab Emirates, Oman and Saudi Arabia. All of these factors meant that the parastatal was ripe for conversion to a company that provided socially useful goods. In fact, during the Covid-19 pandemic in South Africa, Denel announced its intention to produce medical ventilators with other state institutions, given the drastic shortage globally. The parastatal also indicated that it was looking at options to produce sanitizers for industrial and medical uses, and converting Casspir mine-protection vehicles into ambulances (Reuters 2020). These plans showed just how possible it was for an arms manufacturer to repurpose itself to produce socially useful good during a national crisis, and raised questions about why this approach could not form part of its diversification strategy once the crisis abated.

Developing a vision beyond the ubiquitous surveillance society and state should also include thinking through what should happen to the manufacturers of surveillance technologies, including which aspects should be allowed to continue and which should be shut down. As argued in previous chapters, an anti-capitalist response would most likely emphasize defunding and shrinking surveillance capabilities, rather than expanding them. Untargeted surveillance should be a particular focus of activism, as it presents the greatest potential for abuse, and is an instrument for the maintenance of global inequalities. Although a targeted capability, lawful interception too can be replaced by a far less invasive form of surveillance for broader society in the form of lawful hacking, although it will be far more invasive for those targeted.

Shrinking surveillance capabilities, and the industries that produce them, in this way, will inevitably have job consequences; but as the Lucas Aerospace experience showed, with some imagination, there are many possibilities for putting these skills to more purposeful uses. Whether they are based in the US, the UK, Europe, China or Israel, the major surveillance manufacturers have become bigger and wealthier, and have contributed to growing inequality. In order to curb these abuses of monopoly power, anti-capitalists would need to address the issue of control. In other words, these companies would need to revert to public control, and that control would need to be socialized – what the Lucas Aerospace workers were trying to achieve back in the 1970s. Doing so would create conditions for people to enjoy non-exploitative, anti-surveillance and privacy-centred communications. It would also create the basis for the industrial capabilities that remain to manufacture surveillance equipment to be directed towards serving real public safety needs, as there would be less scope for abuse. For-profit surveillance capabilities, on the other hand, are hard-wired for abuse, as there is a financial incentive to sell these capabilities to governments irrespective of the potential for abuse. At the same time, the domestic markets for dual-use surveillance technologies would need to be shrunk rather than grown. However, as domestic policing becomes increasingly intelligence-led, the demand for these technologies has grown, while controls over police uses have not: a problem I will discuss in the next chapter.

Chapter 6

POLICE AS SPIES

SECURITIZATION OF PROTESTS AND INTELLIGENCE-LED POLICING

Introduction

In 2015, university campuses across South Africa erupted in protests against student fee increases. Soon, the protests escalated into demands for transformed, decolonized, fee-free higher education. Widely referred to as the #feesmustfall movement after the hashtag that popularized the movement across social media, the protests spread across university campuses and mobilized thousands of students across ideological lines. Many universities responded by seeking and obtaining interdicts to control the spread of disruptive protests, and police came onto campuses to enforce the interdicts. As the protests became increasingly disruptive and then violent, and divided along party political lines, the SSA and the Crime Intelligence Division of SAPS began investigating the protests. Former Minister of State Security David Mahlobo claimed that they had evidence of students undergoing military training, and also that the protests threatened national security. The minister blamed academics for fomenting the violence by promoting Afro-pessimism on the pretext of embracing Afro-centrism, and claimed that the agency had a list of names of these academics (Duncan 2016). The SAPS, too, ramped up intelligence collection and analysis and made strategic arrests of protest leaders. In doing so, it shifted more decisively towards a policing model that it had experimented with in the fight against organized crime, namely, intelligence-led policing.

In this chapter, I use the South African #feesmustfall protests as a case study through which to explore the expansion of intelligence-led policing in southern Africa, and what happens to policing when it acquires a national security mandate. I also examine intelligence-led policing as an example of how security practices travel from the North to the South. I explore the promise of intelligence-led policing and the reality of its implementation on the ground. More specifically, I look at how intelligence-led policing has blurred the boundaries between policing work and intelligence work, and contributed towards a growth of political policing focused on ensuring domestic stability as an element of national security. In the process, surveillance and counter-intelligence techniques have become more central to policing. I will then ask what political and ideological stance anti-capitalists could take towards increasingly intelligence-led policing.

Intelligence-led policing in theory

Law enforcement or Crime Intelligence practised by the police[1] and national security intelligence practised by civilian intelligence agencies are very different, or at least they should be. The former should be the product of an analytic process about crime, crime trends and security threats linked to criminality. The latter should focus on the collection and analysis of information necessary to forewarn policymakers about possible threats to a country's sovereignty, even if there is no criminal investigation, so that threats are not realized. The two forms of intelligence should operate in tandem: for instance, if national security intelligence points to the need for a more targeted criminal investigation, then the agency concerned should pass this intelligence over to the police to conduct their own investigations and conduct arrests, where necessary. This is because national security intelligence is rarely admissible as evidence in court, as the agencies concerned may have used otherwise illegal means to collect it, which may lead to criminal prosecutions failing when they arrive in court. Typically, Crime Intelligence has been backward-looking, focusing on events that have occurred, while national security intelligence is forward-looking, focusing on prediction (Carter 2009: 11–19). However, increasingly, police intelligence is becoming more and more like national security intelligence, focusing on predicting crime problems before they occur, rather than responding to crimes once they have occurred. In fact, increasingly it is difficult to separate the two, particularly in relation to strategic intelligence, which the police use to predict longer-term criminal threats without a specific investigation or target in mind. One of the reasons why national security and policing intelligence have converged is that they have both embraced risk-based approaches to security threats. The increasingly fragmented and complex nature of societies propels governments towards attaining more certainty by building knowledge about those they govern. This knowledge enables them to govern at a distance, including through the surveillance and profiling of populations according to the risks they pose to social order (Ericson and Haggerty 1997: 83–96).

Civilian and police intelligence have also converged because governments have blurred distinctions between internal and external security, allowing them to shift how state violence is organized in society. This blurring is leading to armies becoming more civilianized and professionalized and police forces becoming more militarized. The lines between domestic and foreign intelligence gathering has also become increasingly porous (Andreas and Price 2001). These shifts would not be possible without a discursive reframing by governments of those who are considered to be 'enemies', moving beyond the traditional targets of warfare (such as hostile countries) to non-traditional ones (such as internal populations that threaten domestic stability). This blurring of boundaries has led to practices used in external intelligence gathering, such as excessive secrecy, being imported into internal policing (Kraska 2014). The nature of enemies has shifted: no longer whole nations, but fuzzier constituencies have been profiled as threats. Forms of social control have shifted from who has the most tanks and guns to who has the most intelligence (Andreas and Price 2001: 31–52).

Intelligence-led policing was conceptualized in the US and the UK in the 1990s, but gained currency only after the attacks on those countries in 2001 and 2005 respectively. This model of policing is meant to ensure more efficient uses of policing resources, as the police attempt to predict the future trajectory of crime (Ratcliffe 2010). On the surface of things, intelligence-led policing sounds eminently sensible. As its name implies, it is based on the assessment and management of risk; in other words, the police identify major risk factors, allowing them to intervene and disrupt the drivers of those risk factors, using targeted interventions. Conventional policing, on the other hand, tends to be reactive, responding to crime once it has occurred, and attempts to deter crimes before it happens may lead to them resorting to resource-intensive saturation techniques using visible policing. Intelligence-led policing is related to another form of policing, namely, predictive policing, which uses data analytics to predict likely occurrences of crime based on historic patterns.

Intelligence-led policing represents a broader scientification of policing, ostensibly turning it into an objective practice informed by data analytics rather than subjective police assumptions about crime and its drivers. This form of policing is also managerial. Its proponents use top-down approaches designed and implemented by higher-ranking police officers, rather than relying on more bottom-up, consultative methods favoured by community policing. However, police officers not only aim to interpret crime trends: they also aim to influence policymakers' thinking about crime and its drivers. This is another way in which the lines between crime and national security intelligence have become blurred, as the latter has traditionally been more policy-orientated than the former. The prediction imperative drives Crime Intelligence police to look not just for evidence of crimes but risks or social harms more broadly, which can lead to them collecting intelligence in the absence of a criminal predicate: a dangerous drift in law enforcement (Ratcliffe 2010).

As policing becomes more intelligence-led, the police have begun to draw on the diversity of intelligence disciplines used in national security intelligence. Police rely heavily on informers and surveillance to collect intelligence, and analysts to interpret it. While covert methods of collecting information remain important to crime and national security intelligence, both are making increasing use of open-source intelligence as sources of first resort. However, even information obtained from open sources needs to comply with existing standards governing the retention of criminal data. Intelligence-led policing makes copious use of open-source intelligence from publicly available sources, to cut down on the need for covert collection. Particularly useful for the police are online social media sites, where police officers can analyse social networking, understand and interpret ideologies. This they do by creating false identities to access sites of interest, and identifying actual or threatened criminal activity, and the contacts of those involved. Software is commercially available to track keywords suggestive of conflict, acting as cues for the police to increase their presence at protests that may raise concerns. So important has social media analysis become to intelligence work that it has even evolved into the distinct discipline of Social Media Intelligence (SOCMINT). So, when assessing the potential for protests to turn disruptive and even violent, the police can monitor preparations for protests, using keyword searches or 'threat words' that suggest that disruption or violence was being planned, how many people are likely to attend a protest and what their ideological orientations are (Dencik et al. 2018).

As police work has taken on more of the characteristics of intelligence work, intelligence sharing with other state agencies has also become a more important feature of policing. More police agencies are embracing a fusion logic, where they develop intelligence from diverse sources and harness the expertise and resources of multiple state agencies across the civilian-military-policing divides. Fusion centres facilitate intelligence sharing by bringing together various intelligence agencies in a cooperative enterprise, blending information from a variety of sources, including traffic and banking data, previous criminal records, firearms licences and car rental information (Monahan 2009: 20–1). Fusion centres are different from joint operational centres, where different state agencies cooperate to solve criminal or terrorism cases. Rather, they are support centres that focus on intelligence analysis, using data analytics to understand crime trends to make tactical, operational or strategic decisions (Budhram 2015: 49–55).

In spite of the fact that it is meant to transform policing into something resembling a hard science, intelligence-led policing can, at times, boil down to educated guesswork based on fragments of information assessed according to subjective criteria (Newkirk 2010: 48). Precisely because they bring together multiple policing and intelligence agencies, fusion centres' lines of accountability can be blurred and weak. Their emphasis on pre-crime policing can have (and has had) a major negative impact on civil liberties, as people can become subjects of intelligence interest on tenuous, subjective grounds. This problem is likely to be exacerbated when private sector data brokers are added into the mix, as they are even less accountable publicly than public agencies. The police can use data mining without there being a reasonable suspicion of criminality, owing to the lax controls on these centres (Newkirk 2010: 48).

Police organizations have found intelligence-led policing to be particularly effective in addressing highly organized, transnational crimes, where they need investigations to uncover criminal networks. However, given that this policing model is, by its very nature, more secretive than visible policing, it is particularly susceptible to abuse. Crime intelligence police have used it to profile individuals and organizations, not only those that are suspected of crime but those who are considered to be security threats more broadly. Consequently, extremism has become a major focus of police work, including the origins and spread of extremist ideologies. Yet, policing has not stopped at collecting intelligence:

the police can move (and have moved in some cases) seamlessly from profiling to disruption, where they infiltrate organized crime gangs and terrorist organizations using undercover methods supported by SIGINT, and disrupt them from within. This seamless progression is made possible by the fact that intelligence-led policing focuses on the criminal or the criminal organization, and not the crime, as crime analysis has shown that a small number of repeat offenders tend to commit crimes (Govender 2012: 83). The police have also been known to label young people as gang members too quickly, with no real evidence of criminality, yet with long-lasting negative impacts on the youths concerned: in the process, intelligence-led policing has become integral to the broader governance of what capitalism considers to be problem populations (Fraser and Atkinson 2014: 154–70).

Nowhere has intelligence-led policing been more problematic than in relation to political policing, and more specifically the policing of protests. Intelligence-led public order police have routinely justified the infiltration of protest movements by exaggerating their threats to public safety. By talking up disruptive protestors as domestic extremists – or individuals or groups based inside a country whose ideologies may predispose them to crime and violence – intelligence-led public order policing has tended to move far beyond crime control and into the construction of political threats to the current social order more generally (Schlembach 2018). In the wake of the protestors' shutdown of the World Trade Centre negotiations in Seattle in 1999, the police began to experiment with more risk-based approaches towards public order policing, shifting from incident-led policing of protests during events to pre-event intelligence collection, infiltration, surveillance and at times even the pre-emptive arrest of those considered troublemakers. In these circumstances, it is relatively easy for the police to cross the line from passive intelligence gathering to entrapment, or deliberately luring protestors into committing a crime. In some cases, the police have actually made their intelligence operations known as a deterrent, which has worked in some instances, leading to protestors staying away from protests. In such cases, they used intelligence gathering as a form of covert coercion, often underpinned by a growing intolerance of disruption more generally (King 2006: 40–58). Increasingly, the police have adopted bifurcated strategies to protest policing, using more coercive 'hard-hat' approaches where disruption was suspected, collecting intelligence against the organizers and then engaging in the mass forceful dispersion of protests. In contrast, they reserved 'soft-hat' approaches for protests that they anticipated would be largely peaceful, but where the potential for some disruption by small groups of protestors still existed. 'Soft-hat' approaches involved the police using restrictive permits for protests, coupled with the targeting of individuals considered to be threats, and zero-tolerance shown towards more disruptive elements in the crowd that could not be controlled through micromanagement (Vitale 2007: 403–15). While most closely associated with the US and the UK, these intelligence-led public order policing strategies have been exported to other parts of the world, including to South Africa.

Intelligence-led policing in *practice: Escalating protests*

For SAPS, intelligence-led policing became key to enabling them to 'disturb, disrupt and erupt on crime' (South African Police Service 2014, 2018a). The Crime Intelligence Division of SAPS has become central to this new model of policing, leading to its status being elevated from being a relatively low-level back-end support unit to being at the centre of police strategy. South Africa was one of the earliest adopters of intelligence-led policing in southern Africa. Dating back as far as 1995, the police's leadership experimented with this model to address the growing problem of organized crime syndicates, and they used it to develop a linkage analysis chart of the suspects, associates, previous criminal incidents and those arrested (Govender 2012: 83). Reactive policing was not proving to be an effective strategy to combat crimes, especially the so-called trio crimes of car hijackings, house robberies and business robberies. Case-based investigations were draining resources and the police realized that they needed to become more strategic in their responses, using in-depth and focused research to find longer-term solutions to crime problems. This they could do by shifting from targeting crimes after they had happened to focusing on crimes that were likely to take place in the future. Increasingly, the police recognized that a minority of the population were generally responsible for most of the crimes committed; therefore, it made sense to focus on identifying and tracking those most likely to commit crimes (Zinn 2011). The police leadership began to argue for the need to modernize their policing methods, and intelligence-led policing, which had become ascendant in international policing circles, provided them with an opportunity to do just that.

Southern African police forces were encouraged to adopt intelligence-led policing by the region's political community, the Southern African Development Community (SADC), and specifically its Council of Police Chiefs for Southern Africa Regional Police Chiefs Cooperation Organization (SARPCCO). This entity required every SADC member state to have a Crime Intelligence Unit in their police service to promote a more coordinated approach towards intelligence-led policing and a proactive approach towards crime-fighting (Mugari et al. 2015). Governments also agreed to the establishment of a sub-regional bureau for the international criminal police organization, Interpol, which was involved with SARPCCO's establishment in that the bureau became the secretariat for SARPCCO. Interpol coordinated SARPCCO's programmes (Southern African Regional Police Chiefs Cooperation Organization n.d.) and provided ongoing Crime Intelligence support in the form of training and access to international databases.

At the same time that SAPS was investing resources into becoming more intelligence-led, it was disinvesting in public order policing. Police violence against civilians, especially protestors, is an ongoing problem in southern Africa, where policing grew out of colonial institutions designed to suppress indigenous populations. Intelligence-led policing has not necessarily lessened police propensity for violence against movements, though, but it has created the basis for violence to become more targeted and less visible. The region reached its lowest point in post-colonial, post-apartheid policing in 2012, when a wave of strikes in

South Africa culminated in the police massacre of mineworkers at the Lonmin platinum mine at Marikana. The police shot mineworkers in full view of television cameras in an initial confrontation in an area that has become known as 'scene one', but more were shot away from the cameras as they ran away from the police, at 'scene two'. By that stage, the post-apartheid police had become notorious for excessively militarized policing and violence against protestors, leading to injuries and deaths. After failed attempts with community policing and sector policing, SAPS was clearly in need of a policing model that removed them from critical public scrutiny, reduced criticisms around police militarization and restored their tattered credibility.

At the same time, the South African government had become increasingly concerned about what it considered to be an uptick in violent protests. While it may not be apparent from much of the media coverage, recent gatherings (which include community protests) remain overwhelmingly peaceful. However, there has been an increase in disruptive and even violent community protests (Alexander et al. 2018: 27–42). Yet, the government response has consistently overstated the extent of the problem, and the police have used it to attempt to obtain bigger budgets. Cabinet's Justice, Crime Prevention and Security (JCPS) cluster – the cabinet cluster of ministries responsible for safety, security and criminal justice – has played an important role in framing protests as threats to public safety and even national security, and this framing has provided justification for harsher policing, greater intelligence scrutiny and increased surveillance of protest movements and organizers. Even before the #feesmustfall protests had become a major part of the political landscape, and the government multi-year spending plan, the Medium Term Strategic Framework of 2014–19, drew a link between violent protests and domestic stability. The plan went on to state that the National Prosecuting Authority (NPA) should contribute to domestic stability by successfully prosecuting violent and criminal conduct (National Prosecuting Authority 2016: 18).

The South African higher education sector has been in a funding crunch in the post-apartheid period, despite student numbers increasing. Consequently, universities and technical and vocational colleges have raised fees consistently to make up for the shortfall. The student aid scheme, the National Student Financial Aid Scheme, has not been an appropriate funding vehicle as it has trapped students in debt (Naidu 2020). Owing to these contradictions, protests have been a feature of the higher education landscape for many years; however, many of the earlier protests failed to attract much media attention as they took place at historically Black universities. It was only when students at historically white universities such as the University of the Witwatersrand (or Wits University) and the University of Cape Town started protesting, and the protests swept across the country from 2015 onwards, that they began to receive national attention from government and from the media.

In response to student and community protests, the JCPS cluster developed a four-pillar approach to addressing domestic stability: community and stakeholder engagement; legal and regulatory interventions; safety and security interventions; and mass communication (South African Police Service 2017: 14). SAPS used the student protest as an experiment in tougher policing, opposing the granting of bail when people were arrested for public violence. They also pursued intelligence-led investigations to uncover details about the crimes that had been committed, and prosecution-led investigations in cooperation with NPA prosecutors, to increase their chances of achieving successful prosecutions (South African Police Service 2017). Prosecution-led investigations were still relatively novel in South Africa, having been applied mainly to complex and organized crimes, such as commercial crimes, by a now-defunct unit in the NPA called the Scorpions. Extending this approach to protests was an indication of the seriousness with which SAPS viewed them (Myeza 2019: 135–6). There are dangers in such an approach, though, as the independence of the prosecutor may be compromised, affecting the right of the accused to a fair trial. The SSA also investigated the protests, underscoring the fact that the student protests had been escalated to the level of national security threats.

As struggles over the affordability of higher education spread across university campuses from 2015 onwards, universities sought and were granted wide-ranging interdicts that prohibited disruptive protests, in spite of the fact that the Regulation of Gatherings Act sets the bar for police intervention at serious disruption. Even then, the police must enter into negotiations with convenors before using force to disperse the assembly. Feeling that they lacked the level of force necessary to respond to the protests, universities boosted their on-campus security capacity with private security guards. On several campuses, inappropriately trained private security guards 'policed' protests. This was in spite of the fact that, according to the Private Security Regulatory Industry of South Africa (PSIRA), its members were not trained adequately in crowd control, and its mandate was not meant to extend to these functions. Furthermore, some of their members armed themselves in ways they were not meant to, and some universities even unlawfully employed private security firms that were not their members (Gichanga 2019). Official overreactions, coupled with competition among protesting groups, can escalate protests, and as attitudes harden on all sides of the conflict, violence is likely to become less sporadic and more organized (Della Porta 2013: 76–85).

As if preparing for war, the SAPS invested in what it maintained were less lethal public order policing equipment to use in defending its members in crowd control situations, as though its own members had been the main victims of the Marikana massacre. SAPS bought fourteen Long-Range Acoustic Devices, commonly known as 'sound cannons', which they identified as loudspeaker technology that allowed the operator to broadcast warnings and instructions over a much greater distance (South African Police Service 2016: 153). SAPS bought additional video cameras and accessories to take video footage of protestors, as well as armadillo suits and gas masks to be used in crowd control situations (South African Police Service 2016: 153, 2017: 142–3). They also organized training for their members in crowd control techniques, including in the confrontational French model of public order policing that has been criticized as being inappropriately militaristic for SAPS (Tait and Marks 2011: 15–22). The SAPS indicated its intention to procure more Nyalas (an infantry mobility vehicle), pyrotechnic weaponry, including teargas and stun grenades, more water cannons equipped with red and blue dye, and other surveillance equipment. All of these purchases suggested that the SAPS was preparing for full-scale confrontations with protestors. According to the former head of the Independent Police Investigations Directorate, Robert McBride, SAPS Crime Intelligence also purchased social media monitoring software, known as 'Ripjar', to use against the #feesmustfall protests, as protestors used social media as an organizing and publicity tool. However, they bought the equipment at hugely inflated prices from a company that was being investigated for laundering money to buy votes for former ANC president Jacob Zuma, and apparently the equipment was never used (McBride 2018). For reasons that will be discussed later on in the chapter, it was not difficult for members of Crime Intelligence to talk up security threats to justify the procurement of such equipment, using a secret services account that dates back to apartheid. This account has been hugely controversial, as it has been easy to abuse, providing a cash machine of sorts to Crime Intelligence officers.

The #feesmustfall protests won a massive victory late in 2015, when the government announced that it would scrap the fee increment for 2016. However, the movement began to lose momentum after that, fracturing along party political lines, which had been less visible the year before owing to the emphasis on ideological unity. Typically, when protests escalate, violence may be spontaneous, as a reaction to police violence or a more general closure of democratic space, for instance. As protest cycles decline, violence often becomes more pronounced as the mass base dwindles and smaller groups of protestors hardened by state intolerance and violence assert themselves. As a result, the struggle shifts onto a terrain dominated overwhelmingly by the state and its repressive apparatuses, weakening the movement even more (Della Porta 2013: 112). By 2018, the Ministry of Higher Education estimated that the protests had inflicted R800 million in damage on universities. Buildings were vandalized, and in some cases torched and burnt (Ministry of Higher Education and Training 2018).

However, far from adopting a more targeted approach towards public violence, the police used this term as a catch-all for a range of conduct-related charges, in the process creating the impression that the police considered protests per se to be public violence. By 2017, SAPS had opened 51 cases and made 207 arrests during the #feesmustfall protests (Parliamentary Monitoring Group 2017). Yet very few of these led to successful convictions, despite the JCPS cluster exerting huge effort to achieve them. Only one of the forty protest-related cases that the law clinic, the Socio Economic Rights Institute (SERI), handled after 2014 led to a successful conviction, and these included #feesmustfall-related cases. Most cases were withdrawn once SERI made representations to the NPA (Duncan 2021a: 188). The NPA claimed that it had achieved important successes in the #feesmustfall cases, including of students who were convicted for public violence and assault. However, in most of these cases the NPA was willing to agree to alternatives short of incarceration, which suggests that the NPA did not consider these crimes to be so serious that they would oppose these alternatives. By 2019, the only #feesmustfall activist who remained in prison, Kanya Cekeshe, was released on parole (Mabuza and Savides 2019), and many of the most serious cases of public violence remained unsolved.

Reviewing the number of intelligence products produced by SAPS over the period of the #feesmustfall protests, it is apparent that the Crime Intelligence Division was generating huge numbers of reports, but they used very few of them and failed to raise their conviction rates to hoped-for levels. These patterns pointed to inefficiencies in their intelligence processes, where intelligence was being generated to meet targets, but where much of the intelligence generated proved not to be actionable (Duncan 2021a: 179–94). Protest-related offences are notoriously difficult to prosecute, as it is difficult to identify the perpetrators in large crowds; however, there was little evidence that SAPS's more targeted and prioritized approaches were solving these problems.

What became apparent from the police response to the #feesmustfall protests was that they were seeking to stop the protests, and not just the violent ones. In fact, SAPS made it clear in relation to all the protests taking place over that period that they considered them to represent 'an increase in the threats to the authority of the state' (South African Police Service 2017: 221). SAPS's terminology is revealing, as it suggests that they saw protests per se as threatening the authority of the state, and in any event, threats to its authority did not automatically equate to unlawful conduct. This statement signalled that they were prepared to move far beyond what was needed to counter crime and into the politically loaded area of policing domestic stability. The Right2Protest Project, a network of law clinics and non-governmental organizations devoted to protecting the right to protests, supported this view. The Project handled many of the #feesmustfall cases, and its coordinator, Busi Matabane, had the following to say about the responses of the police and universities:

> We know that the right to protest is enshrined in the Constitution. But, despite this, those seeking to voice their dissent face many hurdles, there are a lot of tactics that are used to harass and intimidate activists, and ultimately to stop them from organizing, and surveillance is one of those tactics, right. So, during the #feesmustfall protests, there were many reports of surveillance. There are many reports from students on the ground of being followed by police cars and private security vans, and reports of conversations being taped by third parties. We now know that spaces that students had organized for themselves to plan were being infiltrated. We also now know that pictures taken at protests were used to target students, and many faced disciplinary action.[2]

At the same time that the JCPS cluster was strategizing to stop the #feesmustfall protests in 2016, possibly the most serious acts of public violence against state infrastructure took place in Vuwani, Limpopo Province. After an unpopular decision to change the demarcation of some wards, unknown people burnt down twenty-nine schools in what has been linked to internal factional battles in the ANC (Van Zyl 2016). Despite the fact that the SSA indicated that it was forewarned about the possibility of the attacks, no one has been prosecuted successfully for the attacks at the time of writing, in spite of over 100 cases having been opened by the police (Shazi 2017). Well-organized acts of public violence continued to escalate, including repeated attacks on trucks driven by foreign nationals and xenophobic killings of foreign nationals, leading to international non-governmental organization Human Rights Watch criticizing the government for a failure to protect foreign truck drivers against attack or to mount effective investigations to stop the attacks (Human Rights Watch 2019). In an interview, Blade Nzimande, who was Minister of Higher Education at the time of the #feesmustfall protests, and who subsequently became Minister of Transport, made the following comment on these intelligence blind spots:

> There are certain things that don't make sense to me . . . [Why] wouldn't you pick up the burning of so many schools in Vuwani? Even with the #feesmustfall [protests], some of the destruction that was happening. You know in one of the universities, I was told that the people who were doing this damage and burning of things, including the library at one institution, were outsiders. They were not students. But they did not pick it up. Does it mean, could it mean . . . Even now you can see now with the burning of trucks and the blocking of the toll road in Mooi River [one of the scenes of the truck attacks] . . . I don't know, but you could hypothesize that the increasing capacity of state security has got more to do with issues of state security than the safety and security [of the people].[3]

Nzimande's comment implies that the intelligence failures around specific acts of public violence were not accidental or episodic. Rather, they suggest a deep structural logic, where the intelligence agencies poured extraordinary efforts into investigating less serious cases of public violence (often with limited results). At the same time, the police and intelligence services failed repeatedly to detect and arrest perpetrators of more serious cases of public violence, if doing so risked eroding or alienating parts of the ANC's support base. In fact, it is difficult not to conclude that there was an element of willful blindness at work in these cases.

Set up for abuse: Crime Intelligence and systemic bias

The Crime Intelligence Division of SAPS provides a graphic example of how an intelligence agency is set up to evade public accountability and enable factional interests rather than the public interest. The government has baked failure into the institution, making it impossible for it to fulfil its mandate consistently, and consequently, Crime Intelligence's significant intelligence failures abound. In possibly the most significant intelligence failure in the post-apartheid period, the division failed to detect and act against state-enabled corruption under the Zuma presidency, which lasted from 2009 to 2018. Corrupt elements in the state used it and the SSA as vehicles to wage disinformation campaigns in favour of the former president and his perceived enemies (Mufamadi et al. 2018; Pauw 2017). The division's top leadership has been unstable, with a high turnover of appointments, making it difficult for any well-meaning official to clean up the division. Members of SAPS stymied investigations by the Independent Complaints

Investigation Directorate – the statutory watchdog body over policing abuses – by over-classifying information (McBride 2018). Over this period, organized crime spiralled, which raised the confounding question of why crime escalated at the same time that police intelligence capabilities expanded. The secret services account, which is used to fund Crime Intelligence operations, is a repeated source of controversy and a honey pot for corrupt elements (Duncan 2021b; Thamm 2020, 2021).

Crime Intelligence has failed repeatedly to provide basic, actionable intelligence on significant crime threats, because it is practically unregulated, leading to the entity operating largely on the basis of trust. It is impossible not to conclude that the government made a deliberate decision to keep regulation loose to make it more susceptible to manipulation. Hence, an agency that has been set up to fight criminality has itself become criminal. The division's mandate is not set out in the primary law governing the police, the South African Police Service Act, although at the time of writing there was a proposal to change that and include a section. The only law that sets out a mandate is the 1994 National Strategic Intelligence Act – one of a trio of intelligence acts passed with the transition from apartheid to democracy – but the mandate is flimsy, lacks important safeguards and has remained static since then. According to the act, the division gathers, correlates, evaluates, coordinates and uses Crime Intelligence in support of the police's objectives as set out in the constitution. It can also institute counter-intelligence measures within SAPS, and supply Crime Intelligence relating to national strategic intelligence to the coordinating body for intelligence, the National Intelligence Coordinating Committee, or NICOC (President of the Republic of South Africa 1994).

More seriously, though, legislative controls on the secret services account are practically non-existent. The secret services account remains rooted in racist, oppressive practices. SAPS administers the account in terms of the Secret Services Act of 1992, an apartheid-era piece of legislation that had its roots in the security abuses under apartheid. Set up in the 1970s to fund the covert operations of the Bureau for State Security against the anti-apartheid movement, the post-1994 government maintained its lax controls. All that SAPS needs to do to access the account is to prove that it intends to undertake covert activities, and that these activities are in the national interest (which is not defined). The vagueness of this term allows SAPS to stretch an already-nebulous concept to justify access to these funds; so it is a small wonder that the fund has become the source of such abuse. While internal controls may exist, it is too easy for them to be set aside. These lax controls have encouraged an entire political economy to grow up around the fund, where corrupt members can talk up or even invent crime and security threats to justify access to funds, with the #feesmustfall protests being a case in point. Lax controls create space for all manner of abuses. These have included inventing sources to pocket the payments, using funds to pay off mortgages on houses belonging to corrupt members but that are registered as safe houses (used by the police to house witnesses whose lives are in danger), invoicing for equipment that is never obtained or used, and inventing non-existent intelligence projects (Duncan 2021b; Thamm 2020, 2021).

These lax controls have become even more problematic as SAPS has embraced intelligence-led policing, as this shift has elevated the status of Crime Intelligence in the police. An additional aggravating factor is that the mandates of the various intelligence agencies have become blurred, with the SAPS claiming more of a national security mandate, while the SSA has acquired more of a crime-fighting mandate. This blurring creates the basis for competition rather than cooperation between the agencies. More importantly, Crime Intelligence can use national security as a pretext to ensure even greater secrecy around its activities. It can also demand even more resources given the gravity of this mandate, and engage in speculative policing. The national security space is a hugely lucrative space for intelligence agencies, so it is a small wonder that more government departments and organs of state vie for a piece of it. (This will be discussed in the next chapter as well.)

Law enforcement intelligence is generally broader and more secretive than conventional policing work, which is why it should be subjected to particularly stringent safeguards (Carter 2009). One of the safeguards that Crime Intelligence lacks is that its mandate fails to state that it should have a bias towards overt intelligence methods as a general principle, with covert methods being the exception. The division is not required to rely on open-source intelligence in the first instance, with its members resorting to secret intelligence only when intelligence is obtained through open means and where it is necessary to complete the intelligence picture. Given the under-regulation of the secret services account, it is likely that operatives will choose covert forms of collection. Reducing the amount of covert intelligence will automatically reduce the calls on the secret services account. However, nothing explicitly prevents the Crime Intelligence Division's members from targeting people purely on the basis of their membership of a particular religious or racial group, or subscribing to a particular ideology. This basic safeguard is missing. The division also operates with an overbroad definition of counter-intelligence, as it includes measures to impede and neutralize the effectiveness of foreign or hostile intelligence operations and to counter any threat or potential threat to national security. These terms are vague and open to abuse (Matthews et al. 2008: 143–6). All these weaknesses can be addressed, and will most likely widen democratic spaces by limiting the scope for secretive policing against anti-systemic movements and others who threaten the interests of the dominant political class, and broadening the scope for policing to be directed against more genuine security threats.

Exploring alternatives: Defunding intelligence-led policing

In modern societies, governments have separated the police from the military and given the former a domestic mandate in order to secure consent from the policed. However, this separation has masked the highly political role of policing in controlling dissent domestically and reproducing inequality. This separation has been convenient for governments as it lends legitimacy to modern capitalism.

They can argue that there are rules-based restraints on the state's coercive capacity domestically, and that they reserve unrestrained violence exclusively for repelling external threats. In reality, though, governments have expanded policing powers massively into many areas of life, criminalizing more and more social problems such as sex work, migration, political dissent and public protests. As the role of the police in domestic political management has become more visible, the police have gradually lost legitimacy as the supposed upholders of law and order. Yet, at the same time as the police busy themselves with managing dissent, crime continues to spiral (Vitale 2007: 197–201).

Police violence against unarmed Black civilians has politicized the role of the police globally. In 2020, protests erupted against the police murder of George Floyd in the US, and rapidly, protests against police violence spread throughout the world. The #Blacklivesmatter movement that developed around these protests, as well as the nationwide movement that coordinated responses to racialized violence, the Movement for Black Lives, raised the demand to defund the police. The movements argued that policing in the US was not politically neutral: rather, it displayed systemic racial and class biases in ways that directed violence against Black working-class communities. The movements escalated these demands through street-based mass action, and these struggles moved mainstream discourse beyond the typical focus during times of crisis on the need for policing reforms. They politicized police violence as being more than just an aberration of a few delinquent police officers, and raised systemic questions about whether the police should even exist. They argued that policing as an institution was irredeemable, and those most affected by police violence should replace state-controlled policing with community-based, self-organized protection. Ideas that had existed for decades, supporting the abolition of the police and prison system, became impossible for even the media mainstream to ignore. As these movements argued, defunding the police is not just about withdrawing funding from the police, and abandoning communities to violence; rather, it embodies the idea that if funding was moved from policing of social ills, to addressing the social ills themselves and eliminating the harms caused to society, then policing could be pared back and, even eliminated. In other words, the movements' ultimate end goal was not to close the police down, but to eliminate the need for policing, and use the money for healthcare, education, jobs and other services that had been devastated by decades of neoliberalism (Kaba 2020). In fact, police violence had become the state's response to social problems created by its own divestment from basic services (Akbar 2020: 1813–21). While cases of crime were still likely to exist, community-controlled safety and security programmes could respond to them.

These movements also linked policing as an institution to the broader crisis of capitalism, where capitalism has organized society in ways that disempower and brutalize Black working-class communities, and the police are a direct instrument of racial capitalist rule where oppression and exploitation are mutually reinforcing. The demand to shift resources from policing to social services most needed by these communities is not possible under the current capitalist system as it presents a direct challenge to how the system is organized: therefore, the call to defund the police is inherently anti-capitalist. They questioned whether reforms would ever be enough to address the systemic prejudices of the police, and criticized the focus on reforms as being a palliative that avoided dealing with the root of the problem. After decades of advocating for reforms, only to see even more police violence make nonsense of these reforms, abolitionists challenged reformists to move away from improving the police to limiting and ultimately eliminating police power, and addressing the transformative question of how else policing could be organized (Kaba 2020; Akbar 2020: 1813–21).

The current controversies about policing and racism have focused mainly on overt violence against Black people, especially during protests and arrests. However, arguments about reducing the powers of the police are as salient for police spying as they are for visible policing. Intelligence gives the police even more power than they had, and this power is exercised largely in secret and with very little accountability. Spying has become integral to the institutional violence of policing in that it can be used to reproduce and reinforce stereotypes about Black communities being more susceptible to crime than white communities. Intelligence-led policing has also made intelligence more central to policing, which means that the police accountability problem has grown. When applying abolitionist views to police intelligence, it becomes possible to see that such abuses are not a departure from modern policing: rather, they are central to what policing is about. It also becomes possible to see that significant intelligence failures – such as the ones in SAPS Crime Intelligence – follow a particular logic. Conventional intelligence theory would argue that intelligence failures are exceptions to the rule, deviations from the norm in agencies that were set up to protect the public interest. Intelligence agencies claim that they are at a distinct disadvantage relative to other areas of the state as they need to keep their successes from public view to maintain operational secrecy (Gill and Phythian 2012: 28–9). Consequently, what usually surfaces through public scandals are the failures and these tend to stick in the public consciousness. As Richard K. Betts has argued, focusing on intelligence failures creates a distorted view where 'particular failures are accorded disproportionate significance if they are considered in isolation rather than in terms of the general ratio of failures to successes; the record of success is less striking because observers tend not to notice disasters that do not happen' (Betts, quoted in Gill and Phythian 2012: 28).

This argument should not be taken at face value, as it may well be possible for the effectiveness of agencies to be evaluated from publicly available information; to the extent that it isn't, then the agencies often have only themselves to blame for excessive secrecy, as argued in Chapter 2. The successes of law enforcement or crime intelligence are much easier to assess than those of national security intelligence, as their performance can be evaluated against Crime Statistics. Failures can have multiple causes, such as weak analytic tradecraft, leading to analysts interpreting raw intelligence incorrectly. Intelligence agencies may also be blamed for failures that are not within their control as they are policy failures. Politicians may fail to listen to intelligence that is politically inconvenient to them, which applies especially to strategic intelligence as it is designed to inform policymaking about longer-term potential threats. In fact, policymakers may expect too much from intelligence (Gill and Phythian 2012: 143–69).

From the intelligence failures around the September 11 attacks and the invasion of Iraq in their wake to the failures of the South African SSA to predict xenophobic attacks and the Mozambiquan intelligence agencies to disrupt the insurgency in Cabo Delgado, significant intelligence failures appear to follow patterns that are impossible to ignore. Understanding those patterns will help activists to develop a structural account of these failures. Repeatedly, agencies achieve notable successes in neutralizing and impeding the activities of anti-systemic movements for change that use disruption and, at times, property damage. However, their successes in combating crime, disrupting terrorism and protecting public security are less clear. Maintaining capitalism and all that goes with it is not a departure from what intelligence agencies do: it is what they do. As argued in Chapter 2, this is not to say that there are no good people in these agencies attempting to serve the public interest and catch criminals, but the logic of intelligence means that their actions become tangential to the system-maintaining role of these agencies. The argument that intelligence agencies are set up as impartial entities, and that spying on and disrupting legitimate social movements is a deviation from the norm, is premised on a liberal view of the state as a neutral institution, capable of mediating competing class interests in society. Governments and activists alike may share the view that failures can be prevented through reforms such as improving independent oversight and other systems. Undoubtedly, reforms matter. As criminologist Alex Vitale has argued: 'Unless the basic mission of the police remains unchanged, none of these reforms will be achievable. There is no technocratic fix. . . . Powerful political forces benefit from abuse, aggressive and invasive policing, and they are not going to be won over or driven from power by technical arguments or heartfelt appeals to do the right thing' (Vitale 2007: 221). This argument applies to criminal intelligence too.

Security and intelligence from below: The case of South Africa

Like in many countries in the region, the history of policing in South Africa is tied to colonialism and apartheid. The architects of the democratic transition intended to transform policing from being an instrument of racist oppression and capitalist exploitation to being a guarantor of community safety and security. Not surprisingly, as this transition is still within the living memory of so many South Africans, there is still a widely held belief that the police can, and even do, serve and protect the public, which makes abolitionist arguments less straightforward than in the US. Furthermore, the extremely high levels of violence and crime in South African society complicate calls to defund and dismantle the police, as the vacuum left in its wake may be too ghastly for many to contemplate. The true history of policing in post-apartheid South Africa, though, shows how superficial and inadequate government-led transformation has been. The SAPS is more lethal than the US police, when adjusted for population size, which may well make the case for the removal of an institution that remains complicit in racism and oppression (although not to the same extent as it was under apartheid). Social services still command the lion's share of the budget, with peace and security projected to be approximately 10 per cent of government spending in the 2021–2 financial year (National Treasury 2021: 3). The SAPS budget has grown exponentially, escalating rapidly between 2006 and 2014, and more slowly after that. Crime Intelligence accounts for a small percentage of the overall budget, although its budget has escalated more than visible policing and the overall SAPS budget, suggesting an outsized growth. Overall, SAPS has ballooned in recent years, having enjoyed a 41.8 per cent increase between 2009 and 2013, allowing it to increase its personnel by 50 per cent (Newham 2013). Yet, since then, murders have increased, although this increase has tapered off in recent years, and robberies and sexual violence remain staggeringly high (Pijoos and Wicks 2020). It is difficult to see the 'value for money' offered by this expenditure. The lack of policing in working-class communities has left a vacuum that affects women disproportionately. The police have too many roles in society, and policing domestic stability is one role that should be removed from the police's remit, as its record of accomplishment in this area is poor. Intelligence-led policing was meant to offer a pathway towards more targeted policing, particularly to infiltrate and disrupt organized crime. But the way the division has been organized prevents it from realizing this promise, and thinking that government is going to organize it more effectively is unrealistic. The political elite have developed stakes in having it remain as their cash dispenser and praetorian guard.

Crime intelligence is rooted in racist apartheid practices, and it has become a conduit for disproportionate policing in the post-apartheid period. Intelligence-led policing has not necessarily led to more efficient, effective or professionalized policing. The demilitarization called for in the wake of the Marikana massacre has not really come to pass, and SAPS has been in denial and resistant to change. Police members are also suffering from high levels of stress and trauma, being themselves targets of violence. The police-community gap is widening, and many police are traumatized. South Africans desperately need proper policing. Better education and training and bigger budgets are not proving to be the answer; they may have limited effects for limited periods, but as an answer to the country's systemic crises of policing it is too limited and offers no vision for how policing should be organized.

In this context, it makes absolute sense to decrease police power and resources and reallocate them to job creation and social services, especially for women, while developing a more forward-looking vision for policing in broader society. In other words, the focus needs to shift from police reform to the societal transformation needed to make policing unnecessary. This is especially so in the wake of the Covid-19 pandemic, which has devastated the country and led to an austerity budget in a global context where countries in the global North are moving in the opposite direction and spending themselves out of the crisis. The government here is defunding communities in real terms, and the social grants that stand between many South Africans and starvation are not keeping up with inflation (Smit 2021).

The government has also cut funding to the higher education sector, likely leading to yet another round of student protests and police violence, and there is no reason to believe that Crime Intelligence will behave any differently to them than previously. SAPS, too, stands to be affected by budget cuts, as part of overall cuts to public sector personnel costs (South African Treasury 2021: 461–76).

As to how to organize policing, South Africa does not even need to look further than itself to find answers to the question of how to ensure community control of these functions as part of solidarity actions more generally, and what a world could possibly look like without policing and prisons as currently constituted. South Africa has a long history of community level, self-organized policing owing to the poor policing of the townships, and these efforts prefigured policing and justice after liberation. At the height of the anti-apartheid struggle in the 1970s and 1980s, many township residents rejected the police, given their complicity with apartheid. However, they needed to respond to the resulting safety and security vacuum, and established street committees in order to do so. These committees were democratically elected structures that acted as watchdogs over a range of local-level issues and provided alternative dispute resolution mechanisms. Some areas established peoples' courts with both policing and adjudicative functions, although many became controversial for acting as poorly controlled vigilante groups, where 'comtsotsis' or criminals masquerading as comrades held sway. These self-defence efforts evolved into more well-organized Self Defence Units (SDUs), which were meant to be governed by a code of conduct developed by the ANC. Although the code was never accepted by the SDUs, nevertheless this code remains relevant to policing to this day. It emphasized that the SDUs were not private armies, and should not be used to further anyone's personal or political ambitions. The ANC envisaged that SDUs should be community protectors and not terrorizers, and that they should use any weapons in their control for self-defence only. The SDUs were meant to be controlled democratically, with its command structures including elected members of the community and members of MK. It was envisaged that the command executive would include an intelligence function, which would collect and distribute intelligence necessary for community protection (African National Congress 1991; Rakgoadi 1995).

These SDUs were flawed from the start, because they assumed that the ANC represented communities, and was the sole and authentic representative of the oppressed. To that extent, they were less democratic than the earlier street committees, which residents often set up and ran irrespective of party political affiliation; but they do provide some instructive lessons about how self-organized defence could work, including pitfalls to avoid. So deep has the safety and security crisis been in Black working-class communities in the post-apartheid period, that some communities have re-established street committees to address the absence of policing, and some have proved to be resilient as they promote collectivist ideas to security and care for neighbours. They also confronted criminals and disciplined them, at times even violently, although some de-escalated violent situations by mediating family disputes and convincing criminals and their families to refrain from violence. In doing so, they offered what Godfrey Maringira and Diana

Gibson have referred to as security from below, made possible by collective action (Maringira and Gibson 2019: 62). Local-level dispute resolution is particularly important in South Africa, where so much violent crime is interpersonal in nature, and where the perpetrator and victim are likely to know one another.[4]

Post-apartheid street committees lack resources and formal recognition, yet do the work of the police in the absence of the police: in these conditions, it is self-evidently important that such structures should be encouraged and supported, including through the budgets that the government is using to support the statutory police (Maringira and Gibson 2019: 68–9). Doing so is entirely achievable within the f, although there are the attendant risks of the state attempting to steer and even control these self-directed community safety efforts. By doing so, defunding the police while promoting community safety and security becomes an achievable aim, rather than an empty slogan, or, worse, an irresponsible demand that risks visiting even more violence on those most affected by it. At the same time, it is also necessary for activists to continue shrinking the mandates of government institutions that claim to be about safety and security. I will discuss this issue further in the next chapter, but in relation to government functions relating to citizenship and immigration.

Chapter 7

FORTRESS SOUTH AFRICA

SECURITIZING IDENTITY AND BORDER MANAGEMENT[1]

Introduction

As discussed in previous chapters, the Arab Spring was a game changer for many governments in Africa and the Middle East, as they saw thousands of people taking to the streets to challenge corrupt, autocratic regimes and austerity. Less well known, though, is the fact that the Arab Spring spread south of the Sahara, inspiring protests movements in many countries across the region (Paret 2017: 3–5). While they were ideologically diverse and highly uneven, these protests were a form of insurgent citizenship where people who typically were marginal to formal politics used their collective agency to claim their rights to be full members of a political community. In other words, they claimed the right to have rights, participate in political life and decide for themselves how society is organized (Brown 2015: 57–63; Branch and Mampilly 2015: 200–16).

In the wake of the Arab Spring, governments fearful of popular power reasserted their authority to decide on what rights and resources people could have access to. Invariably, governments moved citizenship in a more conservative direction, restricting citizenship access and rights to narrowly defined communities: a trend that Guy Ben-Porat and As'ad Ghanem (2017) have referred to as the shrinking of citizenship. In order to win consent for this shrinkage, governments recycled discourses honed in the war on terror to spread fear that uncontrolled immigration or poor identity management threatened public order and, ultimately, national security. They also began to apply risk-based and intelligence-led methodologies to areas of the state that managed legal citizenship and immigration, and these methodologies spread to southern African governments, too. Digital risk technologies, meant to bring certainty to questions of who is a citizen and who isn't, and who should get to enter a country and who shouldn't – such as biometrically based identity systems and advance passenger profiling systems – have become sought-after tools to help governments respond to these perceived emerging threats.

Southern Africa is one of the most peripheral regions in the world, and active citizenship is necessary to change the status quo. With these points in mind, in this chapter, I answer the following question: how has the shift towards risk-based approaches towards citizenship, and the adoption of digital risk technologies, affected the practice of citizenship in the region?

In this chapter, I will explore the trend in southern Africa towards governments securitizing civil functions that typically fall under 'Homeland Affairs' departments, and specifically the management of national identity systems and immigration. I will focus on South Africa, as it is the region's economic powerhouse, and, consequently, the main receiver of migrants. I will look at the ways in which the government is modelling some of these government functions on the US Department of Homeland Security. I will examine this phenomenon against the backdrop of the growing number of right-wing governments and movements around the world, and the backlash against and scapegoating of immigrants in the wake of the 2008 global recession. I will also explore what an anti-capitalist perspective on border control and identity management could look like, drawing on lessons from a struggle against smart ID cards in Mauritius.

Securitizing identity and migration in the post-September 11 environment

South–South migration has been growing more rapidly than South–North migration, including in southern Africa. Spatial inequalities in southern Africa are stark, with South Africa dominating the region. Some countries are migrant-sending and others migrant-receiving. Migrants have left the DRC, Zimbabwe, Botswana and Namibia in large numbers, with South Africa being the most desirable destination for intra-African migration, and the highest outflows being from Zimbabwe (Kitimbo 2015: 85–90). Consequently, the South African government has tightened border controls against immigration, which it has framed increasingly as a national security threat. In 2019, then newly appointed head of the domestic branch of the South African SSA, Mahlodi Muofhe, said that 'The number one domestic threat is to ensure that our borders cease to be so porous. From all over the world there is a perception that our borders are porous from neighbouring countries, but our borders are porous from all over the show ... We need to ensure that those who come into our country, do so lawfully.'[2] Yet, at the same time, immigrants have been complaining about how it has become increasingly difficult to do just that and regularize their status as lawful (Ncube and Tracey 2020: 28–49).

This closing up of South Africa is contrary to the SADC's founding vision, which was to promote a form of regional integration that strengthened and consolidated the long-standing historical, social and cultural affinities among the region's peoples (Declaration and Treaty of SADC 1992: 5). The SADC envisaged a phased approach towards integration, starting with a free trade area, followed by a customs union, a common market and, ultimately, an economic union. However, after an initial period of enthusiasm about free movement within the region, the SADC dragged its heels on adopting an enabling policy framework (Magidimisha 2018: 189). In fact, it seems fair to say that after a period of high mobility of people, the region is de-globalizing. More governments are promoting restrictive immigrant laws and state practices that promote exclusionary citizenship based on indigeneity. Increasingly, these states see migration as a threat, rather than an opportunity. Consequently, they are seeking to protect their labour markets and reduce citizenship rights by making free movement across borders more difficult. They are also erecting higher barriers for individuals and groups to achieve and maintain the benefits of citizenship (Nshimbi et al. 2018: 177; Parshotam 2018: 7–9). Yet, businesses continue to expand their reach across the region, especially South African businesses, prompting the well-deserved accusation that the country is developing an increasingly sub-imperialist relationship to countries further north (Bond 2015: 18–19). Securitized nationalism coexists with free market transnationalism: in other words, the region's governments have embraced a free movement of capital, but not of labour (Moyo 2020: 1–12; Duncan 2015).

Governments can shrink citizenship more easily when they can convince their publics that if they do not control who gets to enter a country, and who gets to be a citizen, then national security could be compromised. However, as national security powers are usually the most stringent and secretive a government can use, lawmakers and policymakers should keep the definition of national security as narrow as possible, and the list of government agencies that defend it as short as possible. Securitization, where a variety of social issues and problems are turned into national security issues, can lead to governments treating symptoms rather than causes of social problems, and often in the most confrontational manner possible (Duncan 2020). Since the September 11 attacks, the US has been a world leader in recasting what were relatively mundane administrative decisions around immigration and citizenship as national security issues, and more governments around the world have followed suit, although to different extents.

Southern African countries could have chosen a different path, and resisted efforts to securitize identity and immigration, given the region's history of colonial powers imposing borders arbitrarily on communities that had histories of intermingling and migration (Moyo 2020: 1–12). However, in South Africa, some securitized discourses and practices of the US in the post-September 11 period have become more apparent. In a key public admission about its intentions in 2017, the country's Minister of Defence, Nosiviwe Mapisa-Nqakula, said that matters of homeland security, although a term borrowed from the US, were central to South Africa's new security management architecture, which includes the establishment of a Border Management Authority (BMA) and an enhanced cyber-capability (Katzenellenbogen 2017). The BMA is a public entity meant to facilitate and manage the flow of people and goods across South Africa's borders. This comment gave important insight into government thinking about the role of its Department of Home Affairs and its new entity, the BMA. By referring to homeland security, she clearly had the US Department of Homeland Security in mind as a model.

Then-president George W. Bush established the US department after the September 11 attacks, in the process centralizing scores of existing government departments into one huge bureaucracy employing close to half a million people

(Mabee 2007: 385–97). The department's primary objective is to use a risk-based model underpinned by extensive anticipatory intelligence capabilities to forecast trends in national security threats, and prepare for and prevent these threats from being realized, whether they originate inside or outside the US. They also promote community awareness about threats, and cooperate with foreign partners to strengthen their counterterrorism capabilities. With regard to external threats, the Department of Homeland Security aims to push US borders outwards, identifying national security risks through screening and vetting inbound travellers, using classified and open-source intelligence, as well as biometric and biographic information and big data, to identify and prevent security risks from entering the country, or even the hemisphere.

The department has relied increasingly on risk methodologies and technologies using calculative models to target pre-emptively suspicious individuals who may intend to attack the country. Using a decision support tool underpinned by mathematical modelling like the Automatic Targeting System, the department assigned travel passengers with a risk score of how safe or risky they appear to be to the country's national security. This they do by using and cross-referencing big data sources to build a profile of their travel habits, including how tickets were purchased, whether the ticket is return or one way, seating records and 'no-show records', as well as checking travellers against terrorism watch lists. However, because travellers never know their scores and the methodologies used to reach them, they cannot challenge them easily if the decisions violate their freedom of movement unduly (Amoore and de Goede 2008: 6). Fusion centres also help the department to integrate its effort with those of other government departments and share intelligence (Amoore and de Goede 2008: 5–14; Department of Homeland Security 2019).

Homeland Security has been criticized for using AI to mine data in uncontrolled ways that take no account of peoples' privacy, creating risks of the department flagging people falsely as security threats. More members of the public are being labelled security threats, leading to the flagging of a wide range of perfectly legitimate individuals and organizations (Mohanan 2010: 50–63; 99–112). Profiling and subsequent criminalization of suspect individuals and groups display a particular hostility towards Muslims, Black people and political activists. The externalization of borders can lead to nationalities being excluded en masse on a discriminatory basis as they are deemed to threaten national security.

Homeland Security has also provided a template for other countries for securitized border controls, to the point where the UN's Special Rapporteur on contemporary forms of racism, Tendayi Achiume, has called for a moratorium on the use of surveillance technologies in border enforcement, saying they can perpetuate discrimination and even lead to border deaths (Achiume 2020b: 20). Increasingly, governments have come to see migrants per se as threats to national security. While distinctions between citizens and non-citizens are permissible in international law, the kinds of profiling used by Homeland Security can move beyond that and into the realm of racial discrimination, as well as 'technocolonialism', where digital technologies reinforce inequalities. People have been systematically excluded from biometric identity systems, especially ethnic minorities. Migrants are particularly vulnerable to technological experimentation, as they may have no means of providing informed consent. Decision-making about visas is becoming increasingly automated or algorithmic. Far from leading to fair and dispassionate decisions, automated decision-making can amplify existing human biases. Risk assessment tools using AI can target minorities and Black people (Achiume 2020a, b)

Homeland Security has turned into a sprawling bureaucracy whose effectiveness is in question. It has spawned a huge Homeland Security-industrial complex where security companies gain lucrative contracts to provide surveillance equipment to a poorly regulated entity that has even operated extra-judicially at times. While the US has not suffered another terrorist attack on the scale of the September 11 attacks, it is no less vulnerable than it was at the time of these attacks, in spite of the growth in the number of security institutions (Duncan 2020; Miller 2014: 243–69; Remnick 2019).

Home Affairs enters the security cluster

In southern Africa, South Africa is at the forefront of embracing a risk-based approach towards identity management and immigration, and the government department responsible is the Department of Home Affairs. The department provides civic services and immigration services, managing the flow of people into the country through ports of entry, immigration, visa facilitation and recognizing refugees and asylum seekers. It also maintains a civil registry of citizens and permanent residents, the National Population Register (NPR) – which was established in 1982 – and issues key identity documents based on their status (Department of Home Affairs 2020: 9). Entry to the NPR is through birth registration, at which point Home Affairs issues a lifelong unique identity number for each individual. The civil registration process is necessary for people to secure their identity, nationality, civil rights and access to social services in South Africa, and includes information about vital events such as marriage and death (Statistics South Africa 2019).

In 2020, after many delays, parliament finally gave the department legal authority to establish the BMA through the Border Management Authority Act. The purpose of the BMA is to integrate border management functions that were dispersed across various government departments, including the management of law enforcement functions at ports of entry and the border, preventing cross-border crimes and managing cross-border risks, and facilitating legitimate trade and travel (President of the Republic of South Africa 2020: 2). South Africa has become notorious in the region for an increasingly hostile approach towards foreigners, demonstrated graphically in its refugee regulations released in 2019. According to the regulations, South Africa would expel a refugee if s/he 'participates in any political campaign or activity related to his or her country of origin or nationality whilst in the Republic without the permission of the Minister'

(Department of Home Affairs 2019b: 11). The regulations went on to say, 'No refugee or asylum seeker may participate in any political activity or campaign in furtherance of any political party or political interests in the Republic [of South Africa]' (Department of Home Affairs 2019b: 11). These regulations made a political appointee, namely, the minister, the arbiter of whether one of the most vulnerable groups in the country can practice basic political rights. This level of control was entirely inappropriate, as it was bound to discourage refugees from practising basic rights and freedoms that Home Affairs cannot withdraw on a whim. The regulations were also inadvisable because they prevented refugees from organizing to change the destabilizing conditions in the countries they fled from. The inability to organize international solidarity campaigns made it more likely that these conditions would continue, contributing to the very problem that the South African government was trying to avoid, namely, an unmanageable influx of refugees.

Home Affairs has also tightened up on its identity management to the benefit of indigenous South Africans, to the point of turning immigration and identity management into national security issues. Emblematic of this shift was the department's integration into the government's security apparatus. Until 2016, and reflecting its largely civil status, Home Affairs fell into the Governance and Administration cluster. However, in that year, cabinet approved the reclassification of Home Affairs as a JCPS cluster member after having approved a plan for the department, indicating that the highest levels of government considered the department to be integral to protecting South Africa's national security (SANews 2016). The government cemented this reframing in late 2019, when President Ramaphosa announced the re-establishment of the National Security Council after a hiatus of some years. Tasked with streamlining all security-related work in the country, the Council included the Home Affairs Minister (South African Broadcasting Corporation 2019).

Putting the cart before the horse, the government released a draft White Paper on Home Affairs for public comment in 2019, only after it had been repositioned as a security institution. The draft set out the new mandate of the department and recognized three elements to its mandate: enabling national sovereignty and national self-determination, ensuring citizens to access their rights, and protecting national security. The department claimed that it is central to national security as it enables citizens and institutions to realize their rights and responsibilities and protect their identities to enable them to vote, for instance. It also allows the state to protect national security by tracking the movements of people who may threaten the country. The department went on to argue that its mandate necessitated a new operating model built around a National Identity System and underpinned by new legislation. Similar to the US Department of Homeland Security, the department indicated its intention to provide the state with responsive reports of risks and threats to national security within the scope of its mandate (Department of Home Affairs 2019b).

The South African government did not aspire to a mandate that was nearly as extensive as Homeland Security's. Nevertheless, the South African constitution is very specific about which institutions can act as security services, and these include the police, the military and any intelligence service established in terms of the constitution. The constitution does include the caveat, though, that other armed services may be established in terms of legislation, but this caveat does not extend to national security institutions (Constitution of the Republic of South Africa 1996: 198–210). The dubious constitutional status of the Home Affairs shift has been glossed over in the public arena, which the government achieved by creating moral panics about immigration and its purported threats to national sovereignty, and preparing the ground for an acquiescent, unquestioning public.

Preparing the public: Discursive dimensions of South Africa's shift to a Homeland Security model

Down the years, Home Affairs has administered essential, but mundane, civil functions like issuing birth and death certificates, maintaining an NPR and managing immigration. But, increasingly, the government has reframed these functions discursively as being central to national sovereignty and, ultimately, national security. Drawing on discursive strategies used by other governments (Nunn 2015), South Africa has framed immigration increasingly as a national security threat that is so imminent that their need to counter it as such so self-evident that citizens may fail to question the institutional underpinnings of the state. They have even warned that South Africans may rise up in revolt against their own government 'if they feel they're in competition with everybody' (Duncan 2020; Bendile 2017). Yet, the government has exaggerated the numbers of undocumented migrants, as it has their contributions to crime and unemployment. In any event, South Africa's crime statistics have been unable to demonstrate a causal link between immigration and crime (Hiropoulos and Landau 2015; Wilkinson 2015; Newham 2017). Nevertheless, South Africa's immigration control system has taken on more of the characteristic of crime control.

Academics Barry Buzan, Ole Waever and Jaap De Wilde have argued that some governments participate in political posturing to securitize issues in an attempt to implement measures not normally acceptable in a low- or no-threat environment, which southern Africa largely is (Buzan et al. 1998). These governments elevate the nature of any threat to reduce pushback from the population, especially if counter-measures involve the potentially controversial expansion of security and surveillance powers and the policing of activities far beyond what criminal behaviour might justify. This they do by conflating threats to national identity with threats to national security, which the government then uses as a means to control and restrict migration. South Africa faces a massive unemployment crisis and rampant crime, and in conditions where employment is scarce and crime is escalating, it becomes tempting for the government to blame foreign nationals for these problems and to frame immigration as an existential threat to national security. In such conditions, xenophobia is almost inevitable, taking root in society largely because the state promotes it and not because society is inherently prejudiced against foreigners (Neocosmos 2008).

One word that has started to creep into Home Affairs statements with increasing regularity is 'modernization', which it has used to refer to its decision to move away from old, fragmented, paper-based systems to more efficient, integrated, digital, paperless ones. The department has also signalled its intention to reposition itself as the 'nerve centre of security' (Reuters 2017), and this new position would move it from the periphery to the centre of government. Such discursive repositioning helps a low-key administrative department with status problems in government to acquire a more high-profile national security mandate. Its leadership has also been working hard to move the department away from what it was under apartheid – namely an administrative entity of petty bureaucrats servicing a minority under apartheid – to one that is on the cutting edge of innovation. In fact, they have even claimed that the Fourth Industrial Revolution would be impossible without a modern, secure Home Affairs Department (Duncan 2020; Department of Home Affairs 2019b: 12, 68). Already, the department has managed to harness technology to increase its efficiency, although mainly to improve the delivery of identity services to South African citizens.

Home Affairs goes digital: Securitizing civic services

According to Benjamin J. Muller, more governments are now using bureaucratized (usually biometric) identity management systems to restrict citizenship access and exclude those considered 'undesirable'. In his view, citizenship is increasingly not about people determining their own positions in society by performing citizenship acts such as claiming rights (Muller 2004: 279–94). Governments can use biometric systems to control who has access the rights and benefits of citizenship, using a supposedly 'objective' technology to decide who is included and who is not. They have sold biometric identification systems to publics for their efficiency gains; yet, in reality, these systems have their own flaws and biases and can be used for exclusionary and restrictive purposes to shut out those considered undesirable or unworthy of citizenship. Claims about biometrics being a fail-safe method of establishing identity are called into question when engineers have programmed facial recognition algorithms with biases towards white and older people, and fingerprint biometrics are more likely to fail when people work with their hands, such as mineworkers or domestic workers.

New digital identity card systems present governments with a moment for the creation of exclusion of those considered undesirable, and the reframing of identity as being necessary for security creates even more opportunities for exclusion. The World Bank has played a role in promoting digital initiatives in Africa, including a subtle shift from promoting digital identity as a means for governments to prevent exclusion (from access to basic services, for instance), to using it to decide who should and should not be allowed to access citizenship rights. This shift has led to a drastic reduction in the number of people granted citizenship, with automatic paths towards citizenship being phased out. Furthermore, digital identity is being weaponized, as citizenship begins to revolve around nativist definitions of indigeneity. Increasingly, citizenship is becoming the preserve of the autochthonous inhabitants of a country, while those considered to be non-indigenous are excluded, stigmatized and persecuted, even violently. Historical state practices may also influence how governments set up identity systems, and the extent of democratic controls they put on these systems. For instance, Anglophone countries have preferred to give the authorities wide discretion to use them, with little meaningful oversight: a tendency that the British promoted as they used identity to divide and rule, and therefore discouraged their subjects from suspecting the executive of malafides.

As a former British colony, South Africa maintained a centralized identification system, and the apartheid and democratic governments have encouraged their citizens not to question the practice of collecting fingerprints and issuing ID documents as foundational practices in the country (Breckenridge 2014). In other words, from colonial times, these practices have become naturalized, which has made it much easier for Home Affairs to obtain consent for more invasive identification practices. The Department of Home Affairs' embracing of a national security mandate has coincided with it using increased surveillance on the basis of identity and citizenship. To that end, the department has introduced several risk management practices, ostensibly to cut down on cross-border crime and fraud by pre-emptively identifying those who pose the most risk to South Africa. These risk practices include identity document (ID) blocking, border externalization, advanced passenger profiling and land border enforcement and administration (smart borders).

The department has experienced ongoing problems with identity fraud. The old ID books, containing a photograph of the person, a barcode and a unique identity number, were relatively easy to forge. Consequently, the department faced the problem of people obtaining IDs fraudulently and using them to commit crimes, and claiming social benefits they were not entitled to, as non-South Africans. Corruption has been a systemic problem in the department, with its own officials colluding with members of the public to obtain fake IDs. Government became increasingly concerned that people were entering the NPR too easily, leading to them reviewing their plans for the NPR and joining the growing number of African countries introducing biometrically based smart identity cards. Some citizens also have two or more identity numbers assigned to them, while some identity numbers have several people assigned to them. These problems led the department to develop plans to clean up the NPR and use biometrics to ensure de-duplication of identity documents.

According to the draft White Paper, the department is establishing a National Identity System (NIS), which will replace the existing NPR and manage the biometric and biographic data of all persons, citizens and non-citizens (Department of Home Affairs 2020: 9). The NIS will include an Automated Biometric Identification System (ABIS), which will replace the existing Home Affairs National Identification System (HANIS) system. The department used

HANIS to capture fingerprints and photos for the NPR, but the system had reached its end-of-life as it was running on old equipment and software. The department also intended to integrate other databases into the NIS. These included the National Immigration Information System, the Movement Control System and the Enhanced Movement Control System. Once the department integrates these databases, then it would be able to issue electronic visas and provide identification services to other government departments and the private sector, but from one large database (Parliamentary Monitoring Group 2019). This integration initiative was part of a modernization programme the department initiated in 2012. The programme involved transforming the department's records from paper-based to digital ones, and the integration of different systems to overcome fragmentation that led to databases not talking to one another and contradictory information being stored in different databases (Department of Home Affairs 2020: 25–6).

The department intends to provide operating units with some operational autonomy, assisted by automated decision-making tools to increase the speed of decision-making about issues affecting citizens and non-citizens.[3] However, if automated decision-making is going to be used to weed out who is worthy of services and who is not, then there needs to be transparency about the basis for these decisions. Otherwise, users of Home Affairs services may find it even more difficult to challenge decisions than they have, as the department has developed a not-unfounded reputation of being difficult to communicate with. This problem may become even more severe as Home Affairs removes its identity management functions from the realm of normal politics and shifts them into the security realm. This shift could lead to the department using national security as a pretext not to provide reasons for decisions about the non-issuing of ID documents.

In fact, evidence is mounting that the department is using its new 'smart' ID card systems as a means of population control and exclusion, where they use the conversion process to block access to IDs on inappropriate grounds and render people stateless in the process. The process intensified from 2016 onwards, when then Home Affairs Minister Malusi Gigaba announced the digitization of birth certificates and other vital documents. For Gigaba, this digitization effort represented an attempt to replace the old, unreliable and problematic system with a new, more efficient system that minimized security risks, allowed for documents to be audited and that, overall, revolutionized the old NPR as it was transformed into the NIS to maintain its integrity.[4] Over the past decade, it has become much more difficult to obtain South African citizenship, and immigration is being tightened. These measures appear to be based on a view that sees 'foreigners' not as a resource but as a threat. Speaking about the Home Affairs efforts to tighten up on who has access to citizenship rights, a former employee of the department who requested anonymity said:

> [It was more about] how do we limit these people from accessing services, that's why the population register became like the holy grail. Because the moment you access the population register you get an ID, the moment you get an ID you get a grant. You get a job. That is what determines insiders and outsiders.

The department established that in 2013, almost 90 percent of asylum claims were rejected as unfounded. So, the overwhelming majority of asylum claims fell outside the Refugees Act. But, there's also a lack of an effective and operative management of asylum seekers . . . and they felt they needed to regulate access to citizenship by foreign nationals. The belief was that there were more people coming in, taking our resources. That's the mentality, which they felt required a modernization process involving the creation of a single national identity system, which is based on biometrics. That's what it was meant to be. There was a JCPS cluster decision that there was a need to balance the inward flow of low skilled labour to curtail the negative impact it has on domestic employment. So these are JCPS cluster decisions or issues.[5]

The department also aimed to provide identification services to other government departments, especially those in the security cluster, and expand beyond collecting fingerprints to collecting other biometrics, including iris prints and photographs for facial recognition purposes. Central identification and verification is becoming increasingly important to other departments in the security cluster, including the police, as well as private sector organizations like banks, and the department has done much to facilitate their access. Commenting on the police's direct access to the database, the Deputy Director General for Institutional Planning and Support, Thulani Mavuso, said the following:

> But, obviously when police are investigating, you remember that they only keep the fingerprints of people who are criminals, but when they get to a crime scene, they need to be able to identify people from the fingerprints they gather, so they'll have to come to us in order for them to verify that particular individual. When someone talks of surveillance, in my own understanding, it's regular monitoring, you know movements of people and all those things, so in our case I think it's not about that, it's about how do you resolve complex crime, how do we service people quickly. Remember that the police have continuous investigations, there are people who don't want to give their identity documents, they give the wrong names, the police should be able to say no, no, no, you are not Thulani, you are Joe, you know, check who you are because some people lie. So we also want a situation where the state does not create multiple databases. So, as Home Affairs we want to be able to offer this service government to government, government to business.[6]

Home Affairs clearly intends to deal with those who have biometric complexities, such as poorly defined fingerprints, by collecting more biometrics. However, there are few controls over improper use of this unlimited access. For instance, there do not appear to be any constraints preventing the police or intelligence services from using Home Affairs data for profiling people for improper reasons, or for conducting warrantless searches where no reasonable suspicion of criminality exists. Once the integrated NIS is established – which will be a civilian rather than a criminal database – and if police access is live and real time, then there are no constraints on how they can use Home Affairs' incredibly rich store of information about peoples' identity status and travel habits. The police and intelligence services could also use the Home Affairs facial database for unregulated facial recognition, which is concerning given the controversies globally about the accuracy of the technology and the ability to track people in public spaces for improper reasons (Swart 2021). In other words, Home Affairs' plans are running ahead of the regulations needed to prevent abuse.

Home Affairs is also using the transition from barcoded to smart IDs to deprive people arbitrarily of citizenship rights, in the process tightening up on who has access to the privileges of South African citizenship. This shift is manifested in the practice of ID blocking, where someone is prevented from transacting with public and private institutions as their ID is flagged as being suspicious and possibly fraudulent. This risk practice is pre-emptive in that it profiles individuals likely to be guilty of identity theft, or a threat to South African identity more generally, and in the process of doing so, it normalizes suspicion and supposition based on physical or geographical characteristics (Ericson 2008). According to Lawyers for Human Rights (LHR), a public interest law clinic in South Africa, IDs are blocked without notice, with people discovering that their IDs have been blocked when attempting to bank or access social services. This practice affects people in the most drastic ways, as they may be unable to access a grant, apply for a job or withdraw funds from their bank accounts, and the fact that the process is automated means that such life-altering decisions are taken by a system, not a person.[7] Also, the fact that there is no notice of intention to block beforehand means that the process lacks administrative justice. The basic principles of administrative justice require that public power is exercised in ways that are fair, legally defensible, reasoned and timeous, and that follow due process. People should be provided with reasons for the deprivation of a right, and should also have a right to appeal decisions which violate these basic principles. Automated decision-making about this most basic of rights – namely the right to identity – makes the exercise of these rights more difficult. Home Affairs' more securitized approach has also made it more difficult to access information on these issues.

The LHR has found that men are vastly more affected than women are. Most of their clients were South African, although Zimbabweans and Mozambiquans were affected too. Affected nationals of other countries include those from Namibia, Nigeria, Palestine, Eswatini, Tanzania and Zambia. The fact that the majority of those affected were South Africans points strongly to arbitrary and unjustifiable deprivation of citizenship from people who could claim citizenship legitimately. As Home Affairs' investigations into these cases could take a year or two, the impact on the everyday lives of those affected is considerable. Clients have approached the department with the assistance of LHR, provide the documents necessary for them to lift the block and the affected person was interviewed to determine their status. However, there were particular difficulties in providing the nationalities of older clients who may not have many of the necessary documents, leading to them being particularly susceptible to protracted blocking.

The number of blocked IDs peaked in 2017–18, when the digitization process and conversion to smart IDs was at its peak, and declined somewhat after that. Presumably, the department used the conversion process as an opportunity to try and clean up the NPR. However, around the same time, the department also became increasingly unresponsive, making it difficult to resolve queries about blocked individuals. In a case that LHR won in court, a South African citizen with a South African mother but with grandparents from Eswatini had his ID blocked and was ordered to leave the country. LHR overturned the block successfully, pending the finalization of his citizenship status.[8] According to the manager of the statelessness unit for LHR, Thandeka Chauke, the Covid-19 lockdown saw an influx of cases to LHR, as people found their IDs blocked but could not follow up with the department as their offices were closed. The department has claimed that they did not have the information about where people whose IDs were going to be blocked were, and so it was impossible to notify them beforehand. However, there are alternative processes they could use, such as publishing details about their intention to block individuals, or use SMSs.[9]

The department has claimed that they only do a 'soft block' in many cases, where someone needs to regularize some aspect of their status, and where they place a marker against someone's name, meaning that people can still transact on the ID. These differ from 'hard blocks' in more serious cases, where someone is suspected of having obtained citizenship illegally. However, LHR has found that in reality, the department applies this distinction inconsistently. Furthermore, it has proved to be extremely difficult to have the department lift these blocks, whether hard or soft, and which to all intents and purposes function as hard blocks. People have committed suicide out of frustration, because they cannot transact with institutions for basic services, and cannot obtain proper redress from the department. Almost exclusively, these blocks affect Black people owing to the apartheid history of poor documentation: birth certificates for older people, for instance, may be difficult to obtain or even not exist. Black people living in border towns and mining towns, as well as those showing regular movement across borders, are at particular risk of being profiled and blocked. Children of migrants have a right to be considered South African citizens, but they may be blocked because they live in a border town and cross the border regularly. Children of blocked parents may be blocked too, showing the trickling effect of blocked IDs. According to Chauke:

> I feel that [ID blocking] affects poor black people, and it affects men more than women, probably because they travel more . . . [I think] this ties back to that history of documentation in South Africa, and the fact that, you know, under apartheid civil registration and identity management systems only existed as a way of controlling the native population. It was not about it being an effective way of capturing people's data, and the population data, and I think it was only in the 1980s that legislation was introduced that actually made it compulsory to do things like birth registration. Before then, many people did not even see the necessity of having things like a birth certificate or an ID, because maybe they lived in remote areas and they worked in an informal sector, when they

cross the border, officials will just ask for money, so they did not see the need of having documentation. We see that even some of the cases we have dealt with, it is clients that were affected during that time. Now they cannot have the block lifted because they do not have that documentary proof, they were just given the ID numbers, they do not have birth certificates, they do not have any other documentary proof. So, I think it is somehow linked to that legacy of, you know, colonialism and apartheid, and that is why I think it affects mainly black people and, you know, black poor people. And, obviously then with xenophobia and the inference of fraud, the inference of you being an illegal foreigner is a bit higher when you are black.[10]

Home Affairs has linked its identification plans to ideas of nationalism and modernization. They have portrayed smart IDs and the move towards a centralized NIS as intrinsically progressive and an innovation that society can benefit from. However, these benefits are spread unevenly across society, and are being distributed in exclusionary ways. As Home Affairs takes on the character of a national security department, it becomes increasingly difficult to hold it to account for these practices, and automated decision-making is aggravating the problem. As the ability to prove one's identity becomes integral to modern life, identity gaps open up between people who have access to a legal identity and those who do not. Those who are most likely to suffer are Black working-class people whose families have histories of regional migration – after all, migration has been central to southern Africa's history. Furthermore, far from being a tool that allows citizens these hard-won rights and freedoms, the smart ID card system and the database that underpins it risk becoming a tool for the centralization of government power and authority. The 'single view of the client' that it enables risks becoming yet another opportunity for surveillance, in spite of the department's protestations to the contrary.

Immigration and border management: Smart borders

In principle, South Africa has aimed at a controlled and managed immigration policy as a pragmatic alternative to a closed, insular society on the one hand, and a completely open society lacking basic controls on the other. In reality, though, the government has tightened restrictions on who is allowed to enter and settle in the country beyond what could be described credibly as a controlled and managed system. While pressures to do so have been largely domestic, relating to the country's mounting unemployment crisis, powerful nations and blocs have also exerted pressure on South Africa to tighten its borders. For instance, in the wake of the Arab Spring and the subsequent flow of migrants from North Africa and the Middle East, the EU has been attempting to curb irregular migration, while recognizing that an ageing population meant that it would have to seek skilled people from outside the union. Through its Global Approach to Migration and Mobility, the EU has focused on strengthening cooperation with global and regional powers, including South Africa (European Commission 2011: 1–9). However, the subtext of these efforts was that the EU wanted to divert unwanted migrants to other countries, including South Africa, and furthermore it wanted South Africa to institute stronger border controls (Department of Home Affairs 2012).

Increasingly, South Africa is following the US Homeland Security model, pushing its borders outwards and making them smarter. The Home Affairs Department is integrating technology-driven and intelligence-led proactive risk management into its decision-making, rather than relying on reactive assessments of compliance with rules. These decisions determine whether individuals are allowed to enter and remain in the country, and often before visitors even enter the country. Foreign missions are expected to screen potential travellers for national security risks through an Advance Passenger Processing System, instituted ahead of South Africa's hosting of the FIFA 2010 World Cup. Immigration officers, too, are replacing physical border controls with virtual border controls by undertaking pre-screening of potential risks and instituting an advanced warning system. In making these changes, Home Affairs has moved increasingly from protection of its borders against military threats to border control to ward off non-military threats. These threats include the unauthorized and illegal movement of people and goods, such as the uncontrolled flow of migrants, smuggling of goods, drug trafficking and arms smuggling, piracy and terrorism. According to the department, the fact that immigration officers take decisions about entry to South Africa has put them on the frontline of national security protection, elevating their status in the security establishment beyond merely facilitating legitimate travel efficiently. The department has also introduced biometrics in immigration control, providing them with an internationally recognized, consistent means of identification. Biometrics allow for easier profiling of travellers, where individual characteristics and profiles are starting to replace fuzzier attributes like nationality as a grounds for determining eligibility for entering the country. To this end, the department had instituted an Enhanced Movement Control System to track movements across the country's borders at various ports of entry, and including biometric capabilities. If a 'hit' is generated on an undesirable person, then the person could be prevented from entering the country (Parliamentary Monitoring Group 2012; Department of Home Affairs 2014).

So, while immigration has not become the responsibility of a security department – which would suggest more complete securitization – Home Affairs itself has become more and more like a security department. As noted earlier, the department has also indicated that it intends to provide the state with early warnings of threats to national security within the scope of its mandate, which is likely to require significant strategic intelligence capabilities. However, legislators have given strategic national security intelligence powers to the SSA only through the National Strategic Intelligence Act, including on matters that fall within Home Affairs' mandate (Duncan 2020; Department of Home Affairs 2019a).

Historically, immigration services was a low-key part of the Home Affairs' mandate, as the department prioritized civic services that commanded the lion's share of resources. However, as immigration to South Africa picked up speed and the number of asylum seekers peaked in 2009 owing to the political crisis in Zimbabwe, the department's priorities shifted towards immigration. In order to justify this shift, they developed a narrative that immigration was integral to the security of the state. Nkosasana Dlamini-Zuma, who was minister between 2009 and 2012, pursued a much more securitized approach towards immigration, and this view sharpened after an embarrassing international incident involving a UK national Samantha Lewthwaite, believed to be a member of the Al Shabaab organization and linked to several terrorism attacks, including one in 2013 on a shopping mall in Nairobi, Kenya. Before that, she lived in South Africa for a while under a false identity and travelled to and from the country repeatedly, raising questions about the integrity of South Africa's immigration system. According to a former Home Affairs employee who requested anonymity:

> The emphasis was always on the civic side. So, the immigration side was falling apart and remember also that in terms of budget allocation, immigration never got what Civics got. I mean there was usually a massive difference. It wasn't prioritized. With Nkosasana [Dlamini-Zuma], you started getting this thing of security and the need to centralize more functions, the population register, naturalization, the concerns about permits, people getting married too easily, the abuses of the late registration of births process. There were key concerns about people entering the nation, and the national population register too easily, and we are not checking who these people are. So, it was all these attempts to clamp down on how to become a citizen. Then, a lot of decisions were centralized, saying don't do it in the provinces because we have no control, people's permit applications were stuck in drawers, never submitted unless they paid for the application to be. So a lot of that started happening.[11]

However, in attempting to clamp down on corruption in the provinces and bring uniformity to decision-making, the increasing centralization of functions saw immigration being deprioritized and demoted, as much of the expertise brought to bear on the centralized functions actually lay in civic services. The lack of resources for immigration management, coupled with the absence of a deep appreciation of the issues, led to this function being hollowed out, and drifting away from a rights-based approach to immigration to one emphasizing control.[12]

In an attempt to make it more difficult for foreigners to enter the country, the government decided to establish the Border Management Authority (BMA), falling under Home Affairs. The BMA will include a border guard of commissioned officers to enforce the law at the border (Republic of South Africa 2020: 10). The BMA grew out of the Border Control Coordinating Committee, which sat in the tax collection agency, the South African Revenue Service, until the government relocated this entity to Home Affairs. In a departure from the classic securitization model, the government took time to establish the BMA, which was a protracted affair. Its genesis can be traced back to 1996, when the government undertook an assessment of border policing, informed by a US team, which found that illegal smuggling of goods and people was widespread. The assessment offered two pathways for dealing with these problems: either a single border control agency or a cooperation venture with different government departments. Not all countries follow an integration model, but significantly, the Five Eyes countries do. This model follows a front office-back office approach, where staff in the back office identify risks that the front office staff prioritize, through the compliance and inspection functions.

It was only in 2013 that cabinet decided to establish the BMA following a NICOC feasibility study the year before and a National Intelligence Estimate that motivated for it after finding that existing institutional structures were inadequate. Cabinet wanted to move away from a silo-based approach to border management and control, where various government departments had different responsibilities, and coordination of these responsibilities was becoming complex and difficult. Rather, it decided to move towards an integration model, where one dedicated entity with clear lines of accountability became responsible, using what it referred to as modern techniques and technology to deliver its mandate (Department of Home Affairs 2015a). The BMA would assume control over the country's ports of entry, and adopt an intelligence-driven and integrated structure to manage risks at the border and facilitate the movement of goods and people, replacing the old gatekeeping approach towards border management (Department of Home Affairs 2015b). In the same way that the NIS is intended to establish a single view of the citizen, the BMA is meant to establish a single view of the traveller.

One of the dangers presented by the BMA is that it may lead to function creep with other government departments. Already, SAPS has expressed concern that the BMA has been granted policing powers that should rightfully have remained with them, but their concerns were given short shrift during parliamentary debates (South African Police Service 2018b: 12–15; Parliamentary Monitoring Group 2019). Mirroring Homeland Security, the agency also wished not only to screen travellers for known suspects, and profile travellers but also to identify unknown risks based on passenger profiles, too. To that end, the agency resolved to establish a National Border and Risk Management and Targeting Centre, which would act as an early warning system relating to risks and threats in the border environment, and complement the existing Advance Passenger Processing System. The department also envisaged establishing a trusted traveller programme, where it would allow low- to no-risk travellers to proceed through e-gates without being inconvenienced by cumbersome manual immigration checks (Parliamentary Monitoring Group 2016a, b; BusinessTech 2020). While the United Nations Security Council has called on its member countries to establish such systems for terrorism screening (Privacy International 2018b). South Africa's plans risked tilting over into profiling of potential threats based on unclear characteristics, with limited transparency or scope for being challenged. Basic democratic rights of notification, correction and appeal against adverse decisions are likely to be difficult to exercise.

Progressive alternatives to centralized identification systems: The case of Mauritius

South Africa has a long tradition of registration and identification of its citizens, and the need to do so has proved to be relatively uncontroversial, notwithstanding the apartheid history of the 'dompas', the internal passport to control the movements of Black people. In contrast, the US, the UK and other countries in the global North have rejected national ID systems as being unacceptable violations of basic rights and freedoms. In fact, biometric civil and voting registration systems have a colonial dimension, as they are concentrated in the global South and in former colonies (Breckenridge: 2014: 17). These realities show that centralized national identity systems are not essential to development or security: in three Five Eyes countries (the UK, Australia and the US), citizens have rejected centralized biometric databases outright. Any struggle against exclusionary identity and citizenship needs to be a political struggle: after all, in a post-capitalist, socialist society people should not only be equal but also free.

When citizenship is equated with legal nationality, governments can claim the power to determine who can claim rights and who cannot, and what the terms of one's membership of society are. In class societies, governments can use citizenship to divide the working class and keep the benefits of citizenship exclusive. Rights are individualized, which makes it more difficult for the class to win these rights for itself. Identification systems also provide governments with the ability to identify and track the citizenry, and shift the terms and conditions of membership of society from society to governments. While they provide real benefits, national identity systems are becoming integral to the maintenance of uneven development. Governments such as South Africa's are using them to identify insiders from outsiders, and barricade more fortunate countries from less fortunate ones. What is particularly significant about South Africa's immigration system is that it targets low-skilled labour especially, and Home Affairs' emerging systems are exclusionary specifically for them. Furthermore, there are dangers of only one document being needed to establish identity, as this system is likely to increase identity theft. A centralized database such as the NIS – which will be a critical database of the personal information for the entire South African population – is vulnerable to hacking, corruption and manipulation. While they may not start out as being internal passports, tracking and even restricting domestic movement, ID cards could gradually become just such a system as, once established, it is unlikely to be restricted to its original purpose. In fact, the card's purpose could move far beyond identification and extend into a central registry documenting many aspects of citizens' lives, leading to more citizenship rights being subjected to whether or not they have the card, and leading to the system becoming mandatory rather than voluntary. So while in theory, citizens would have the right to opt out of such a massive tracking system, in reality it would become de facto mandatory.

There is no reason why multiple identity systems cannot operate effectively. There are benefits to unconnected data silos, as they can prevent government or companies from being able to access a person's complete profile. In contrast, the more services require an ID to be shown, and the more Home Affairs registers the ID as having been accessed by service providers, the more possible tracking becomes. Such tracking can lead to 360-degree profiling, and raises the question of whether government can maintain large amounts of personal data and keep it safe and error free. In a centralized system, errors could have catastrophic consequences for the individuals concerned. These features of South Africa's identity system provide some of the intellectual and political foundation for opposition.

Important lessons can be learnt from another southern African country with a history of coercive population registration, namely, Mauritius. In a struggle against government attempts to create a smart ID card system linked to a centralized national population database, social movements and technical experts developed ideas about how alternatives could be constructed. Colonial administrations in Mauritius forced slaves on the sugar plantations to carry identity cards on pain of arrest. Because of this history, and the resulting sensitivities about population registration, Mauritius did not really have a national population register until the 1980s, when it set up a paper-based system. It was only in 2013 that the Mauritian government instituted a smart ID card system, involving the collection of fingerprints and facial photographs for facial recognition purposes. Different and disparate campaigns sprung up organically, and while they coalesced at different points in time, largely they remained separate.[13] The paper-based system was run by the Civil Status Office, which fell under a government ministry, but when smart IDs were rolled out, the responsibility was transferred to the presidency, suggesting that the project had been elevated in importance from being a relatively low-status administrative matter to being a national security matter requiring direct presidential control.

Fearing that the populace would not accept the smart ID card system, the Mauritian government took over a decade to initiate it, and when they did, they went on a massive public education drive. In an attempt to gain acquiescence, the government portrayed the ID card as a one-stop shop, where people would only need to carry one card to transact with a wide range of institutions, from banks to education and health services. Thus, the card and its centralized database represented the government's attempt to address discrepancies in the existing system, where different government departments held records that, at times, contained inaccurate and conflicting information. Strategically, they also understated the possible security uses of the card, as they feared that people would come to see the card as a social control tool. The public was suspicious of the government's intentions but did not know enough about the system to oppose it. In fact, according to Mauritian information technology specialist and open-source advocate Ish Sookun, the system was a 'black box for them, they didn't know what was inside'.[14]

However, as discomfort spilled over into opposition against the smart ID card system from a variety of different perspectives and ideologies, campaigns became more organized. One of the organized opponents was the internationalist socialist political organization born out of Mauritius's mass movements, Lalit de Klas. The organization argued that those without ID cards would be at a disadvantage relative to those with them, and those in the working class would be most disadvantaged. Not only did the organization attack the central database, however, they also attacked the oppressive system that underpinned it, and argued that opposition needed to be part of a broader political struggle for more freedom, less surveillance and less oppression (Lalit 2017). Lalit member Rajni Lallah made the point that the campaign against smart ID cards politicized the system and raised the costs for the government in taking it forward. It became a factor in the electoral victory of Militant Socialist Movement leader Pravind Jugnauth, who challenged the lawfulness of the system and who subsequently became prime minister. According to Lallah:

> When we started the campaign against the biometric ID and database, we were alone as a political force. And what happened was, through our campaign we saw various leaders of traditional political parties and parliamentary parties gradually taking a stance against the biometric ID card system, with its centralized database. So, in a way, it started being a political victory, because we started out being the first political force, the only political force, and then they became a majority of political forces. After a while, after the campaign started gaining ground . . . And when Pravind Jugnauth who actually launched the case in the Supreme Court, it was a reflection of the strength of the campaign. So, there was a general election in 2014, and [the smart ID card system] was one of the major points in the electoral campaign, and the party of Pravind Jugnauth won the election. So, in a way, that was a political victory, before the Supreme Court judgements.[15]

There were important differences in the strategic goals of the campaign; some were systemic and some anti-systemic. Privacy was not a particularly successful argument from a legal perspective. For Sookun, a population register is a necessary part of modern society, so he was not against population registration as such. What he opposed was the government's blindness to the flaws in their proposed system, and the dangers of it falling under the president's office, which gave the most sensitive database of personal information to the most powerful political authority in the country.[16]

After the Supreme Court judgement, the system was converted from a one-to-many identification system – where a search could be conducted on the fingerprints of an unknown person to identify them – to a one-to-one system verification system, where a smart ID card bearer could use it to verify that they were who they said they were. The government still collected fingerprints, stored them for a short time to allow for the processing of the card and then destroyed them. All relevant information would then be stored on the card, including the fingerprint, and a department or service provider would use a card reader to verify the bearer's biometrics on the card against their actual biometrics. While this concession was undoubtedly a partial victory for the campaign, it made very little sense from an identity management point of view as the card could be forged. People still needed to carry their birth certificate and proof of address to transact with a bank, for instance.

The danger of a centralized biometrically based national identity system is that it creates a single point of failure. One option to mitigate the dangers of centralization is to create a more distributed identity management system, where updating of information takes place automatically across government departments. Speaking about some of the principles that should underpin a more secure identity management system, Sookun suggested the following:

> I would not prefer a central population register, I will prefer a distributed system, where each of them is to have their responsibilities and checks to do whenever something is updated. They get the notification when something is updated, and they have the validation process to go through. A modern distributed system would be that the data consistency does not become the responsibility of one team in the government. A modem system would be where you have the different ministries, having their applications, their database, they are recording their data, and all of these are being automatically updated, while going through different checks ... [Let's] look at how identity systems work. It works on something which is based on trust ... [It] does not cater for how the system can be compromised, and whether there are checks for those different means of compromising the system ... [Give] me a computer and tell me this computer's fully secured. I'm going to have a smile on my face and say no. There are different ways to circumvent modern information technology (IT) systems.

> So for me, to have a modern identification system for the government, for the population, it would it need to have both [human and automated interventions]. You need to have the parts of IT to facilitate things to make things go fast, but different ministries and government agencies need to be able to talk to each other and get information, not have to make people wait for three, four months for their applications to process. But at the same time, the trust cannot be put completely on the systems, there needs to be a sort of process or procedure where the trust is human based.[17]

However, Lalit was of the view that not even a distributed system was needed. Noting the fact that Mauritius survived very well without a national identity management system, they opposed such a system in principle. For Lallah, the country had the experience of using more basic identity documents, such as birth certificates, to transact with the government and businesses such as banks.[18] The Mauritian experience gives an indication of effective anti-surveillance activism that can be pursued even in the context of capitalism, and activism that can unite a broad range of social forces for maximum effectiveness.

Beyond Afrophobia: From open borders to no borders

Struggles against centralized national identification systems cannot be waged in isolation of struggles against restrictive, anti-working-class immigration systems, as the former underpin the latter. As a regional hub, South Africa is a destination for thousands of migrants from the region. Yet, the government is becoming increasingly hostile towards migration, promoting xenophobic discourses and practices and 'othering' non-nationals, and it is using identity systems to achieve these goals. In doing so, it is dismantling an earlier, important political project of pan-African unity, and failing to provide thought leadership on the need for free movement as the only socially just solution to the region's problems. It is also using identity management and border controls to cement its role as a neoliberal sub-imperialist power, by discouraging the free movement of labour while championing the free movement of capital, and specifically its own capital in the form of South African companies.

States in Africa were often based on colonial boundaries that imposed irrational divisions in previously united communities: divisions that had to be sustained by force by colonial regimes. Nowhere is the arbitrariness of borders more evident than in southern Africa, where competing colonial powers settled territorial disputes over the heads of indigenous populations. While Portugal and Germany maintained important footholds in the region, the UK dominated to the point where at one stage, it even supported the idea of a union of southern Africa countries under its rule. Territorial boundaries were really settled in the region only once South Africa, Zimbabwe, Zambia, Botswana and Mozambique obtained independence from these colonial powers. South Africa inherited its external border from the UK's 1910 establishment of the Union; yet, cross-border mobility remained high, especially between Zimbabwe and South Africa. Their respective post-apartheid, post-colonial administrations maintained the borders established by colonial and white minority rule, and used them to impose the terms of bounded citizenships on their populations; yet, it was only quite recently that these administrations began to circumscribe relatively free cross-border movement through official regulations (Klotz 2016: 180–94).

What are the alternatives to increasingly securitized borders and identity systems? Regional integration implies moving beyond the official obsession with borders, because the destiny of the most oppressed and exploited – including in South Africa – is likely to be a shared one that lies in regional unity rather than division. As even a cursory understanding of the history of the region shows, nation-states as currently constituted are very recent historical artefacts. However, regional integration must take place on terms set by labour and the unemployed, not by capital. Capitalism is not necessarily hostile to open borders: in fact, there is a pro-capitalist argument for open borders, which is that free movement of labour allows employers to address skills shortages, removes the number of border crossings by undocumented migrants and encourages regional trade (Kitimbo 2015: 92–5). However, this perspective tends to favour a pan-Africanism of capital, but not of labour, and to the extent that workers are allowed to migrate, then they do so on terms set by capital. Capital's support for open borders tends to extend to promoting a high-skill, high-wage regional integration, where governments allow those with scarce skills more mobility than workers with more generic skills, or semi-skilled or unskilled workers. These immigration policies inevitably advantage middle-class workers in niche sectors and disadvantage the rest.

Open borders are undoubtedly more desirable than closed borders and barricaded countries. To that extent, it is an important transitional demand that a broad range of progressive social forces could unite around, whether anti-capitalist or not. In doing so, though, they would need to promote open borders for labour, rather than open borders for capital. Anti-capitalists would need to argue for a pro-working class perspective to become dominant in any open borders movement. However, even the idea of open borders does not seem to be aspirational enough, as it still recognizes the existence of borders and the regulatory role they play in keeping migrants insecure and exploitable. Open borders can still be closed and fortified at some stage in the future, and as such the idea does not offer a longer-term solution to the problem of anti-working-class border controls. In other words, this perspective fails to question the basis of the regulatory system that gave rise to borders in the first place (King 2016: 19). Yet, there is nothing natural or inevitable about nation-states and their artificial, often arbitrary, territorial boundaries. Instead, a no-borders perspective – which does not recognize borders at all – means refusing to acknowledge the legitimacy of borders, on the basis that they interfere with the freedom of movement and peoples' right to self-determination more generally.

No borders builds on the anarchist tradition of taking a principled stance against the state, although it may be necessary to engage with the state to secure further freedoms. A struggle for freedom of movement is inherently a struggle against the state and capitalism, as borders define the outer limits of state power (King 2016: 19). Migration practiced autonomously by people involves a form of escape from the state, as the state is unable to control their movements. Decolonial theory also understands borders as a form of imperialism and encourages anti-capitalists to prefigure a borderless society that is non-oppressive and non-hierarchical. Western imperialism and capitalism are major causes of displacement and migration as they make it impossible for migrants to survive in their homelands. Yet, they also criminalize migration and define migrants as aliens and illegals. They racialize migration by constructing whiteness and Western nations as inherently superior, and make migrants exploitable by maintaining them in precarious conditions (Walia 2013: 27–36).

It is also possible to read a no-borders perspective into more anti-capitalist versions of pan-Africanism, which represented a multiplicity of attempts – in theory and in practice – to overcome colonial divide-and-rule legacies and promote a vision of a self-reliant and united Africa. Pan-African thought has straddled multiple perspectives, from outright capitalist to radical nationalist, anti-capitalist and socialist. In fact, African political thought is rich in perspectives that make the case for inclusive approaches towards nationality, which are not tied to primordial markers of identity but are understood as political communities that can be made and re-made. These perspectives reject essentialist definitions of nationality that were so evident in European thought. For instance, German theorists J. G. Herder and J. G. Fichte maintained that a nation is defined by its culture and mainly its language, while Joseph Stalin infamously defined a nation as a historically evolved stable community of people based on community of language, territory, economic life and psychological make-up manifested in a community of culture. The inescapable conclusion of these definitions is that groups that do not share certain characteristics (like language or race) are to be excluded from the definition of who constitute the nation (Duncan 2007).

African theorists of nationality have had to grapple with the concrete conditions of nation-formation to develop an inclusive theory of nationality that breaks decisively from essentialist definitions (Duncan 2007; No Sizwe 1979: 181). Much depends, though, on which class is ascendant in the struggle for nationality. In developing an anti-colonial critique of 'official nationalism', Frantz Fanon recognized that nationalism has both a revolutionary and a reactionary potential. It was revolutionary in that it could be used to mobilize the masses of colonized people against colonial regimes, and reactionary in that – once independence was realized – it could be used by an emergent indigenous bourgeois leadership to suppress the very masses that had waged the national liberation struggle. The only way of countering these divisive tendencies is for the masses to mount claims on the state based on a common nationhood, and not based on particular racial, ethnic or religious identities. Such an approach would be a recipe for class disunity, which would ultimately be in the interests of the capitalist class (Fanon 1963: 191). Pan-African integration would need to transcend narrow nationalism and be international in outlook in ways that pan-Europeanism has failed to achieve. In fact, the pan-European political experiment has created an inward-looking and provincializing Europe that seeks to protect its own from external 'invaders', especially migrants from Africa, while pan-Africanism needs to be international in outlook and embrace migrants (Ndlovu-Gatsheni 2018: 29). Political elites have become wedded to received borders – in spite of their often colonial and racist histories – because they have benefitted from them, creating perverse incentives to promote citizenship founded on indigeneity (Neocosmos 2008: 10). Yet, some more opportunistic elements in the indigenous bourgeoisie have been willing to absorb African nationalism to the extent that they could use it to undermine more radical African claims (Ndlovu-Gatsheni 2018: 29).

In the case of South Africa, which despite a recent economic decline remains the region's economic powerhouse that attracts the lion's share of intra-African immigrants, the struggle against apartheid was, in part, a struggle to establish an inclusive national identity. South African socialist and political theorist Neville Alexander argued that this struggle could well create the path to regional integration and the development of supra national identities in time to come, leading to a greater sense of regional belonging. Alexander argued that every South African should be open to having his or her identity – including national identity – extended 'should historical evolution point in the direction of regional or continental, and even global unification' (Alexander 2002: 109). The end result may be a very different identity to that of being a South African, but citizens should be open to this process of historical development and not feel threatened by it. However, for Alexander, the material basis for the wide-scale development of supranational identities does not exist yet. He argued that 'as long as the national state is the political and economic entity in terms of which international relations are structured, even if only on the surface, [national] identity is an inescapable one' (Alexander 2002: 109). But, that does not mean to say that socialist movements should not aspire to this objective in the long term.

Free movement on a no-borders basis is also a form of reparation: a giving back to the region by a South African government that has become increasingly dominant. South Africa is using its regional might to extract surplus from the region while serving as a stabilizing force for capitalism. The post-apartheid South African state has been highly successful in dividing the region's working class against itself through the promotion of official exclusionary practices that amount to Afrophobia, or xenophobia targeting Africans only. In this context, migration could become a politically transformative act that brings into being an entirely different community in the region that recognizes its common destiny rather than its apart-ness. This sort of free movement would also be claimed and practised from below, rather than being granted from above by official institutions such as governments, or government and state-centric pan-African institutions such as the SADC or the African Union (AU).

The predecessor to the AU, the Organization of African Unity (OAU), accepted the boundaries of the 1884–5 Berlin conference that formalized the scramble for Africa by European powers, and rather committed itself to facilitating free movement on the continent. Consequently, Home Affairs could argue that South Africa does not deal with immigration on a terrain of its own making, and, furthermore, that the country has finite resources. However, in order to claim the policy space to think about immigration differently, at the very least, Home Affairs needs to remain in the realm of normal politics rather than becoming integrated into security politics. South Africa's existing security institutions have enough accountability problems already, without the government creating another one. Home Affairs should not be part of the JCPS cluster, and national security should be stripped out of its mandate. Even from a limited reformist perspective, it is not necessary for the department to be repositioned as a national security institution for its functions that impact on national security to be secured. South Africa can and should make a different, conscious political choice to those ethno-nationalist states seeking to promote racist and classist notions of citizenship, defining themselves according to who they exclude. Afrophobia is turning South Africa into a pariah of the region. Thankfully, the country does not face any major conventional national security threats at the moment. However, if it continues on the path that Home Affairs is on, then it should surprise no one if this threat picture changes. This is because security politics have a nasty way of boomeranging on the very countries that practice them.

CONCLUSION

Beyond national security surveillance

The most difficult challenge of writing this book has been to understand the patterns in national security surveillance in southern African countries, move beyond them and attempt to envision alternatives without falling into the trap of empiricism. The region's peoples cannot afford to remain prisoners of prevailing adverse conditions. On the one extreme, by focusing on current realities, I faced the danger of restricting alternatives to what appears to be 'realistic'. On the other, I risked engaging in unrealizable, utopian, thought experiments. The challenge I faced was to offer a basket of reforms, without lapsing into reformism; in other words, to be both pragmatic and visionary at the same time. It would be highly demoralizing to argue only for those changes that could be achieved beyond capitalism, as the system may remain with us for some time to come given the weaknesses of left forces and anti-systemic movements, including in southern Africa. At the same time, as pre-revolutionary moments have taught us, when and how social explosions with huge transformative potential are likely to occur are almost impossible to predict. The bridge between what exists and what should exist needs to be built from material that connects the present to the future, linking democratic demands that are achievable before the overthrow of capitalism, to alternatives to capitalism in the future. Once this work is done, then it becomes easier to respond to openings for more radical change with speed when they do occur.

Southern Africa is inserted into the global economy on terms that are profoundly unfavourable to it, and the Covid-19 pandemic is likely to worsen the problem, as is the vaccine apartheid playing out across the globe at the time of writing this book. The pandemic and ensuing lockdowns have also made mass organizing so much more difficult, and the practically unchallenged dominance of security services in enforcing these lockdowns has added to these problems. There is little doubt that the protest movements that sprang up in the region in the wake of the 2007–8 global recession will emerge from this period weaker than they were: and this at a time when they are more needed than ever before.

In this conclusion, I draw the threads of the various chapters together and conclude with suggestions for an anti-capitalist programme setting out how national security surveillance could be challenged and re-imagined in non-prescriptive ways. These alternative capabilities would not use mass surveillance or mass criminalization as ways of achieving social control, but would pursue regionally relevant versions of what criminologist Meghan McDowell (2017: 43–55) has termed 'insurgent safety', or safety that is locally determined and anti-capitalist. This form of safety would involve ordinary people re-imagining what it means to feel safe and secure, and how freedom from fear and want – the essence of the human security definition of national security – can be achieved without giving the main authority to the state to do so. The programme will outline suggestions that anti-capitalists could use to pursue reforms – while not making reforms the end goal of their activism, or non-reformist reforms – while dismantling national security surveillance powers, and pursuing ways of creating safety collectively that could form the basis of security powers in a socialist society.

In each chapter, I explored different dimensions of security and surveillance powers and practices, and alternatives to them. I prioritized intelligence and surveillance powers on national security matters, and particularly communication surveillance. This focus was deliberate: an examination of the full gamut of security powers, from visible policing and military security, was too broad a scope for this book. In any event, I was interested in exploring what to do about the less visible or invisible national security powers, as they are often more pernicious given the high levels of secrecy around them, and therefore more difficult to organize around and challenge. I was also uncomfortable with the lack of left scholarship on intelligence and wanted to address that gap.

The main arguments chapter by chapter

What follows is a sketching out of the arc of the main arguments and the chapters that took these arguments forward, to show why I chose them and how they relate to one another and the overall arguments. While classical imperialism and colonial rule may have come to an end in southern Africa, newer forms of imperialist domination ensure that the former imperial powers continue to exert indirect control over their former dominions. One of the ways this is done is by the major surveillance powers organized into the Five Eyes alliance championing expanded definitions of national security and intelligence, covering not only threats but also interests. This expansion has allowed them to bend national security surveillance to pursue their economic interests abroad. The continued relevance of imperialism becomes apparent when examining Lenin's five features of imperialism, which are evident in how surveillance is practised by the Five Eyes countries. While the emergence of new sub-imperialist 'middle powers' such as China has complicated the situation, making a simple assertion of the continued existence of classical imperialism difficult, the term still has considerable explanatory power in explaining how the region continues to relate to its former colonial dominators (Chapter 1).

Not only have imperialist and former colonial countries promoted expansive definitions of national security around the world, they also have encouraged the establishment of unaccountable intelligence agencies in southern Africa. This becomes apparent through an examination of agencies established in Anglophone southern Africa, and there I focused particularly on Zimbabwe, Botswana and Namibia. Largely, these agencies are weak in the sense that they cannot challenge the continued domination of the means of surveillance by their former colonizers, and their entanglements with policing – a colonial legacy that post-colonial governments have perpetuated – have weakened them even further. However, these agencies are also strong in the sense that they have access to an increasingly sophisticated arsenal of tools and practices to police restive local populations, thereby making sure that the limited incorporation of the region into the global economy can continue relatively unchallenged. Multilateral institutions such as the UN and OECD have not helped matters by promoting a purportedly alternative vision for national security – namely human security – that has securitized more and more social issues and legitimized the massive expansion of national security powers into more and more areas, such as food and water security. However, historically, the former liberation movements demonstrated that intelligence powers do not automatically belong to the state; they are functions that society needs, even if they are currently bent towards serving capitalist class interests. So, while there are strong arguments for shutting these agencies down as there is limited evidence of them serving the functions they claim to serve, alternatives still need to be found for how these powers are to be organized in society. However, alternatives to national security and all its current institutional arrangements would need to engage with the complex question of what an ideal society or alternative social order should look like (Chapter 2).

I turned to discussing the most prominent national security surveillance practices in the region, diagnosing the problems with them, and answering the following questions: what should an anti-capitalist perspective be on these practices, and in a post-capitalist, socialist society, should these practices continue to exist, and if so, in what forms? Surveillance practices and tools honed in the war on terror and developed for military uses allow the major imperial powers to monitor their interests (and threats to them) remotely and gain diplomatic advantages through the theft of other countries' trade secrets, rendering direct colonial occupation unnecessary. Mass SIGINT surveillance extends far beyond the stated purposes of fighting organized transnational crime and terrorism and extends into reproducing and reinforcing global racial and class hierarchies. Such surveillance has made global social relations between former colonizers and the colonized more unequal. At the same time, southern African countries lack the same capacities to surveil the Five Eyes countries, while they are always finding innovative ways to practice mass surveillance on their own citizens. Even if they cannot afford the state-of-the-art equipment available to the major surveillance powers, they have learnt how to create the fear of surveillance in broader society – even if it is not taking place – creating a self-disciplining effect where people police themselves.

Global South countries have attempted to correct the continued control of world affairs by the major imperialist powers, in the form of the BRICS alliance of countries. However, increasingly this alliance has become sub-imperial in nature, with China especially using surveillance to extend its hegemony across the region, given its growing importance as a resource base for the country's continued expansion. Russia has also been very active in exporting its 'colour revolution' national security doctrine to the region, and former liberation movements in government in the region have embraced it with relish, as it provides them with a doctrinal justification to engage in domestic political policing of dissent. An anti-capitalist approach would endorse the need for global South cooperation, but on the basis of a 'BRICS-from-below' (Bond 2015), and one that overcomes xenophobic and localistic tendencies, as well as the surveillant tendencies of the major BRICS powers. There would be no place in a post-capitalist, socialist society for mass surveillance powers, as they contribute to the weaponization of the internet. While there should be a highly limited place for targeted surveillance, the lawful interception model promoted by the US and the EU is too invasive and promotes insecure communications to the advantage of these major surveillance powers. There is a much less invasive way of conducting surveillance, involving targeted hacking that exploits existing software and hardware vulnerabilities, rather than creating new vulnerabilities (Chapters 3 and 4).

After decades of peripheralization, parts of southern Africa are becoming increasingly important to the global economy. Southern Africa especially is rich in natural resources, and the region's commodities and land are at a premium. These realities mean that surveillance is likely to increase, as the major imperialist powers seek to extend their influence and ultimately control over the region's resources. The region also provides a huge but still relatively untapped market for surveillance technologies. As anti-austerity protests spread across the region, and new social and political actors take to the streets and social networks, governments already panicked by the Arab Spring are scrambling to acquire data-driven surveillance tools. There is an arms race in the region, where the countries with mature arms economies compete with emerging BRICS superpowers (especially Russia and China) for new markets. Largely, southern Africa has become a net importer of surveillance equipment, creating technological dependence on the major surveillance powers. However, if surveillance capabilities are pared down massively, then what is to become of the surveillance industry? An anti-capitalist programme would focus on the fact that the scientific and engineering expertise used in the manufacturing of this equipment is being misdirected, and argue for divestment from the surveillance industry to free up public funds for more life-enhancing, socially useful and ecologically sustainable work. In that regard, the current campaigns against the arms trade should be extended to dual-use goods, including surveillance technologies, which would mean broadening these campaigns beyond their historical focus on conventional arms (Chapter 5).

The Five Eyes alliance has encouraged southern African countries to fuse military, intelligence and policing capabilities, with policing becoming more militarized and intelligence-led, as this shift creates domestic markets for military equipment. In the process, internal security has become framed increasingly as a national security concern, with the police playing more of a role in achieving national security. This reframing of policing mandates has become more visible in southern Africa, too, although this is in addition to an already-existing problem of many intelligence agencies themselves having internal policing powers. Using the South African police's responses to the student #feesmustfall protests as a case study, I showed how intelligence-led policing has made the police even less accountable for their actions than they were, in part because this form of policing has blurred the lines between law enforcement and national security. Bearing in mind the growing calls internationally to defund and abolish the police as part of efforts to dismantle racialized oppression, I argued for the need to re-envision how policing functions are to be organized in society, where basic state functions are taken over by community structures organized on the principles of mutual solidarity. However, the South African experience with self-organized policing through self-defence units has highlighted some of the dangers, and the need for strong but non-partisan democratic controls by organized sections of the working class. A world without prisons, policing or mass criminalization of social problems will most likely have very little need for surveillance powers anyway (Chapter 6).

I then turned to one final expanding area of national security surveillance powers, namely, the civil functions that typically fall under 'Homeland Affairs' departments, and particularly the management of national identity systems and border security. Using the South African Department of Home Affairs as a case study, and its introduction of a biometrically based 'smart' ID card, as well as its initiatives to tighten South Africa's borders, I showed how increasingly the government is using digitally based risk practices to fortify the country against the region's increasingly desperate and mobile working class. When civic identity functions become national security functions, and when surveillance based on citizenship is heightened, the government can use citizenship to divide and disempower a working class that has been regionalized for much of its history, and turn the working class on itself. Imperialism has a stake in promoting the free movement of capital, but not of labour. Consequently, the EU is promoting tighter border controls in Africa and encouraging greater surveillance of borders as part of fortification efforts. In the process, borders have become securitized, and the government agencies tasked with border management have appropriated national security mandates. While most of these efforts have focused on North Africa, they have also promoted fortification of borders in southern African countries, too. Surveillance is being used to keep 'invaders' from majority Black countries out of the north at the empire's periphery, and keep them trapped in conflict zones. Using risk technologies honed in the war on terror, South Africa is engaging in similar exclusionary practices in the region, in the process helping to keep the region's most marginalized people at bay.

At the same time, migration from the region to South Africa continues notwithstanding, as people refuse to recognize borders and practice living freely without official restraints. Based on a rich tradition of southern African scholarship, including Marxist scholarship, that demonstrates the artificiality and arbitrariness of the region's borders, I argued that a no-borders perspective, rather than open borders, coupled with programmes to eliminate inequalities within and between states, is the only socially just perspective. Borders reinforce historical global colonial disparities, and a no-borders perspective would render national security surveillance of citizenship inside countries and at their borders superfluous. Struggles around identification systems and surveillance more generally in Mauritius have provided some practical pointers as to how these functions can revert into the civil realm, and point to a world that does not even need centralized national identification systems (Chapter 7).

Returning to racial capitalism as a lens through which to view national security surveillance, it is apparent that the colonial powers and apartheid regime institutionalized racism in order to justify exploitation of, and controls over, the Black working class. South Africa did so on a regional basis, relying on migrant labour from the region to accumulate profits. The colonial and apartheid powers encouraged over-policing and over-surveillance, and once they had established the architecture of exploitation and oppression, they could dispense with these race-based systems of domination. This was because the architecture would continue to exist, although run by a new class of post-colonial, post-apartheid elites represented by political parties that could continue to dominate with relative ease.

Surveillance perpetuates social and historical disadvantage in various ways. It provides deeply entrenched ruling parties with the means to track any emerging opposition, by continuing colonial-era practices of domestic political surveillance, including by using more contemporary digital surveillance tools. These ruling parties act as regional police, containing dissent in these countries by targeting those perceived to be leading protests, and stabilizing imperialism by neutralizing emergent threats to the system before they escalate into full-blown challenges. Imperialist countries continue to profit from repression as these countries offer markets for their arms and surveillance companies, and the nominal trappings of democracy, such as multiparty elections, allow them to continue selling surveillance tools to them without fear of a political backlash. In any event, southern African countries can always turn to China or Israel to provide surveillance tools if there is a political backlash in the US or Europe, as these countries have even fewer controls over their surveillance exports. The former colonial powers can blame surveillance abuses – which are almost inevitable given the intelligence architecture of the region – on weak or dysfunctional states, which absolves them over their own roles in promoting unaccountable surveillance. Transfers have not stopped at surveillance technologies, though. They have also extended to a range of intelligence and surveillance ideas and practices transported from the North to the South, and they have also contributed to pervasive surveillance of whole populations. Some practices, such as SIM card registration and centralized identity systems, are not even considered acceptable for the global North; yet they are implemented with abandon in southern African countries.

As a general rule, surveillance exporting countries fail to practice meaningful due diligence on the extent of controls in southern African target markets, as though their citizens are not deserving of data protections. In fact, there appears to be a data free-for-all in the region, with lax to no controls. At the same time, imperialist countries use their superior surveillance capabilities to keep a watch on southern African countries to maintain their own interests, ensuring their continued predatory relationships with these countries. Doing so in invisible ways allows them to maintain the legitimacy of the system, preventing them from being accused of continued exploitation of majority Black countries. The racial hierarchies that were established violently through colonialism can continue to exist through the global distribution of power and resources. In other words, pervasive surveillance is not an aberration of the global capitalist system, but integral to it.

Envisioning alternatives to national security surveillance

It would be entirely inappropriate to prescribe the content of anti-surveillance struggles in southern Africa as this would 'mock democracy from the beginning' (Raptis 1980: 8); however, while a blueprint would be inappropriate, it is necessary to have at least some notion of the basic principles to guide the transition to a post-capitalist, socialist society. As FRELIMO's founder Eduardo Mondlane recognized, it is no easy task to conceive of a transition to socialism and establish political institutions and ideological tools to bring it about, under conditions of severe underdevelopment (Mondlane 1983: xi). Much depends on the strength of social and political movements in the region, something that is beyond the scope of this book to explore in detail. What also needs to be acknowledged are the deep feelings in large parts of the region about the 'Marxism' of FRELIMO, MPLA and other former liberation movements–turned–political parties, and the ways in which this distortion of socialism was imposed on the region's peoples in highly undemocratic and oppressive ways. Any anti-capitalist programme would need to distance itself from this legacy, in case it is opposed on the basis that the region has already had one failed experiment with socialism. Aspirational principles that could form the basis of a more enduring collective security project could include the following:

- *Complete equality of all nations and languages, to eliminate global and regional disparities* – Such equality will be possible only if existing national boundaries are broken down. While it is important to promote linking languages to encourage mutual intelligibility of the region's peoples, this cannot be forced, and must emerge organically from the languages that the majority of people speak. Almost certainly, this position is not likely to be conceded under capitalism, as it presents a fundamental challenge to the existence of states and the class interests that have grown up around them. Also, a world with no borders is possible only if there is no state, and no state and no borders mean no professional standing armies. National security as the dominant collective security project of our times falls away.
- *Work for all* – Full employment should not involve universalizing poor quality jobs. Rather, it is poor quality, unfulfilling, unskilled work that should be

eliminated, which is entirely possible through automated production. The interests of the working class should provide the normative foundation of the new society.

- *Property relations and the profit motive* – Existing property relations, where the commanding heights of the economy remain in private hands, are incompatible with an equal society. If no one owns the means of production, then capitalism ceases to exist: an approach that avoids the dangers of state ownership and even social ownership (Albert 2004: 90). The destruction of private ownership, and in fact of ownership per se, would put an end to the private appropriation of surplus as profit and the class distinctions that go along with this system.

- *Self-management of the basic functions of society* – People are capable of running their own economic, social and political lives in all spheres and at all levels, and the generalization of self-management will create conditions for the democratic organization of social life. It will also eliminate the dangers of distorted 'socialism' that becomes bureaucratized and state-run. In order for there to be personal participation in managing the affairs of society, illiteracy would need to be wiped out and popular education run on how to manage those aspects of society that currently fall under the state. At the same time, self-management also places an onus on people to be constructive and active members of society. Collective associations could be organized for the delivery of social and economic goods (Albert 2004: 92–3). Such self-management would necessitate the destruction of the state as it is currently constituted, to the extent that the capitalist state is the vehicle through which members of the capitalist class pursue their interests. Whether there will be a need for a state in a socialist society is a difficult issue; most likely there will be, although on a drastically reduced basis. This is because, no matter how much planning takes place at local level, there will still be a need for a level of central coordination (Brenner et al. 2002).

- *Political diversity and respect for dissent* – There needs to be a broadening of political democracy, not a restriction. One of the main reasons why the official 'socialism' of the region's former liberation movements failed was because they shunned political diversity. Imperialism and international solidarity movements alike designated certain national liberation movements the sole and authentic representatives of the oppressed, in the process trampling on the diversity of political traditions within these liberation struggles. These movements then used the security levers of the state to entrench their dominant positions once they were in power. Respect for political diversity is of the utmost importance if any transition to socialism is to succeed. It will also reduce the scope for opportunistic politicians and ethnic entrepreneurs to misuse differences.

- *Self-management and popular security* – A socialist society needs security capabilities that are more adapted to the real needs of the people. From the popular militias of working-class movements to the intelligence capabilities of older national liberation movements and contemporary social movements, history abounds with examples of self-organized and self-managed defence and intelligence functions that have not lapsed into private armies of factional interests. Much depends on the level of political maturity and democratic organization of the movements that run them. One of the most difficult issues for any revolutionary movement is when to use the coercive capacities of society to suppress counter-revolutionary forces that oppose popular societal changes to protect their own vested class interests. As uncomfortable as it is to think about and plan for, there may be an inescapable need to use force to prevent capitalism from being restored by the capitalist class, or sections of it. However, these issues are not impossible if the other principles form the basis of these new institutions, and these principles are necessary to avoid a transition beyond capitalism from descending into despotism. During Mozambique's struggle for liberation, for instance, FRELIMO promoted village- and district-level political institutions supported by popular militias. As they liberated parts of the country through armed struggle, they found it necessary to resolve questions of defence, health, education, governance and administration, using the liberated and semi-liberated areas as what Samora Machel referred to as 'our laboratory for the creation of a society' (Mondlane 1983: 126–30; Machel 1983: 76–7). However, the party's efforts to build institutions were authoritarian (Alexander 1997), and their lack of respect for democracy and political diversity meant that these structures morphed into neocolonial 'spy on your neighbour' institutions of surveillance akin to the East European Stasi, as discussed in Chapter 3.

Once there is clarity on the principles that are to guide the transition beyond capitalism, then the question becomes how to get there. Any such programme would need to be based on a strategic logic that includes some goals that have reasonable prospects of being achieved (Wright 2015). Some suggestions in this regard are made herein, based on the conclusions made in each chapter.

Towards an anti-capitalist programme on national security surveillance

Preamble

Societies need intelligence capabilities to forewarn them of possible threats and to defend themselves against hostile actors. Mass movements in struggle need these capabilities to defend themselves against their adversaries, just as the southern African liberation movements needed them during the historic struggles against colonialism and apartheid. In fact, it would be impossible to realize alternatives to capitalism without them. However, the capitalist class has distorted these necessary societal functions to serve their interests. They are augmenting human intelligence capabilities with digital surveillance capabilities to spy on social movements, journalists and civil society organizations on the pretext of protecting national security. In order to justify mass dragnet surveillance, where no reasonable suspicion of criminality exists, they have stretched the definition of national security to include all manner of issues that may threaten their interests.

The major imperialist powers are using dragnet surveillance, principally through the Five Eyes alliance, not just to protect themselves against threats, but to continue imperialism and colonialism by other means. National security surveillance is perpetuating the historic marginalization and disadvantage of the region and its peoples; however, it is not correct to assert that the working class is affected equally. Intelligence agencies target some sections of the working class more than others, or their inaction contributes to their insecurity, especially Black people and women. Oppression on the basis of nationality, especially of nations based in the global South, is also a major problem. Anti-capitalists should take racism, sexism and national oppression as seriously as class oppression. National security is not the same thing as collective or insurgent security, which is aimed at protecting those most marginalized and oppressed by capitalism through the self-activity of their legitimate organizations.

At the same time, former liberation movements–turned–ruling parties are misusing their ever-expanding intelligence and surveillance capabilities to act as regional policemen for their own class interests and imperialism more generally. They have not done enough to transform intelligence agencies and practices from the colonial and apartheid periods, because it has served them not to do so. The BRICS alliance of countries has not necessarily provided alternatives, either. Spying on social movements, opposition political parties and journalists is not an aberration or departure from what intelligence agencies do: it *is* what they do. Intelligence and surveillance have become, and in fact have always been, instruments of capitalist class power, and national security is the fig leaf behind which they hide. Any potential good that intelligence agencies are delivering is distorted by their system-maintaining role and the excessive secrecy with which they operate.

The system-maintaining role of intelligence under capitalism requires a political response embedded in broader struggles against oppression and exploitation, and not just a rights-based response emphasizing privacy, freedom of expression and other violations. This political response should include movements identifying the security functions that will remain in a socialist society, and that are analogous to the present functions of the state.

National security intelligence

There are gains to be made from calling for reforms to the state on national security matters, as these can be achieved within the constraints of the current capitalist system. However, strategically, the response needs to move beyond reforms and focus on shrinking, defunding and ultimately eliminating the state's national security intelligence and surveillance capabilities. At the same time, movements can prefigure future intelligence capabilities by drawing on the historic memories of previous liberation struggles, and develop bottom-up security policies and strategies, encouraging people to engage in open conversations and debates about real threats and strategies needed to counter them, demystifying intelligence in the process. Reforms in and of themselves are unlikely to change these secretive, powerful areas of the state. However, reforms may increase collective security in the short to medium term, and may even save lives. Some may also be conceded quite readily by the capitalist class, especially if factions of the capitalist class themselves become targets of intelligence agency spying. Therefore, there is no reason why such reforms cannot be pursued even under capitalism. However, campaigns for carefully chosen reforms could precipitate political crises if they are unlikely to be conceded by the current system. At every stage, state intelligence agencies should be forced to justify their existence by demonstrating what they have actually done to protect collective security. They should be challenged to roll back excessive and unjustifiable secrecy, which may be self-defeating in situations where these agencies are actually delivering a real public service, as this service will remain invisible to sceptical publics. Intelligence agencies cannot be allowed to argue 'trust us' when justifying their existence, and asserting their successes in protecting national security.

Struggles to shrink and defund intelligence agencies need to focus on doctrinal issues, mandates, powers and functions and effectiveness.

- *National security doctrine* – National security is a dead-end concept that is too tied up with the capitalist state and narrow national interests to be of any use to movements. While human security is well-meaning, and has been taken up as a rallying cry for reforms in southern Africa, it is individualistic and inadequate to the task of realizing collective security. Human security forces people to look for security to the very state that has made them insecure. It is also dangerous in that state intelligence agencies can (and do) use it to claim bigger budget and more powers. Collective security, on the other hand, needs to focus on threats to the working class which capitalism has differentiated along several (fault)lines, including race (or colour), gender, nationality and class; but it should also focus on societal needs as a whole as the intention is to transcend these divisions and truly create institutions that serve the general interest.
- *Mandates* – Intelligence mandates should be narrowed to strip out domestic political intelligence – which state intelligence agencies are incapable of using in politically impartial ways – as well as intelligence that focuses on national interests. Economic intelligence needs to be limited to the most destabilizing economic threats that threaten everyone irrespective of their class positions, such as preventing proliferation of nuclear weapons. There can be no justification for espionage, as these actions escalate global conflicts.
- *Internal structures and controls* – Giving intelligence agencies policing powers is a colonial legacy that has no place in democratic societies of any description. It dates from the times when colonial authorities used intelligence to spy on and repress anti-colonial movements. Policing must be separated from intelligence, as intelligence agencies that act on the intelligence they collect suffer from intolerable conflicts of interest. They can

also use enforcement powers in secret, which can (and does) lead to people disappearing without trace. As a temporary measure, offensive counter-intelligence functions could be relocated either to the police or to the military. Intelligence agencies should be decentralized and removed from the control of the presidency, as this institutional structure leads to intelligence agencies protecting the sitting president first and foremost.

- *Professionalization and unionization* – Anti-capitalists have a vested interest in encouraging conditions for whistle-blowing in intelligence agencies, as much of the information about intelligence and surveillance abuses has come from internal whistle-blowers. One of the ways of doing so is to promote measures that separate the political and management layers of intelligence agencies from workers, pointing out that workers inside these agencies should have common cause with workers outside them. Promoting the professionalization of intelligence may also be important to support for tactical reasons, as it encourages people of principle to act as whistle-blowers when spying violates their professional principles. While rarely recognized in state intelligence, trade union rights are also important as they can provide collective support for whistle-blowers. Anti-capitalists should support the right of intelligence officers to join or form independent trade unions.

- *Oversight* – State oversight is a contradiction in terms, as one part of the state will never challenge another part of the state to desist from being an instrument of class rule. However, in moments of political crisis, the state and the capitalist class more generally may be divided, and anti-capitalists can use these divisions to push for reforms. Parliamentary oversight is vastly preferable to executive oversight, as parliaments are often multiparty platforms and may include parties that have the interests of the working class at heart. Parliament is also more likely to hold its proceedings in public than the executive, although not on intelligence matters. Parliaments should be pushed to perform meaningful oversight over intelligence agencies, and open hearings should be the default position. Parliamentary oversight committees should have powers to enquire into operational matters of intelligence agencies. These committees should be supported by an independent inspector general for intelligence that is functionally and structurally independent from the agencies they are overseeing.

Lawful communication interception

While the powers to intercept communications on a targeted basis have developed under capitalism, there is little doubt that a socialist society would need them, too. While crime will most likely decrease greatly – as such a society would have addressed many of the conditions that drive criminality – no doubt it will not disappear entirely. However, the major imperialist powers have promoted a form of lawful interception that introduces new vulnerabilities into communication networks that their intelligence agencies have exploited. Global South countries, including in southern Africa, are particularly vulnerable to espionage as they are net importers of this equipment whose standards are controlled by the US and Europe. Lawful interception as currently practised should be opposed on the basis that it is not politically neutral, and there are other ways of undertaking targeted surveillance that exploits existing vulnerabilities, such as lawful hacking. Developing a form of targeted surveillance that focuses on legitimate criminal suspects, rather than risking the security of whole populations, is undoubtedly a worthwhile challenge for anti-capitalists, and broader society, to rise to in the short term.

Just as movements do not campaign for intelligence reforms because of any inherent faith in state intelligence to act in the public interest, but as part of defensive strategies to protect the working class, so too could this be applied to surveillance reforms. Movements could consider some of these reforms as part of their campaigns.

Possibly the most important reform is user notification, where intelligence agencies must notify surveillance subjects that they have been under surveillance once investigations reach a non-sensitive stage. Making sure that judges take decisions about who should be placed under surveillance and who shouldn't would be an advance on executive decision-making, as potentially, the judiciary is more likely to take decisions independently of the bureaucratic layer of the executive than a section of the executive itself. However, the judiciary may or may not open political spaces that movements can use. Much depends on the character of the judiciary, though, which only movements on the ground can assess in their respective localities.

Bulk SIGINT surveillance

This form of surveillance has become a tool of imperialism and neocolonialism, as it collects and analyses data on an untargeted basis. Anti-capitalists should oppose this power in principle and call for these capabilities to be discontinued. Unlike targeted lawful interception, no meaningful reforms are possible to these powers, owing to their breadth and secrecy. Opposing these powers is a matter of principle.

Bulk SIGINT surveillance is a highly developed, resource-intensive intelligence discipline that is practised most by the world's major surveillance powers. Southern African intelligence agencies are using other bulk powers, some of which have been opposed by global North countries for 'their own' citizens as they are considered too invasive. It is difficult not to arrive at the conclusion that these powers are considered more acceptable for the global South as majority Black countries are somehow less deserving of privacy. These powers should be opposed in principle, and include the following:

- *SIM card registration* – This practice is overwhelmingly a global South one, and activists could politicize this fact. Anti-capitalists should oppose SIM card registration, as it violates the right to communicate anonymously and indiscriminately and is a form of mass surveillance, and the available evidence points to it having limited utility in crime fighting. Boycotting SIM card registration could be a powerful political mobilizing tool, but only if there is a critical mass of people behind the campaign: otherwise, being cut off from the network for failing to register a SIM card will be a politically symbolic, but ultimately self-defeating, act.

- *Mandatory data retention* – Storing communication data for long periods of time should also be opposed, as this practice targets criminal suspects and the innocent alike. Instead, judicially authorized targeted preservation orders could ensure that communication service providers store only that data where someone is reasonably suspected of having committed a crime.

Global trade in surveillance

Whether they are based in the US, the UK, Europe, China or Israel, the major surveillance manufacturers have become bigger and wealthier, and have contributed to growing inequality. Shrinking national security surveillance capabilities, and the industries that produce them, will inevitably have job consequences. However, as the Lucas Aerospace workers showed in the 1970s, with some imagination, the scientific and engineering skills of defence industry personnel could be put to more purposeful uses. Arms manufacturing, including the production of dual-use goods and surveillance technologies, can be converted to socially useful work, including the production of renewable energy and health technologies, and the Covid-19 pandemic has increased the urgency of doing so. There will still be a need for surveillance technologies, though, for targeted surveillance. However, in order to curb these abuses of monopoly power, the remaining manufacturers would need to be removed from private ownership and placed under worker and broader public control, which would create conditions for people to enjoy non-exploitative, anti-surveillance and privacy-centred communications. It would also create the basis for the industrial capabilities that remain to manufacture surveillance equipment to be directed towards serving real public safety needs.

Policing and law enforcement intelligence

Increasingly, police forces are becoming intelligence-led, which is making them even less accountable and more abusive than they were. From the US, where police target and kill Black people, to the UK where undercover police infiltrate social movements and trick women into relationships to provide them with cover, and South Africa, where the police talk up and even invent national security threats to milk secret services funds, policing has abused the very people it has claimed to serve and protect. There is no doubt that policing needs intelligence capabilities, but the more the police claim a national security mandate, the more secretive, abusive and unaccountable they become. In the circumstances, it is entirely correct for movements to argue for the police to be defunded, and for these funds to be reallocated to job creation and social services, especially for women, while developing a larger vision for policing in broader society. In other words, the focus needs to shift from police reform to the political, economic and social transformation needed to make policing unnecessary.

It is not necessary to look to the US for alternative models of community safety; the region has its own examples to draw on. For instance, South Africa offers useful lessons in organizing bottom-up policing under apartheid and even in the post-apartheid period, including street committees and Self Defence Units. These initiatives lack resources and formal recognition, yet do the work of the police in the absence of the police. In these conditions, it is self-evidently important that such structures should be encouraged and supported, including through the budgets that the government is using to support the statutory police. By doing so, defunding the police while promoting community safety and security becomes an achievable aim, rather than an empty slogan, or an irresponsible demand.

National identity systems and immigration

Countries may be tempted to follow the path of the US Department of Homeland Security, and turn what were civil functions into national security functions. These include basic registration of the citizenry such as issuing birth, marriage and death certificates, to deciding who is a citizen and who is not, or who is deserving of refugee status or who isn't. The more these civil functions become securitized, the more the capitalist class uses them to divide the working class, turning it on itself through the promotion of state-sanctioned xenophobia. It can blame 'foreigners' for the lack of jobs and services, thereby deflecting the blame from itself. Centralized national identity systems allow the capitalist class to take back control of citizenship from a working class that has long insisted on practising active citizenship-from-below, in the process defining the terms and conditions of their membership of society. Anti-capitalists must fight against attempts to politicize national identity and to use border controls to prevent people from seeking a better life. People have an inalienable right to flee from the very countries that have been destabilized by imperialism's wars of aggression, conducted most recently in the name of the war on terror, global security and 'promoting democracy' worldwide. Recognizing their right to do so is a form of reparation. Overwhelmingly, Black people and women are affected, turning them into criminals and national security threats merely for wanting to escape conditions of poverty and violence.

- *Civil registration functions* – Anti-capitalists should reject the repositioning of home affairs or internal affairs departments as security departments and campaign for civil identity management and immigration functions to remain civil functions. This is another way of shrinking national security surveillance, as these departments will start to use risk management functions, including digital surveillance, as part of their everyday work when they become security departments.

- *Centralized biometric identity management systems* – Identity management
  systems that centralize peoples' personal information create a honey pot
  of data that can be misused, not only by the state but also by private actors
  that can hack or obtain the information illicitly. They should be opposed as
  anti-democratic and dangerous. Distributed systems are much less risky, but
  even they should not be taken for granted as being necessities. Unnecessary
  collection and processing of personal information should be opposed,
  whether at the hands of the state or the private sector. Usually there are
  alternative options for verifying a person's identity, such as birth certificates.
  People should be given a choice as to how to identify themselves, and not
  be forced into accepting identity systems that are becoming increasingly
  invasive as they embrace 'smart', biometrically based technologies. In any
  event, centralized smart ID card systems are most in evidence in global
  South countries, suggesting that it has become a globally accepted reality that
  citizens who are more likely to be Black have less right to bodily integrity
  than citizens who are more likely to be white, including control over their
  biometrics.
- *Borders and immigration* – As there is nothing natural or inevitable about
  borders as they exist today, people should have a right to move wherever they
  want, without restraint, in search of a better life. The struggle for freedom
  of movement is inherently a struggle against capitalism, which through the
  state and in its own interests tries to control how people move and where.
  Recognizing the right to freedom of movement while addressing the massive
  disparities in how wealth is distributed in the region should create conditions
  for the Rwandan saying 'humanity is others' to become a lived reality.

Final thoughts: National security surveillance and the need for politics

As noted in the introduction, imperialism politicized struggles in southern Africa,
leading to struggles in the colonies reaching far beyond their geographic boundaries
and destabilizing the global capitalist system. If surveillance is contributing to
the maintenance of empire, then anti-surveillance struggles need to change their
character and become an integral part of the broader struggles against all forms
of contemporary imperial domination, whether practised by the established or
emergent imperial powers. In that way then perhaps southern Africa could be
spared from becoming a theatre of conflict between the globe's major surveillance
powers – a conflict that will most likely not be in the best interests of the region's
peoples or the working class around the world.

In view of Snowden's exposure of widespread abuses of the SIGINT capabilities
of the NSA, GCHQ and others, one would have expected more sustained
resistance to mass surveillance. Yet in spite of Snowden's disclosures, it appears
to be 'business as usual' in the signals intelligence community, and in fact, more
countries are expanding their mass surveillance capabilities (Privacy International
2016b). Understanding the contributions of SIGINT to the maintenance of global

inequality is important because it challenges official claims about how necessary these powers are to ensuring global stability and security. Politicizing SIGINT in this way creates the basis for widespread resistance in those parts of the world that are most likely to be disadvantaged by the worldwide spread of digital surveillance.

Such politicization will be possible only if scholars and activists move beyond criticizing surveillance as a danger to privacy, which has been the most important organizing concept in the fight against surveillance up to this point. Identifying the struggle as primarily a struggle for privacy is a very narrow and individualized understanding of the problem, and can lead to paralysis as governments argue that as an individual right, privacy must give way to a collective right, such as national security. Rather, if anti-surveillance activism is to be broadened into a mass movement, then activists have to demonstrate how surveillance has become central to the control of marginalized communities and the maintenance of dominant interests (Hintz et al. 2019). So, a more politicized understanding of the problem that focuses on how surveillance has become increasingly important to the appropriation of resources, for instance (Couldry and Mejias 2019), could be much more galvanizing. This is because it could provide the basis to escalate anti-surveillance struggles beyond being niche concerns, and generalize them by linking them to the need to change society. Re-imagining national security as collective security could offer the world a different model of security and of society.

NOTES

Introduction

1 Author's interview with Domingos da Cruz, Google Meet interview, 19 September 2021.
2 Joseph Cannataci speaking at a Council of Europe webinar entitled 'Setting Democratic Global Standards for Intelligence Agencies: The Way Forward', 9 November 2020. Available online: https://www.coe.int/en/web/data-protection/video -recording-setting-democratic-global-standards-for-intelligence-agencies-the-way -forward (accessed 11 May 2021).
3 Sophie in 't Veld speaking at a Council of Europe webinar entitled 'Setting Democratic Global Standards for Intelligence Agencies: The Way Forward', 9 November 2020. Available online: https://www.coe.int/en/web/data-protection/video-recording-setting -democratic-global-standards-for-intelligence-agencies-the-way-forward (accessed 11 May 2021).
4 Please see Chapter 2 for a discussion of the political complexities of the term 'terrorism' and why I choose to use it in this book.
5 I define surveillance as the collection and analysis of information and the accessing of a person's physical characteristics for the purposes of social control. In narrowing the definition to social control purposes, I agree with Christian Fuchs that including non-coercive forms of observation into the definition of surveillance is too broad and empties the term of meaning. See Fuchs 2010a: 1–22.
6 The archive is available at the following URL: https://snowdenarchive.cjfe.org/ greenstone/cgi-bin/library.cgi.

Chapter 1

1 S.5(a)(2) of the Regulation of Interception of Communications and Provision of Communications-related Information Act No 70 of 2002, (Republic of South Africa 2002).
2 Susan Landau, 'Lawful Hacking: Using Existing Vulnerabilities to Wiretap Internet Communications', lecture delivered at Duo Tech Talk, 30 September 2016, available online: https://www.youtube.com/watch?v=QcwmH0-6E2s (accessed 28 March 2020).
3 The following was the title of an edited volume assessing Lenin's legacy in the contemporary period. See Budgen et al. (2007).
4 Edward Snowden in discussion with Kumi Naidoo at the 'Privacy Right, Surveillance Wrongs: An Activist's Dialogue' conference, co-hosted by the Legal Resources Centre and the International Network of Civil Liberties Organizations, Johannesburg, 31 October 2016.

Chapter 2

1 Here I refer to the fact that in African countries, colonial powers like the UK withdrew from direct physical and military control of 'their' colonies. Using this term in no way discounts the existence of neocolonialism, or the use of capitalist economic relations to perpetuate unequal exchange after the withdrawal of physical control.

2 Author's interview with researcher on intelligence matters in Zimbabwe who requested anonymity (Zoom interview), 27 October 2020.

3 Author's interview with Jeremy Brickhill, Google Meet interview, 26 August 2021.

4 Author's interview with Nompilo Simanje, legal officer, Zimbabwe Chapter of the Media Institute for Southern Africa, WhatsApp interview, 13 November 2020.

5 Author's interview with Nompilo Simanje, legal officer, Zimbabwe Chapter of the Media Institute for Southern Africa, WhatsApp interview, 13 November 2020; interview with researcher on intelligence matters in Zimbabwe who requested anonymity (Zoom interview), 27 October 2020.

6 The Gukurahundi was a massacre of Ndebele civilians in the southern Matabeleland of Zimbabwe carried out by the Zimbabwean National Army between 1983 and 1987. The massacre took place after the ZANU-PF government had assumed office, and the party continued to remain threatened by dissidents from the rival liberation movement, the Zimbabwe African Peoples' Union (ZAPU).

7 Author's interview with Jeremy Brickhill, WhatsApp interview, 19 February 2021.

8 Author's interview with Tachilisa Balule, MS teams interview, 2 March 2021.

9 Author's interview with Frederico Links, MS Teams interview, 15 February 2021.

10 Author's interview with Frederico Links, MS Teams interview, 15 February 2021.

11 Testimony of former Minister of State Security, David Mahlobo, at the Commission of Enquiry into State Capture, 9 April 2021. Available online: https://www.statecapture.org.za/site/hearings/date/2021/4/9 (accessed 12 May 2021).

12 Author's interview with Frederico Links, MS Teams interview, 15 February 2021.

13 I am grateful to the director of the Afro-Middle East Centre, Na'eem Jeenah, for having made this point. Signal conversation with Na'eem Jeenah, 26 February 2021.

14 Author's interview with researcher on intelligence matters in Zimbabwe who requested anonymity (Zoom interview), 27 October 2020.

15 S. 32 of the Namibia Central Intelligence Service Act of 1997 (Republic of Namibia 1997).

16 S. 32 of the Namibia Central Intelligence Service Act of 1997 (Republic of Namibia 1997).

17 S. 11 of the National Central Intelligence Service Act of 1997 (Republic of Namibia 1997).

18 Author's interview with researcher on intelligence matters in Zimbabwe who requested anonymity (Zoom interview), 27 October 2020.

19 Author's interview with Jeremy Brickhill, WhatsApp interview, 25 February 2021.

20 Author's interview with Jeremy Brickhill, WhatsApp interview, 25 February 2021; written answers to author's interview questions from Munyaradzi Nyakudya, 25 February 2021.

21 Author's interview with Jeremy Brickhill, WhatsApp interview, 25 February 2021.

22 Written answers to author's interview questions from Munyaradzi Nyakudya, 25 February 2021.

23   Author's interview with researcher on intelligence matters in Zimbabwe who requested anonymity (Zoom interview), 27 October 2020.
24   Author's interview with researcher on intelligence matters in Zimbabwe who requested anonymity (Zoom interview), 27 October 2020.
25   Author's interview with Nompilo Simanje, legal officer, Zimbabwe Chapter of the Media Institute for Southern Africa, WhatsApp interview, 13 November 2020.
26   When I refer to post-capitalist society, I am referring specifically to a socialist society. There are many possible post-capitalist futures, including ones that may not be emancipatory. A socialist future clearly is emancipatory as it aims for a classless society. See Albo (2020).
27   Author's interview with Jeremy Brickhill, Google Meet interview, 26 August 2021.

Chapter 3

1   Susan Landau, 'Lawful Hacking: Using Existing Vulnerabilities to Wiretap Internet Communications', lecture delivered at Duo Tech Talk, 30 September 2016, accessed from https://www.youtube.com/watch?v=QcwmH0-6E2s (accessed 28 March 2020).
2   Susan Landau, 'Lawful Hacking: Using Existing Vulnerabilities to Wiretap Internet Communications', lecture delivered at Duo Tech Talk, 30 September 2016, accessed from https://www.youtube.com/watch?v=QcwmH0-6E2s (accessed 28 March 2020).
3   Susan Landau, 'Lawful Hacking: Using Existing Vulnerabilities to Wiretap Internet Communications', lecture delivered at Duo Tech Talk, 30 September 2016, accessed from https://www.youtube.com/watch?v=QcwmH0-6E2s (accessed 28 March 2020).
4   Author's interview with Nompilo Simanje, legal officer, Zimbabwe Chapter of the Media Institute for Southern Africa, WhatsApp interview, 13 November 2020.
5   Author's interview with Tachilisa Balule, MS teams interview, 2 March 2021.
6   Author's interview with Tachilisa Balule, MS teams interview, 2 March 2021.
7   Author's interview with Frederico Links, MS Teams interview, 15 February 2021.
8   s. 24(2) of the Namibia Central Intelligence Service Act of 1997 (Republic of Namibia 1997).
9   Part 6 of the Communications Act (Republic of Namibia 2009).
10 Author's interview with Frederico Links, MS Teams interview, 15 February 2021.
11 This phrase was used by Rui Verde to describe the situation in Angola. Author's interview with Rui Verde. MS Team interview on 18 March 2021.
12 Author's interview with Ernesto Nhlanhle, Google Meet interview, 6 April 2021.
13 Author's interview with Ernesto Nhlanhle, Google Meet interview, 6 April 2021.
14 Author's interview with Ernesto Nhlanhle, Google Meet interview, 6 April 2021.
15 Section 1, National Security Act of 2002 (Lei Segurança Nacional 2002).
16 Section 1, National Security Act of 2002 (Lei Segurança Nacional 2002).
17 Author's interview with Rui Verde, MS Teams interview, 17 March 2021.
18 Susan Landau, 'Lawful hacking: using existing vulnerabilities to wiretap internet communications', lecture delivered at Duo Tech Talk, 30 September 2016, accessed from https://www.youtube.com/watch?v=QcwmH0-6E2s (accessed 28 March 2020).

Chapter 4

1   Author's interview with Duncan Campbell, Brighton, United Kingdom, 31 May 2018.
2   Author's interview with Duncan Campbell, Brighton, 31 May 2018.
3   Ministry of State Security, the Office for Interception Centres, the National
    Communications Centre and the State Security Agency, 'amaBhungane Centre
    for Investigative Journalism and Stephen Patrick Sole v the Minister of Justice
    and Correctional Services and Nine Others: Second, Seventh, Eighth and Tenth
    Respondent's Answering Affidavit', case number 25078/2017, pp. 57–63.
4   Ministry of State Security, the Office for Interception Centres, the National
    Communications Centre and the State Security Agency, 'amaBhungane Centre
    for Investigative Journalism and Stephen Patrick Sole v The Minister of Justice
    and Correctional Services and Nine Others: Second, Seventh, Eighth and Tenth
    Respondent's Answering Affidavit', case number 25078/2017, pg. 58, paragraph 132.
5   S.198(a), Constitution of the Republic of South Africa, Act 108 of 1996 (Constitution
    of the Republic of South Africa 1996: 12).
6   Author's interview with Moe Shaik, Pretoria, 17 April 2018.
7   Author's interview with Moe Shaik, Pretoria, 17 April 2018.
8   Author's interview with Moe Shaik, Pretoria, 17 April 2018.
9   Author's interview with Nompilo Simanje, legal officer, Zimbabwe Chapter of the
    Media Institute for Southern Africa, WhatsApp interview, 13 November 2020.
10 Author's interview with Frederico Links, MS Teams interview, 15 February 2021.
11 Author's interview with Rui Verde, MS Teams interview, 17 March 2021.
12 MSNBC, 'Full interview with Edward Snowden on Trump, privacy and threats
    to democracy'. The 11th Hour. Accessed from https://www.youtube.com/watch?v
    =e9yK1QndJSM on 28 March 2021.

Chapter 5

1   Author's correspondence with Leon Labuschagne, Manager: Marketing and
    Technology Research, Vastech, 6 April 2017.
2   Author's interview with Nompilo Simanje, legal officer, Media Institute of Southern
    Africa, Zimbabwe, WhatsApp interview, 13 November 2020.
3   Author's interview with Rajni Lallah, interview over Signal, 4 February 2021.
4   Information obtained from the Security Assistance Monitor, which aggregates data
    from four different US security datasets. It includes data about US economic aid,
    security aid, security training and arms sales to other countries.
5   Arms sales, Security Assistance Monitor, http://securityassistance.org/content/arms
    -sales-dashboard (accessed 27 March 2020)
6   Author's interview with Rui Verde, MS Teams interview, 17 March 2021.

Chapter 6

1   'Law enforcement intelligence' is a term that is more in use in the US, while 'crime
    intelligence' is a more familiar term in southern Africa. Hence, I will refer to crime
    intelligence.

2   Busi Matabane speaking at 'Human Rights and Civil Society: the State's Abuse of Power and Activists' Stories of Violence and Surveillance, seminar hosted by Greenpeace Africa, 24 March 2021.
3   Blade Nzimande quoted in Duncan (2021a): 191–2.
4   This point was made by Kelly Gillespie in a seminar held on Instagram by Cops are Flops and STB Debating, 6 August 2021. The seminar was called 'Abolitionism: A South African Perspective' (Cops are Flops and STB Debating 2020).

Chapter 7

1   This chapter expands on an opinion piece I wrote for the *Daily Maverick* entitled 'South Africa's emerging Department of Homeland Security' and integrates some of the text from this piece (Duncan 2020).
2   eNCA interview with Mahlodi Muofhe, 14 August 2019. Available at https://www .enca.com/news/illegal-immigration-threat-says-new-spy-boss (accessed 25 August 2020).
3   Department of Home Affairs. 'White Paper on Home Affairs'. 18 January 2019, pp. 43–82. Available at https://www.gov.za/sites/default/files/gcis_document/201901 /42162gon08.pdf (downloaded 25 March 2020).
4   Unpublished memorandum to the author on ID blocking from Lawyers for Human Rights, 10 December 2020.
5   Author's interview with former Department of Home Affairs employee who requested anonymity, Johannesburg, 30 August 2020.
6   Author's interview with Thulani Mavuso, Deputy Director of Institutional Planning and Support, Department of Home Affairs, Pretoria, 28 November 2017, published in Duncan (2018: 177).
7   Unpublished memorandum to author on ID blocking from Lawyers for Human Rights, 10 December 2020.
8   Unpublished memorandum to author on ID blocking from Lawyers for Human Rights, 10 December 2020.
9   Author's interview with Thandeka Chauke, manager, Statelessness Project, Lawyers for Human Rights, MS Teams interview, 25 January 2021.
10   Author's interview with Thandeka Chauke, manager, Statelessness Project, Lawyers for Human Rights, MS Teams interview, 25 January 2021.
11   Author's interview with former Department of Home Affairs employee who requested anonymity, Johannesburg, 30 August 2020.
12   Author's interview with former Department of Home Affairs employee who requested anonymity, Johannesburg, 30 August 2020.
13   Author's interview with Ish Sookun, interview on Google Meet, 4 February 2021.
14   Author's interview with Ish Sookun, interview on Google Meet, 4 February 2021.
15   Author's interview with Rajni Lallah, interview over Signal, 4 February 2021.
16   Author's interview with Ish Sookun, interview on Google Meet, 4 February 2021.
17   Author's interview with Ish Sookun, interview on Google Meet, 4 February 2021.
18   Author's interview with Rajni Lallah, interview over Signal, 4 February 2021.

REFERENCES

Achiume, E. T. (2020a), 'Racial Discrimination and Emerging Digital Technologies: A Human Rights Analysis. Report of the Special Rapporteur on Contemporary Forms of Racism, Racial Discrimination, Xenophobia and Related Forms of Intolerance', Report presented to the forty-fourth session of the Human Rights Council.

Achiume, E. T. (2020b), 'Report of the Special Rapporteur on Contemporary Forms of Racism, Racial Discrimination, Xenophobia and Related Intolerance', Report, prepared for the seventy-fifth session of the United Nations General Assembly, 10 November.

African National Congress. (1991), 'A Code of Conduct for the SDUs'. Available online: https://www.csvr.org.za/index.php/publications/1466-the-role-of-the-self-defence -units-sdus-in-a-changing-political-context.html (accessed 15 April 2021).

Akbar, A. A. (2020), 'An Abolitionist Horizon for (Police) Reform', *California Law Review*, 108 (6): 1781–1846.

Albert, M. (2004), *Parecon: Life after Capitalism*, London: Verso Books.

Albo, G. (2020), 'Post-Capitalism: Alternatives or Detours?', in L. Panitch and G. Albo (eds), *Beyond Digital Capitalism*, 387–411, London: The Merlin Press.

Alexander, J. (1997), 'The Local State in Post-War Mozambique: Political Practice and Ideas about Authority', *Africa*, 67 (1): 1–26.

Alexander, J. and J. McGregor. (2017), 'African Soldiers in the USSR: Oral Histories of ZAPU Intelligence Cadres', *Journal of Southern African Studies*, 43 (1): 49–66.

Alexander, N. (1985), *Sow the Wind: Contemporary Speeches*, Johannesburg: Skotaville Publishers.

Alexander, N. (2002), *An Ordinary Country: Issues in the Transition from Apartheid to Democracy in South Africa*, Durban: University of KwaZulu-Natal.

Alexander, P., C. Runciman, T. Ngwane, B. Moloto, K. Mokgele and N. van Staden. (2018), 'Frequency and Turmoil: South Africa's Community Protests 2005–2017', *South African Crime Quarterly* 63. Available online: https://journals.assaf.org.za/sacq/article/view /3057 (accessed 17 April 2021).

Al Jazeera. (2020), *Targeted by a Text* [documentary film], 14 February. Available online: https://www.aljazeera.com/programmes/faultlines/2019/05/targeted-text -190514054646147.html (accessed 8 April 2020).

Alt.advisory and Right2Know Campaign. (2019), 'Submission to the United Nations Special Rapporteur on the Promotion and Protection of Freedom of Opinion and Expression: The Surveillance Industry and Human Rights'. Available online: https:// altadvisory.africa/wp-content/uploads/2019/07/Submission-The-Surveillance-Industry -and-Human-Rights-ALT-Advisory-and-R2K.pdf (accessed 20 April 2020).

Amnesty International. (2014), 'On the Streets of America: Human Rights Abuses in Ferguson', 24 October. Available online: http://www.amnestyusa.org/research/reports/ on-the-streets-of-america-human-rights-abuses-in-ferguson?page=4 (accessed 5 April 2021).

Amnesty International. (2019), 'The Surveillance Industry and Human Rights: Amnesty International Submission to the UN Special Rapporteur on the Promotion and

Protection of Freedom of Opinion and Expression', 22 February. Available online: https://www.ohchr.org/Documents/Issues/Opinion/Surveillance/AMNESTY %20INTERNATIONAL.pdf (accessed 13 April 2020).

Amnesty International. (2020), 'Media Freedom in Ashes: Repression of Freedom of Expression in Mozambique', (report), London: Amnesty International. Available online: https://www.amnesty.org/download/Documents/AFR4129472020ENGLISH .pdf (accessed 24 February 2021).

Amoore, L. and M. de Goede. (2008), 'Introduction', in L. Amoore and M. de Goede (eds), *Risk and the War on Terror*, 5–19, London: Routledge.

Andreas, P. and R. Price. (2001), 'From War Fighting to Crime Fighting: Transforming the American National Security State', *International Studies Review*, 3: 31–52.

Andrews, W. and T. Lindeman. (2013), 'The Black Budget', *Washington Post*, 29 August. Available online: http://www.washingtonpost.com/wp-srv/special/national/black -budget/ (accessed 20 January 2020).

Anderson, C. (2015), 'Considerations on Wassenaar Arrangement Control List Additions for Surveillance Technologies'. Available online: https://www.accessnow.org/cme/assets /uploads/archive/Access%20Wassenaar%20Surveillance%20Export%20Controls %202015.pdf (accessed 27 April 2019).

Anderson, D. (2016), 'Report of the Bulk Powers Review', August. Available online: https:// terrorismlegislationreviewer.independent.gov.uk/wp-content/uploads/2016/08/Bulk -Powers-Review-final-report.pdf (accessed 17 March 2021).

Anonymous. (2020), *Drifting towards Darkness: An Exploratory Study of State Surveillance in Zimbabwe*, Johannesburg: Media Policy and Democracy Project. Available online: https://www.mediaanddemocracy.com/uploads/1/6/5/7/16577624/zimbabwe_report _2nd_pages.pdf (accessed 4 May 2020).

Ansorg, N. (2017), 'Security Sector Reform in Africa: Donor Approaches Versus Local Needs', *Contemporary Security Policy*, 38 (1): 129–44.

Ball, K. and L. Snider. (2013), 'The Surveillance-Industrial Complex: Towards a Political Economy of Surveillance?', in K. Ball and L. Snider (eds), *The Surveillance Industrial Complex: A Political Economy of Surveillance*, 1–13, New York: Routledge.

Balule, B. T. and B. Otlhogile. (2016), 'Balancing the Right to Privacy and the Public Interest: Surveillance by the State of Private Communications for Law Enforcement in Botswana', *Statute Law Review*, 37 (1): 19–32.

Bamford, J. (2015), 'A Death in Athens', *The Intercept*, 29 September. Available online: https://theintercept.com/2015/09/28/death-athens-rogue-nsa-operation/ (accessed 28 April 2020).

Beckett, A. (2015), 'Is Britain's Arms Trade Making a Killing?', *The Guardian*, 18 February. Available online: https://www.theguardian.com/world/2013/feb/18/britains-arms-trade -making-killing (accessed 26 April 2019).

Bellamy Foster, J. and R. McChesney. (2014), 'Surveillance Capitalism: Monopoly-Finance Capital, the Military-Industrial Complex, and the Digital Age', *Monthly Review*, 66 (3). Available online: http://monthlyreview.org/2014/07/01/surveillance-capitalism/ (accessed 23 April 2020).

Bellovin, S. M., M. Blaze, S. Clark and S. Landau. (2014), 'Lawful Hacking: Using Existing Vulnerabilities for Wiretapping on the Internet', *Northwest Journal for Technology and Intellectual Property*, 12 (1): 1–63.

Bendile, D. (2017), 'Home Affairs Minister: SA Must Tighten its Immigration Policies', *Mail & Guardian*, 1 June. Available online: https://mg.co.za/article/2017-06-01-home -affairs-talks-tough-on-borders/ (accessed 4 January 2021).

Ben-Porat, G. and A. Ghanem. (2017), 'Introduction: Securitization and Shrinking of Citizenship', *Citizenship Studies*, 21 (8): 861–71.

Blue Coat. (n.d.), 'The Blue Coat Security Platform', (post on company website). Available online: https://www.bluecoat.com/products-and-solutions/encrypted-traffic-management (accessed 23 April 2020).

Bond, P. (2015), 'BRICS and the Sub-Imperial Location', in P. Bond and A. Garcia (eds), *BRICS: An Anti-Capitalist Critique*, 15–26, Johannesburg: Jacana Media.

Born, H., I. Leigh, and A. Wills. (2015), 'Making International Intelligence Cooperation Accountable', (report), Geneva: Geneva Centre for Security Sector Governance. Available online: https://www.dcaf.ch/sites/default/files/publications/documents/MIICA_book-FINAL.pdf (accessed 24 March 2021).

Boulanin, V. (2013), 'Arms Production Goes Cyber: A Challenge for Arms Control', (report), Stockholm International Peace Research Institute, 30 May. Available online: https://www.sipri.org/node/361 (accessed 27 October 2020).

Branch, A. and Z. Mampilly. (2015), *Africa Uprising: Popular Protest and Political Challenge*, Cape Town: BestRed.

Breckenridge, K. (2014), *Biometric State: The Global Politics of Identification and Surveillance in South Africa, 1850 to the Present*, Cambridge: Cambridge University Press.

Brenner, R., J. Dewar and S. Murray. (2002), 'Anticapitalist Manifestos: Monbiot, Albert and Callinicos', League for the Fifth International. Available online: https://fifthinternational.org/content/anticapitalist-manifestos-monbiot-albert-callinicos?q=content/anticapitalist-manifestos-monbiot-albert-callinicos (accessed 6 May 2021).

Brincat, S. (2020), 'The Insurgency in Cabo Delgado', *Africa is a Country*, 30 April. Available online: https://africasacountry.com/2020/04/the-insurgency-in-cabo-delgado (accessed 24 February 2021).

British-US Communication Intelligence Agreement. (1946), 'Agreement between London Signal Intelligence Board and State-Army-Navy Communication Intelligence Board', Signed on 5 March.

Bromley, M. (2016), 'ICT Surveillance Systems: Trade Policy and the Application of Human Security Concerns', *Strategic Trade Review*, 2 (2): 37–52.

Bromley, M. (2017), 'Human Rights, the European Union and Dual-Use Export Controls', *SIPRI Yearbook 2017: Armaments, Disarmament and International Security*, Stockholm: SIPRI. Available online: https://www.sipri.org/sites/default/files/SIPRIYB17c15sV.pdf (accessed 5 April 2020).

Bromley, M. (2018), 'Export Controls, Human Security and Cyber-Surveillance Technology', (report), Stockholm: Stockholm International Peace Research Institute. Available online: https://sipri.org/sites/default/files/2018-01/sipri1712_bromley.pdf (accessed 11 April 2020).

Brown, J. (2015), *South Africa's Insurgent Citizens: On Dissent and the Possibility of Politics*, Chicago: University of Chicago Press.

Budgen, S., S. Kouvelakis and S. Žižek, eds (2007), *Lenin Reloaded*, Durham, NC: Duke University Press.

Budhram, T. (2015), 'Intelligence-led Policing: A Proactive Approach to Combatting Corruption', *South African Crime Quarterly*, 52: 49–55.

BusinessTech. (2014), 'BRICS Must Take Control of the Internet', *BusinessTech*, 7 July. Available online: https://businesstech.co.za/news/internet/63093/BRICS-must-take-control-of-the-internet/ (accessed 27 July 2018).

BusinessTech. (2020), 'New Plans to Bring Smart ID and Passport Applications to Post Office Branches', *Mybroadband*, 3 March. Available online: https://mybroadband.co.za

/news/it-services/341023-new-plans-to-bring-smart-id-and-passport-applications-to
-post-office-branches.html (accessed 19 January 2021).

Buzan, B., O. Waever, and J. De Wilde. (1998), *Security: A New Framework for Analysis*,
Boulder: Lynne Rienner Publishers.

Çağlı, E. (2009), 'On Sub-Imperialism: Regional Power in Turkey', *Marxist Tatum*, 28
July. Available online: http://en.marksist.net/elif_cagli/on_sub_imperialism_regional
_power_turkey.htm on 26 April 2019 (accessed 20 March 2021).

Calzada, I. and E. Almirall. (2019), 'Barcelona's Grassroots-Led Urban Experimentation:
Deciphering the "Data Commons" Policy Scheme', accepted paper in the Data for Policy
2019 International Conference, London, 11–12 June. Available online: https://www
.compas.ox.ac.uk/wp-content/uploads/Barcelonas-grassroots-led-urban-experimentation
-Deciphering-the-data-commons-policy-scheme.pdf (accessed 31 March 2021).

Campaign Against Arms Trade. (2014), 'Arms to Renewables: Work for the Future',
(research report). Available online: https://www.caat.org.uk/campaigns/arms-to
-renewables/arms-to-renewables-background-briefing.pdf (accessed 17 April 2020).

Campaign Against Arms Trade. (2020), 'BAE Systems', (blog post), 6 March. Available online:
https://www.caat.org.uk/resources/companies/bae-systems (accessed 8 April 2020).

Campbell, D. (2014), 'NSA: Inside the Five-Eyed Vampire Squid of the Internet', *The
Register*, 5 June. Available online: https://www.theregister.co.uk/2014/06/05/how_the
_interenet_was_broken/ (accessed 17 February 2020).

Campbell, R. (2019), 'Beleaguered Defence Group Denel Looking for Diversification
Opportunities', *Engineering News*, 22 August. Available online: https://www
.engineeringnews.co.za/article/beleaguered-defence-group-denel-looking-for
-diversification-opportunities-2019-08-22/rep_id:4136 (accessed 17 April 2021).

Camps-Febrer, B. and G. Farres-Fernandez. (2019), 'Power and the Security Sector:
Thoughts on the Sociology of Power', *Contemporary Arab Affairs*, 12 (1): 3–18.

Cannataci, J. (2017), 'Report of the Special Rapporteur on the Right to Privacy', *Thirty
Fourth Session of the United Nations Human Rights Council*, 24 February. Available
online: http://www.ohchr.org/Documents/Issues/Privacy/A_HRC_34_60_EN.docx
(accessed 9 May 2020).

Carmody, P. (2016), *The New Scramble for Africa*, Cambridge: Polity Books.

Carmody, P. and G. Hampwaye. (2016), 'The Asian Scramble for Investments and Markets:
Evidence and Impacts in Zambia', in P. Carmody (ed.), *The New Scramble for Africa*,
195–214, Cambridge: Polity Books.

Carter, D. L. (2009), 'Law Enforcement Intelligence: A Guide for State, Local, and Tribal
Law Enforcement Agencies', US Department of Justice. Available online: https://fas.org
/irp/agency/doj/lei.pdf (accessed 6 August 2020).

Casola, C. and A. Iocchi. (2020), 'The "Faceless Evildoers" of Cabo Delgado: An Islamist
Insurgency in Mozambique', (blog post), 3 August. Available online: https://nupi.brage
.unit.no/nupi-xmlui/bitstream/handle/11250/2711439/Casola%2C+Iocchi+-+The
+Faceless+Evildoers+of+Cabo+Delgado+an+Islamist+Insurgency+in+Mozambique+-
+ISPI+2020.08.03.pdf?sequence=1 (accessed 24 February 2021).

Choudry, A. (2019), *Activists and the Surveillance State: Learning from Repression*, London:
Pluto Press.

Christie, R. (2010), 'Critical Voices and Human Security: To Endure, to Engage or to
Critique?', *Security Dialogue*, 41 (2): 169–90.

Communications Assistance for Law Enforcement Act. (1994), 'Public law 103–414', 25
October. Available online: https://www.congress.gov/103/statute/STATUTE-108/
STATUTE-108-Pg4279.pdf (accessed 13 March 2021).

Constitutional Court of Germany. (2020), 'Headnotes to the Judgment of the First Senate of 19 May 2020, 1 BvR 2835/17'. Available online: https://www.bundesverfassun gsgericht.de/SharedDocs/Downloads/EN/2020/05/rs20200519_1bvr283517en.pdf?__blob=publicationFile&v=1#page=1 (accessed 24 March 2021).

Constitutional Court of South Africa. (2021), amaBhungane Centre for Investigative Journalism NPC and Another v Minister of Justice and Correctional Services and Others; Minister of Police v amaBhungane Centre for Investigative Journalism NPV and Others CCT278/19 & CCT279/19.

Cops are Flops and STB Debating. (2020), 'Abolitionism: A South African Perspective', *[Instagram broadcast]*, 6 August. Available online: https://www.instagram.com/p/CDmGLwEpviv/ (accessed 16 April 2021).

Couldry, N. and U. A. Mejias. (2019), 'Data Colonialism: Rethinking Big Data's Relation to the Contemporary Subject', *Television and New Media*, 20 (4): 336–49.

Davis, R. (2015), 'What's South Africa's Anti-Human Rights Game at the UN?', *Daily Maverick*, 29 March. Available online: https://www.dailymaverick.co.za/article/2015 -03-29analysis-whats-south-africas-anti-human-rights-game-at-the-un/ (accessed 24 July 2020).

De Capitani, E. (2015), 'State Surveillance: The Venice Commission Updates its 2007 Report'. Available online: https://free-group.eu/2015/04/14/state-surveillance-the -venice-commission-updates-its-2007-report/ (accessed 26 April 2021).

De Fundo, T. (2016), 'Governo de Moçambique está a ouvir e a ler as comunicações de todos os cidadãos', *Verdade*, 4 May. Available online: http://www.verdade.co.mz/tema -de-fundo/35/57818 (accessed 8 April 2020).

Della Porta, D. (2013), *Clandestine Political Violence*, Cambridge: Cambridge University Press.

Dencik, L., A. Hintz and Z. Carey. (2018), 'Prediction, Pre-emption and Limits to Dissent: Social Media and Big Data Uses for Policing Protests in the United Kingdom', *New Media and Society*, 20 (4): 1433–50.

Denel. (2019), 'Presentation to the Portfolio Committee on Defence and Military Veterans', *Powerpoint Presentation*, 27 November. Available online: http://pmg-assets.s3 -website-eu-west-1.amazonaws.com/191127Denel.pdf (accessed 17 April 2020).

Department of Home Affairs. (2012), 'South Africa–European Union Joint Cooperation Report: Migration', (unpublished report), Pretoria: Department of Home Affairs, 16 July.

Department of Home Affairs. (2014), 'Pre-Feasibility Report: Towards the Establishment of a Border Management Agency in South Africa', (unpublished report), February.

Department of Home Affairs. (2015a), 'Border Management Agency Business Case', (unpublished report), 29 July.

Department of Home Affairs. (2015b), 'Border Management Agency Project Overview', *Powerpoint Presentation*, 20 October. Available online: https://static.pmg.org.za /151020BMA_Project.pdf (accessed 11 January 2021).

Department of Home Affairs. (2019a), 'Proclamation No. 60 of 2019', 27 November.

Department of Home Affairs. (2019b), 'White Paper on Home Affairs', 18 January. Available online: https://www.gov.za/sites/default/files/gcis_document/201901 /42162gon08.pdf (accessed 5 January 2021).

Department of Home Affairs. (2020), 'Draft Official Identity management Policy: Public Consultation Version', Pretoria: Government Gazette, 22 December. Available online: https://static.pmg.org.za/Draft_Official_Identity_Management_Policy_Version_with _Call_for_Comments.pdf?utm_campaign=request-for-comment-from-department &utm_source=transactional&utm_medium=email (accessed 12 January 2021).

Department of Homeland Security. (2019), 'Department of Homeland Security Strategic Framework for Countering Terrorism and Targeted Violence'. Available online: https://www.dhs.gov/sites/default/files/publications/19_0920_plcy_strategic-framework -countering-terrorism-targeted-violence.pdf (accessed 23 October 2020).

Department of International Relations and Cooperation. (n.d.), 'Wassenaar Arrangement: History and Present Status'. Available online: http://www.dirco.gov.za/foreign/ Multilateral/inter/wasse.htm (accessed 8 April 2020).

Detzner, S. (2017), 'Modern Post-Conflict Security Sector Reform in Africa: Patterns of Success and Failure', *African Security Review*, 6 (2): 116–42.

Directorate General for External Policies Policy Department. (2015), 'Dual Use Export Controls', (report). Available online: http://www.europarl.europa.eu/RegData/etudes/ STUD/2015/535000/EXPO_STU(2015)535000_EN.pdf (accessed 20 April 2020).

D'Souza, R. (2018), 'The Surveillance State: A Composition in Four Movements', in A. Choudry (ed.) *Activists and the Surveillance State: Learning from Repression*, 23–52, London: Pluto Press.

Duncan, J. (2015), 'Fortress South Africa', *South African Civil Society Information Service*, 8 May. Available online: https://sacsis.org.za/site/article/2369 (accessed 26 November 2020).

Duncan, J. (2016), 'Keep the Spies out of Snooping on Protests', *Daily Maverick*, 7 November. Available online: https://www.dailymaverick.co.za/article/2016-11-17-op -ed-keep-the-spies-out-of-snooping-on-protests/ (accessed 1 August 2020).

Duncan, J. (2017), 'Why South Africans Should be Worried about ANC Talk of a Colour Revolution', *The Conversation*, 14 November. Available online: https://theconversation .com/why-south-africans-should-be-worried-by-anc-talk-of-a-colour-revolution -87019 (accessed 23 February 2021).

Duncan, J. (2018), *Stopping the Spies: Constructing and Resisting the Surveillance State in South Africa*, Johannesburg: Wits University Press.

Duncan, J. (2019a). 'Accountable State Spying: Hacking Needs to be Regulated', *Daily Maverick*, 14 October. Available online: https://www.dailymaverick.co.za/article /2019-10-14-accountable-state-spying-government-hacking-needs-to-be-regulated/ (accessed 8 June 2020).

Duncan, J. (2019b), 'Bulk Communication Surveillance in South Africa: Fix it or Nix It?', *Daily Maverick*, 30 September. Available online: https://www.dailymaverick.co.za/ article/2019-09-30-bulk-communication-surveillance-in-south-africa-fix-it-or-nix-it/ (accessed 18 March 2021).

Duncan, J. (2020), 'South Africa's Emerging Department of Homeland Security', *Daily Maverick*, 20 January. Available online: https://www.dailymaverick.co.za/article /2020-01-20-south-africas-emerging-department-of-homeland-security/ (accessed 26 November 2020).

Duncan, J. (2020), 'Spying for Profit: The Dangers of Economic Intelligence', *Daily Maverick*, 18 March. Available online: https://www.dailymaverick.co.za/article/2020 -03-18-spying-for-profit-the-dangers-of-economic-intelligence/ (accessed 5 June 2020).

Duncan, J. (2021a), 'The Enemy Within: Securitising Protests as Domestic Instability', in M. Williams and V. Satgar (eds), *Destroying Democracy: Neoliberal Capitalism and the Rise of Authoritarian Politics*, 179–94, Johannesburg: Wits University Press.

Duncan, J. (2021b), 'Why SAPS Crime Intelligence is a Hot Mess', *Daily Maverick*, 1 February. Available online: https://www.dailymaverick.co.za/article/2021-02-01-why -saps-crime-intelligence-is-a-hot-mess/ (accessed 6 April 2021).

Durham, R. B. (2015), *Supplying the Enemy: The Modern Arms Industry and the Military-Industrial Complex*, Morrisville: Lulu.com.

Dzinesa, G. A. (2012), 'Zimbabwe's Constitutional Reform Process: Challenges and Prospects', Cape Town: Institute for Justice and Reconciliation. Available online: http://ijr.org.za/home/wp-content/uploads/2017/05/IJR-Zimbabwe-Constitutional-Reform-OP-WEB.pdf (accessed 20 January 2021).

Elaman. (n.d.), 'Governmental Security Solutions (Information Brochure)', *Document leaked by Wikileaks*. Available online: https://wikileaks.org/spyfiles/files/0/187_201106-ISS-ELAMAN2.pdf (accessed 20 April 2020).

Electronic Privacy Information Centre. (2015), 'Slight Decrease in Wiretaps in 2014, Encryption not a Barrier to Investigations', (blog post), 2 July. Available online: https://epic.org/2015/07/slight-decrease-in-wiretaps-in.html (accessed 17 March 2021).

Ellis, S. (2012), *External Mission: The ANC in Exile*, Johannesburg: Jonathan Ball.

Emmerson, B. (2014), 'Statement by Mr. Ben Emmerson, Special Rapporteur on the Promotion and Protection of Human Rights and Fundamental Freedoms while Countering Terrorism to the 69th session of the General Assembly Third Committee, Item 68 (b and c)', United Nations Human Rights Office of the High Commissioner, 23 October. Available online: http://www.ohchr.org/EN/NewsEvents/Pages/DisplayNews.aspx?NewsID=15454&LangID=E (accessed 9 May 2018).

Ericson, R. and K. Haggerty. (1997), *Policing the Risk Society*, Oxford: Oxford University Press.

Ericson, R. V. (2008), 'The State of Pre-emption: Managing Terrorism Risk through Counter Law', in L. Amoore and M. de Goede (eds), *Risk and the War on Terror*, 58–76, London: Routledge.

European Commission. (2011), 'The Global Approach to Migration and Mobility', Communication from the Commission to the European Parliament, the Council, the European Economic and Social Committee and the Committee of the Regions.

European Court of Human Rights. (2006), 'Weber and Saravia vs German, Application no. 54934/00'. Available online: https://hudoc.echr.coe.int/eng#{%22itemid%22:[%2201-76586%22]} (accessed 23 March 2021).

European Court of Human Rights. (2018), 'Case of Big Brother Watch and others v. the United Kingdom', 13 September. Available online: https://hudoc.echr.coe.int/eng#{%22itemid%22:[%2201-186048%22]} (accessed 28 March 2021).

European Union Agency for Fundamental Rights. (2015), 'Surveillance by Intelligence Services: Fundamental Rights Safeguards and Remedies in the EU', Volume II: Field Perspectives and Legal Update. Available online: https://fra.europa.eu/en/publication/2015/surveillance-intelligence-services-volume-i-member-states-legal-frameworks (accessed 22 May 2020).

Fabricius, P. (2017), 'When "Democracy" Becomes "Regime Change"', *ISS Today*, 15 December. Available online: https://issafrica.org/iss-today/when-democracy-becomes-regime-change (accessed 12 May 2021).

Fanon, F. (1963), *The Wretched of the Earth*, London: Penguin Books.

Farries, E. and E. King. (2018), 'Unanswered Questions: International Intelligence Sharing', (report), Geneva: International Network of Civil Liberties Organizations. Available online: https://www.inclo.net/pdf/iisp/unanswered_questions.pdf (accessed 24 March 2021).

Finkel, E. and Y. M. Brudny. (2012), 'No More Colour! Authoritarian Regimes and Colour Revolutions in Eurasia', *Democratization*, 19 (1): 1–14.

Five Eyes Ministerial. (2018), 'Official Communique on National Security'. Available online: https://www.homeaffairs.gov.au/about-us/our-portfolios/national-security/security-coordination/five-country-ministerial-2018 (accessed 12 February 2021).

Foreign Intelligence Surveillance Court. (2010), 'Exhibit F: In the Fatter of Foreign Governments, Foreign Factions, Foreign Entities and Foreign-based Political Organizations', *Certification 2010 A*. Available online: https://snowdenarchive.cjfe.org/greenstone/collect/snowden1/index/assoc/HASH013a/5df62e85.dir/doc.pdf (accessed 11 February 2021).

Forensics for Justice. (2019), 'Forensic Report Regarding Alleged Botswana Vote Rigging'. Available online: https://www.forensicsforjustice.org/wp-content/uploads/2019/12/01-FINAL-REPORT-Botswana-Elections-2019-12-04_Redacted.pdf (accessed 3 May 2021).

Fraser, A, and C. Atkinson. (2014), 'Making up Gangs: Looking, Labelling and the New Politics of Intelligence-led Policing', *Youth Justice*, 4 (2): 154–70.

Fuchs, C. (2010a). 'How Can Surveillance Be Defined?', *Unified Theory of Information Research Group*. The internet and surveillance research paper series. No. 1: 1–22.

Fuchs, C. (2010b). 'Critical Globalization Studies and the New Imperialism', *Critical Sociology*, 36 (6): 839–67.

Fuchs, C. (2013), 'Societal and Ideological Impacts of Deep Packet Inspection (DPI) Internet Surveillance', *Information, Communication and Society*, 16 (8): 1328–59.

Geneva Centre for Security Sector Governance. (2019), 'Zimbabwe SSR Background Note', 28 May. Available online: https://issat.dcaf.ch/Learn/Resource-Library/Country-Profiles/Zimbabwe-SSR-Background-Note (accessed 21 May 2020).

Gichanga, M. W. (2019), *Barriers for Control: The Private Security Industry and Student Protests in South Africa 2019*, Pretoria: Private Security Industry Regulatory Authority of South Africa.

Gill, P. and M. Phythian. (2012), *Intelligence in an Insecure World*, Cambridge: Polity Press.

Goldstein, D. M. (2009), 'Rights and Security: Contradictory or Complementary?', *Anthropology Now*, 1 (3): 43–51.

Gondwe, G. (2020), 'Nine Years of a "Spy Machine"', *The Nation*, 23 May. Available online: https://www.mwnation.com/nine-years-of-a-spy-machine/ (accessed 22 March 2021).

Good, K. (2010), 'The Presidency of General Ian Khama: The Militarization of the Botswana "miracle"', *African Affairs*, 109/435: 315–24.

Goodwin, B. (2016), 'Bulk Surveillance Review is "Fiction", Claims Former NSA Technical Director', *Computer Weekly*, 4 October. Available online: https://www.computerweekly.com/news/450400247/Bulk-surveillance-review-is-fiction-claims-former-NSA-technical-director (accessed 28 March 2021).

Govender, D. (2012), 'Information Management Strategies to Prevent Crime and Combat Losses', *Acta Criminologica*, 25 (12): 79–96.

Government of the United Kingdom. (2016), 'Investigatory Powers Act'. Available online: https://www.legislation.gov.uk/ukpga/2016/25/part/2/chapter/1/crossheading/power-to-issue-warrants/enacted (accessed 5 June 2020).

Groenewald, Y. (2011), 'SA Firm "Helped" Gaddafi Spy on the People of Libya', *Mail & Guardian*, 2 September. Available online: http://mg.co.za/article/2011-09-02-sa-firm-helped-gaddafi-spy (accessed 25 April 2020).

GSM Association. (2016), 'Mandatory Registration of Prepaid SIM Cards: Addressing Challenges through Best Practice', London: GSM Association. Available online: https://www.gsma.com/publicpolicy/wp-content/uploads/2016/04/Mandatory-SIM-Registration.pdf (accessed 13 May 2021).

Gürses, A., A. Kundnani and J. Van Hoboken. (2016), 'Crypto and Empire: The Contradictions of Counter-Surveillance Advocacy', *Media, Culture and Society*, 38 (4): 576–90.

Gutheil, M., Q. Liger, A. Heetman, J. Eager and M. Crawford. (2017), 'Legal Framework for Hacking by Law Enforcement: Identification, Evaluation and Comparison of Practices', Report produced for the European Parliament's Committee on Civil Liberties, Justice and Home Affairs. Available online: https://www.europarl.europa.eu/RegData/etudes/STUD/2017/583137/IPOL_STU(2017)583137_EN.pdf (accessed 17 March 2021).

Gwatiwa, T. (2015), 'The Polemics of Security Intelligence in Botswana: Real or Imagined Security Threats?', *African Security Review*, 24 (1): 43–4.

Hacking Team. (n.d.), 'Remote Control System', (information brochure). Surveillance Industry Index, *Privacy International*. Available online: http://sii.transparencytoolkit.org/docs/Hacking-Team_Remote-Control-System_Product-Descriptionsii_documents (accessed 27 April 2020).

Hager, N. (1996), *Secret Power*, Nelson: Craig Potton Publishing.

Harvey, D. (2003), *The New Imperialism*, Oxford: Oxford University Press.

Harvey, D. (2005), *A Brief History of Neoliberalism*, Oxford: Oxford University Press.

Harvey, D. (2015), *Seventeen Contradictions and the End of Capitalism*, London: Profile Books.

Hawkins, A. (2018), 'Beijing's Big Brother Tech needs African Faces', *Foreign Policy*, 24 July. Available online: https://foreignpolicy.com/2018/07/24/beijings-big-brother-tech-needs-africanfaces/ (accessed 16 November 2020).

Hintz, A., L. Dencik and K. Walh-Jorgensen. (2019), *Digital Citizenship in a Datafied Society*, Cambridge: Polity Press.

Hiropoulos, A. and L. B. Landau. (2015), 'Fighting Crime or Using Immigrants as Scapegoats? ', *Daily Maverick*, 2 October. Available online: https://www.dailymaverick.co.za/article/2015-10-02-op-ed-fighting-crime-or-using-immigrants-as-scapegoats/ (accessed 4 January 2021).

Hopkins, N. and J. Borger. (2013), 'Exclusive: NSA Pays £100m in Secret Funding for GCHQ', *The Guardian*, 1 August. Available online: https://www.theguardian.com/uk-news/2013/aug/01/nsa-paid-gchq-spying-edward-snowden (accessed 24 March 2021).

Hove, M. (2017), 'The Necessity of Security Sector Reform in Zimbabwe', *Politikon*, 44 (3): 425–45.

Hoyos, C. (2013), 'Thales Chief Laments Groups' International Market Prowess', *Financial Times*, 16 September. Available online: https://www.ft.com/content/56d3d05c-1b03-11e3-b781-00144feab7de (accessed 6 April 2020).

Human Rights Watch. (2019), 'Deadly Attacks on Foreign Truck Drivers', (blog). Available online: https://www.hrw.org/news/2019/08/26/south-africa-deadly-attacks-foreign-truck-drivers (accessed 16 April 2021).

Hunter, M. and A. Mare. (2020), 'A Patchwork for Privacy: Mapping Communications Surveillance Laws in Southern Africa', Report commissioned by the Media Policy and Democracy Project, May. Available online: https://www.mediaanddemocracy.com/uploads/1/6/5/7/16577624/patchwork_for_privacy_-_communication_surveillance_in_southern_africa.pdf (accessed 21 March 2021).

Hutton, L. (2009), 'Intelligence and Accountability in Africa', *Institute for Security Studies Policy Brief*, 2, June. Available online: https://www.files.ethz.ch/isn/112461/JUL09INTELLIGENCEACCOUNT.pdf (accessed 23 February 2021).

INCM. (2017), 'Registro de Cartões "SIM" Garante ao Publico Segurança e Serviços de Valor Acrescentado', *25 anos do INCM – Instituto Nacional das Comunicações*

de Moçambique. Available online: https://www.arecom.gov.mz/index.php/sala-de
-imprensa/telecomunicar/154-suplemento-25-anos-do-incm-edicao-especial-1/file
(accessed 21 March 2021).

Kaba, M. (2020), 'Yes, We Mean Literally Abolish the Police', *New York Times*, 12 June.
Available online: https://static1.squarespace.com/static/5856b4a5e6f2e1189ab6e82a/t
/5ee6483c13797867358dc675/1592150076501/Yes%2C+We+Mean+Literally+Abolish
+the+Police+-+The+New+York+Times.pdf (accessed 12 April 2021).

Kane, A. (2016), 'How Israel Become a Hub for Surveillance Technology', *The Intercept*,
17 October. Available online: https://theintercept.com/2016/10,'I how-israel-became-a-
hub-for-surveillance-technology/ (accessed 19 April 2020).

Kasrils, R. (1993), *Armed and Dangerous: My Undercover Struggle Against Apartheid*,
Oxford: Heinemann.

Kasrils, R. (2017), *A Simple Man: Kasrils and the Zuma Enigma*, Johannesburg: Jacana
Media.

Katz, C. (2015), 'Capitalist Mutations in Emerging, Intermediate and Peripheral
Neoliberalism', in P. Bond and A. Garcia (eds), *BRICS: An Anti-Capitalist Critique*,
70–98, Johannesburg: Jacana Media.

Katzenellenbogen, J. (2017), 'Border Management Authority, Defence Review Need Larger
Budget', *DefenceWeb*, 18 October. Available online: https://www.defenceweb.co.za/
security/border-security/border-management-authority-defence-review-need-larger
-budget/ (accessed 25 August 2020).

Kaye, D. (2019), 'Surveillance and Human Rights: Report of the Special Rapporteur on
the Promotion and Protection of the Right to Freedom of Opinion and Expression',
Presented to the forty-first session of the Human Rights Council, 28 May. Available
online: https://www.ohchr.org/EN/HRBodies/HRC/RegularSessions/Session41/
Documents/A_HRC_41_35.docx (accessed 8 April 2020).

King, M. (2006), 'From Reactive Policing to Crowd Management?: Policing Anti-
Globalization Protest in Canada', *Jurisprudencija*, 1 (79): 40–58.

King, N. (2016), *No Borders: The Politics of Immigration Control and Resistance*, London:
Zed Books.

Kirsch, T. G. (2016), 'On the Difficulties of Speaking Out Against Security', *Anthropology
Today*, 32 (5): 5–7.

Kitimbo, A. (2015), 'Is it Time for Open Borders in Southern Africa? The Case for
Free Labour Movement in SADC', in T. McNamee, M. Pearson and W. Boer (eds),
Africans Investing in Africa: Understanding Business and Trade, Sector by Sector, 85–99,
Basingstoke: Palgrave Macmillan.

Klotz, A. (2016), 'Borders and the Roots of Xenophobia in South Africa', *South African
Historical Journal*, 68 (2): 180–94.

Kniep, R. (2016), 'From the Five Eyes to the "SIGINT Seniors Europe": The Intelligence
Community as a Transnational Field', Unpublished paper from selected papers of AoIR
2016: The 17th Annual Conference of the Association of Internet Researchers, Berlin,
Germany, 5–8 October 2016.

Korosteleva, E. (2012), 'Questioning Democracy Promotion: Belarus' Response to the
"Colour Revolutions"', *Democratization*, 19 (1): 37–59. Available online: https://www
.tandfonline.com/doi/abs/10.1080/13510347.2012.641294 (accessed 26 April 2021).

Kraska, P. (2014), 'Militarization and Policing – Its Relevance to 21st Century Policing',
Policing l: 4.

Kwadjo, J. and S. Africa. (2009), 'Introduction', in J. Kwadjo and S. Africa (eds), *Changing
Intelligence Dynamics in Africa*, 1–14, Birmingham: GFN-SSR. Available online: http://

epapers.bham.ac.uk/1526/1/AfricaKwadjo_-2009-_IntelligenceAfrica.pdf (accessed
20 June 2020).

Lalá, A. (2007), 'Mozambique', in G. Cawthra, A. du Pisani and A. Omari (eds), *Security
and Democracy in Southern Africa*, 108–22, Johannesburg: School of Public and
Development Managemet, Wits University.

Lalit. (2017), 'New Phase in Long Battle Against ID Cards', (blog post), 20 March.
Available online: https://www.lalitmauritius.org/en/newsarticle/1946/new-phase-in
-long-battle-against-id-cards/ (accessed 13 January 2021).

Lancaster House Agreement. (1979), 'Southern Rhodesia Constitutional Conference Held
at Lancaster House, London, September – December 1979', (report), 21 December.
Available online: https://sas-space.sas.ac.uk/5847/5/1979_Lancaster_House
_Agreement.pdf (accessed 20 January 2021).

Landau, S. (2010), *Surveillance or Security? The Risks Posed by New Wiretapping
Technologies*, Cambridge, MA: MIT Press.

Law Reform Commission of Hong Kong. (1996), *Regulating Surveillance and the
Interception of Communications* (consultation paper). Available online: https://www
.hkreform.gov.hk/en/docs/intercept-e.pdf (accessed 20 June 2020).

Lee, S. (2016), 'International Reactions to US Cybersecurity Policy: The BRICS Undersea
Cable', *The Henry M. Jackson School of International Studies* (blog), University of
Washington. Available online: https://jsis.washington.edu/news/reactions-u-s
-cybersecuritypolicy-bric-undersea-cable/ (accessed 17 November 2020).

Lei da Política de Defesa e Segurança, in Boletim da Republica 40, Ia Serie, 3oSuplemento,
07/10/97 (Defence and Security Act 17 of 1997). Maputo. Available online: https://
www.resdal.org/Archivo/d000009a.htm (accessed 8 March 2021).

Lindeke, B., P. Kaapama, and L. Blaauw. (2007), 'Namibia', in G. Cawthra, A. du Pisani and
A. Omari (eds), *Security and Democracy in Southern Africa*, 123–41, Johannesburg:
School of Public and Development Management, Wits University.

Links, F. (2018), 'The Rise of the Namibian Surveillance State, Part 3', *The Namibian*,
15 March. Available online: https://www.namibian.com.na/175475/archive-read/The
-rise-of-the-Namibian-surveillance-state (accessed 17 February 2020).

Links, F. (2019), *Spying on Speech: The Threat of Unchecked Communications
Surveillance*, Democracy Report Special Briefing No. 28, June. Available online:
https://ippr.org.na/wp-content/uploads/2019/06/IPPR-surveilance-web.pdf (accessed
24 April 2020).

Links, F. (2021), 'Social Media Surveillance and the Overreaction to Youth Activism', *The
Namibian*, 25 February.

Leistert, O. (2012), 'Resistance Within Social Movements Against Surveillance and How
Surveillance Adapts', *Surveillance & Society*, 9 (4): June 20. Available online: https://
ojs.library.queensu.ca/index.php/surveillance-and-society/article/view/cyber_resist
(accessed 4 May 2020).

Lenin, V. I. ([1916] 1963), 'Imperialism, the Highest Stage of Capitalism', in Lenin's (ed.),
Selected Works, 667–766, Moscow: Progress Publishers.

Lucas Aerospace Combine Shop Steward Committee. (n.d.), 'Corporate Plan', *Summary*.
Available online: https://www.dropbox.com/s/o2sqxvhams2ywup/Lucas-Plan-53pp
-alternative%20corporate%20plan.pdf?dl=0 (accessed 10 May 2020).

Luxemburg, R. (1951), *The Accumulation of Capital*, London: Routledge and Kegan Paul.

Mabee, B. (2007), 'Re-Imagining the Borders of US Security after 9/11: Securitization,
Risk and the Creation of the Department of Homeland Security', *Globalizations*, 4 (3):
385–97.

Mabuza, E. and M. Savides. (2019), '"Very Happy": Fees Must Fall Activist Kanya Cekeshe is Paroled from Prison', *Sunday Times*, 24 December. Available online: https://www .timeslive.co.za/news/south-africa/2019-12-24-feesmustfall-activist-kanya-cekeshe-is -paroled-from-prison/ (accessed 7 April 2021).

MacAskill, E. (2016), 'Does the Berlin Attack Make the Case for Increased Surveillance?', *The Guardian*, 22 December. Available online: https://www.theguardian.com/world /2016/dec/22/berlin-terrorist-attack-surveillance-intelligence-agencies (accessed 19 April 2020).

Machel, S. (1983), 'Speech to the Arusha Conference', in R. V. Sears (ed.), *The Arusha Conference*, 67–80, London: Socialist International.

Madsen, W. (2014), 'Five Eyes Assault on Social Media: Big Brother Now Rules the Internet', *Wayne Madsen Report*, 15 July. Available online: https://www .waynemadsenreport.com/articles/20140715_3 (accessed 11 May 2021).

Magidimisha, H. H. (2018), 'Migration Policies in the Region: Thinking Beyond the Enclaved Political Economy', in H. H. Magidimisha, N. E. Khalema, L. Chipungu, T. Chirimambowa and T. Chimedza (eds), *Crisis, Identity and Migration in Post-Colonial Southern Africa*, 187–203, Cham: Springer.

Mahlobo, D. (2017), 'Input by the South African Minister of State Security Honourable David Mahlobo on National Security and Development at the 7th BRICS Meeting of High Representative for Security Issues, Beijing, China: 28 July 2017'. Available online: http://www.ssa.gov.za/LinkClick.aspx?fileticket=0CDkIoCl4dQ%3D&tabid=56 &portalid=0&mid=763 (accessed 26 April 2021).

Mandaza, I. (1986), 'The State in Post-White Settler Colonial Situations', in I. Mandaza (ed.), *Zimbabwe: The Political Economy of Transition*, 1980–1986, 21–30, Dakar: CODESRIA.

Mandel, E. [as E. Germain]. (1955), 'The Marxist Theory of Imperialism and its Critics', *Two Essays on Imperialism*, Marxists.org. Available online: https://www.marxists.org/ archive/mandel/1955/08/imp-crit.html (accessed 19 May 2020).

Mann, M. and A. Daly. (2019), '(Big) Data and the North-in-South: Australia's Informational Imperialism and Digital Colonialism', *Television and New Media*, 20 (4): 379–95.

Marczak, B., J. Scott-Railton, S. McKune, B. A. Razzak and R. Deibert. (2018), 'Hide and Seek: Tracking NSO Group's Pegasus to Operations in 45 Countries', (report), 18 September. Available online: https://citizenlab.ca/2018/09/hide-and-seek-tracking -nso-groups-pegasus-spyware-to-operations-in-45-countries/ (accessed 8 April 2020).

Mare, A. (2019), 'Communication Surveillance in Namibia: An Exploratory Study', (research report). Johannesburg: Media Policy and Democracy Project. Available online: file:///C:/Users/jduncan/OneDrive%20-%20University%20of%20Johannesburg /Downloads/namibia_report_3rd_pages.pdf (accessed 17 February 2020).

Maringira, G. and D. Gibson. (2019), 'Maintaining Order in Townships: Gangerism and Community Resilience in Post-apartheid South Africa', *African Conflict and Peacebuilding Review*, 9 (2): 55–74.

Martin, C. (2015), 'Witness statement of Ciarin Martin of GCHQ', Greennet Limited and others v Secretary of State for Foreign and Commonwealth Affairs, Investigatory Powers Tribunal, 16 November. Available online: https://privacyinternational.org/sites/ default/files/2018-03/2015.11.16%20CM_Witness_Statement_Signed_2015_11_16.pdf (accessed 17 March 2021).

Martin, G. (2019), 'Denel Optimistic about Turnaround', *DefenceWeb*, 18 November. Available online: https://www.defenceweb.co.za/featured/denel-optimistic-about -turnaround/ (accessed 17 April 2020).

Mason, S. (2020), 'A Plan to Turn Back the Clock – Defence Diversification', *MedAct blog*, 22 February. Available online: https://www.medact.org/2020/blogs/defence -diversification/ (accessed 1 April 2020).

Matthews, J., F. Ginwala and L. Nathan, 'Intelligence in a Constitutional Democracy: Final Report to the Minister for Intelligence Service, the Honourable Mr. Ronnie Kasrils', 10 September. Available online: https://assets.publishing.service.gov.uk/ media/57a08baae5274a31e0000cc8/ReviewComm.Sept08.pdf (accessed 13 April 2021).

Maundeni, Z. (2008), 'Vision 2016 and Reforming the Intelligence in Botswana', *Botswana Notes and Records*, 40: 135–46. Available online: https://www.jstor.org/stable/41236039 (accessed 4 March 2021).

McBride, R. (2018), 'First Respondent's Answering Affidavit and Founding Affidavit in the Counter-application', Vuma and others v The Executive Director: Independent Police Investigations Directorate, Case no. 49791/18. Available online: https://www .documentcloud.org/documents/6929093-Answering-Affidavit-and-Founding -Affidavit-in.html#document/p10/a565395 (accessed 7 April 2021).

McCormack, T. (2010), 'The Limits to Emancipation in the Human Security Framework', in David Chandler and Nik Hynek (eds), *Critical Perspectives on Human Security: Rethinking Emancipation and Power in International Relations*, 99–113, London: Taylor and Francis.

McDowell, M. G. (2017), 'Insurgent Safety: Theorising Alternatives to State Protection', *Theoretical Criminology*, 23 (1): 43–59.

Mendel, T. (2013), 'Defining the Scope of National Security: Issues Paper for the National Security Principles Project'. Available online: https://www.right2info.org/resources/ publications/mendel-on-defining-national-security (accessed 21 April 2021).

Mendes, P. (2015), 'Nurturing Political Consensus – Advancing Against the Odds in Zimbabwe' (blog post), 4 December. Available online: https://issat.dcaf.ch/Share/Blogs /ISSAT-Blog/Nurturing-political-consensus-advances-against-the-odds-in-Zimbabwe (accessed 21 May 2020).

Milan, S. and E. Treré. (2019), 'Big Data from the South(s): Beyond Data Universalism', *Television & New Media*, 20 (4): 319–35.

Miller, T. (2014), *Border Patrol Nation: Dispatches from the Frontlines of Homeland Security*, San Francisco: City Light Books.

Ministry of Higher Education and Training. (2018), 'National Assembly for Written Reply Question 2070', Memorandum from the Parliamentary Office, Republic of South Africa. Available online: https://press-admin.voteda.org/wp-content/uploads/2018/08/ RNW2070-2018-08-07.docx (accessed 7 April 2021).

MISA Zimbabwe. (2019), 'High Court Sets Aside Internet Shutdown Directives' (press release), 21 January. Available online: https://zimbabwe.misa.org/2019/01/21/high -court-sets-aside-internet-shut-down-directives/ (accessed 22 April 2020).

Mmeso, P. (2016), 'Botswana's Most Serious Internal Threat', *The Patriot on Sunday*, 8 August. Available online: http://thepatriot.co.bw/news/item/2956-botswana%E2%80 %99s-most-serious-internal-threat.html (accessed 22 February 2021).

Mogalakwe, M. (2013), 'Deconstructing National Security: The Case of Botswana', *Sacha Journal of Politics and Strategic Studies*, 3: 17–18.

Monahan, T. (2009), 'The Murky World of "Fusion Centres"', *Criminal Justice Matters*, 75 (1): 20–1.

Mohanan, T. (2010), *Surveillance in the Time of Insecurity*, New Brunswick: Rutgers University Press.

Monahan, T. (2017), 'Regulating Belonging: Surveillance, Inequality and the Cultural Production of Abjection', *Journal of Cultural Economy*, 10 (2): 191–206. Available online: http://publicsurveillance.com/papers/Abjection.pdf (accessed 30 April 2020).

Mondlane, E. (1983), *The Struggle for Mozambique*, London: Zed Press.

Moyo, I. (2020), 'On Decolonised Borders and Regional Integration in the Southern African Development Community (SADC) region', *Social Sciences*, 9 (4): 1–12.

Mufamadi, S. et al. (2018), 'High Level Review Panel on the State Security Agency', *Pretoria: Presidency of the Republic of South Africa*. Available online: https://www.gov.za/sites/default/files/gcis_document/201903/high-level-review-panel-state-security-agency.pdf (accessed 8 April 2021).

Mugari, I., M. Maunga and T. Chigariro. (2015), 'Embracing Intelligence-led Policing in the Republic of Zimbabwe', *International Journal of Innovative Research and Development*, 4 (2): 87–94.

Muller, B. (2004), '(Dis)qualified Bodies: Securitization, Citizenship and "Identity Management"', *Citizenship Studies*, 8 (3): 279–94.

Murakami Wood, D. and S. Wright. (2015), 'Surveillance and security intelligence after Snowden', *Surveillance & Society*, 13 (2): 132–8.

Murhula, P. (2020), 'RDC : L'atteinte à la Liberté d'Expression sur les Réseaux Sociaux Entame la Démocratie', *JamboRDC.info*, 13 April. Available online: https://jambordc.info/17294/ (accessed 23 March 2021).

Murray, M. (1987), *South Africa: Time of Agony, Time of Destiny*, London: Verso Books.

Mustafa, T. (2015), 'Damming the Palestinian Spring: Security Sector Reform and Entrenched Repression', *Journal of Intervention and Statebuilding*, 9 (2): 212–30.

Myburgh, P. L. (2017), *The Republic of Gupta: A Story of State Capture*, Cape Town: Penguin Books.

Myeza, N. W. (2019), 'An Analysis of the Prosecution-led Investigation Model in Murder Cases', Thesis submitted for the degree of Doctor of Philosophy in Criminal Justice, University of South Africa. Available online: http://uir.unisa.ac.za/bitstream/handle/10500/25685/thesis_myeza_nw.pdf?sequence=1&isAllowed=y (accessed April 2021).

National Constitutional Assembly. (2001), 'Draft Constitution for Zimbabwe'. Available online: http://archive.kubatana.net/docs/demgg/ncaconst0201.pdf on 20 January 2021.

National Conventional Arms Control Committee. (2004), 'Policy for the Control of Trade in Conventional Arms'. Available online: http://www.armscor.co.za/wpcontent/uploads/2016/09/NCACC-Policy-2004.pdf (accessed 13 July 2020).

National Planning Commission of Namibia. (2014), 'The Root Causes of Poverty', (report). Available online: https://www.npc.gov.na/?wpfb_dl=303 (accessed 16 February 2021).

National Prosecuting Authority. (2016), 'Annual Report: National Director of Public Prosecutions 2015/16'. Available online: https://www.npa.gov.za/sites/default/files/annual-reports/NPA%20Annual%20Report%201516.pdf (accessed 6 April 2021).

National Security Agency. (2007), 'United States SIGINT System January 2007 Strategic Mission List', Leaked document, Snowden Surveillance Archive. Available online: https://snowdenarchive.cjfe.org/greenstone/collect/snowden1/index/assoc/HASH013b/bacb1518.dir/doc.pdf (accessed 16 February 2020).

National Security Agency. (2008), 'X-Keyscore', (leaked powerpoint presentation). Snowden Surveillance Archive. Available online: https://snowdenarchive.cjfe.org/greenstone/collect/snowden1/index/assoc/HASH01d3/6ab1650d.dir/doc.pdf (accessed 15 February 2020).

National Security Agency. (2012), 'Exploiting Foreign Lawful Intercept Roundtable', *Powerpoint Presentation*. Electronic Frontier Foundation. Available online:

https://www.eff.org/document/20150928-intercept-exploiting-foreign-law-intercept
-roundtablepdf (accessed 28 April 2020).

National Treasury. (2021), *#RSABudget2021* (booklet). Available online: http://www
.treasury.gov.za/documents/National%20Budget/2021/guides/2021%20Peoples
%20Guide%20English.pdf.

Naidu, E. (2020), 'A Glimpse into the Heart of Student Unrest', *University World News Africa Edition*, 12 March. Available online: https://www.universityworldnews.com/post
.php?story=20200312074655799 (accessed 7 April 2021).

Ncube, W. and C. Tracey. (2020), *Monitoring Policy, Litigious and Legislative Shifts in Immigration Detention in South Africa*, Johannesburg: Lawyers for Human Rights, May. Available online: https://www.lhr.org.za/wp-content/uploads/2020/06/Detention
-Report-Final-Final-Digital-1.pdf (accessed 25 November 2020).

Ndlovu-Gatsheni, S. J. (2018), 'Decolonising Borders, Decriminalising Migration and Rethinking Citizenship', in H. H. Magidimisha, N. E. Khalema, L. Chipungu, T. C. Chirimambowa and T. L. Chimedza (eds), *Crisis, Identity and Migration in Post-Colonial Southern Africa*, 23–37, Cham: Springer.

N'dungu, S. K. (2003), *The Right to Dissent: Freedom of Expression, Assembly and Demonstration in South Africa*, Johannesburg: Freedom of Expression Institute.

Nehanda Radio. (2011), 'Chinese Building Military Base in Zimbabwe', *Nehanda Radio*, Available online: https://nehandaradio.com/2011/03/03/chinese-building-military
-base-in-zimbabwe/ (accessed 31 March 2021).

Neocleous, M. and G. S. Rigakos. (2011), *Anti-security*, Ottawa: Red Quill Books.

Neocosmos, M. (2008), *From 'Foreign Natives' to 'Native Foreigners': Explaining Xenophobia in Post-apartheid South Africa*, Dakar: CODESRIA.

Newham, G. (2013), 'Institute for Security Studies Comments on the 2013/14 Budget', *Sangonet Pulse*, 28 February. Available online: http://www.ngopulse.org/article/
institute-security-studies-comments-20134-budget (accessed 13 April 2021).

Newham, G. (2017), 'Do Foreigners Really Commit SA's Most Violent Crimes?', *ISS Today*, 29 November. Available online: https://issafrica.org/iss-today/do-foreigners-really
-commit-sas-most-violent-crimes (accessed 4 January 2021).

Newkirk, A. B. (2010), 'The Rise of the Fusion-intelligence Complex: A Critique of Political Surveillance after 9/11', *Surveillance and Society*, 8 (1): 43–60.

Nhanale, E. (2021), *Electronic Surveillance in Mozambique: The Risks and Suspicions in a Context of Authoritarianism and Military Conflict*, Johannesburg: Media Policy and Democracy Project.

No Sizwe. (1979), *One Azania, One Nation: The National Question in South Africa*, London: Zed Press.

NSA and GCHQ. (1946), 'British-US Communication Intelligence Agreement 1946'. Available online: https://www.nsa.gov/newsfeatures/declassified-documents/ukusa/
assets/files/agreement outline 5mar46.pdf (accessed 12 March 2020).

Nshimbi, C. C., I. Moyo and T. Gumbo. (2018), 'Between Neoliberal Orthodoxy and Securitization: Prospects and Challenges for a Borderless Southern African Community', in H. H. Magidimisha,; N. E. Khalema, L. Chipungu, T. C. Chirimambowa and T. L. Chimedza (eds), *Crisis, Identity and Migration in Post-Colonial Southern Africa*, 167–86, Cham: Springer.

NSO Group. (n.d.), 'Governance', *Company Website*. Available online: https://www
.nsogroup.com/ (accessed 8 April 2020).

NSO Group. (2019), 'NSO Group Acquired by its Management', *Company Press Release*, July. Available online: https://www.nsogroup.com/wp-content/uploads/2019/07/NSO
_Group_Acquired_by_its_Management_Feb142019.pdf (accessed 8 April 2020).

Nunn, C. (2015), '"Securitization" Presents Challenges for Migrant Settlement and Integration', *The Conversation*, 16 July. Available online: https://theconversation.com /securitization-presents-challenges-for-migrant-settlement-and-integration-43618 (accessed 5 January 2021).

Nyakudya, M. (2010), 'Security Sector Reform in Zimbabwe: Prospects and Challenges', unpublished paper. Available online: http://www.solidaritypeacetrust.org/download/ sptarticles/security_sector_reform.pdf (accessed 26 May 2020).

O'Brien, K. (2011), *The South African Intelligence Services: From Apartheid to Democracy 1948–2005*. London: Routledge.

Office for the Coordination of Humanitarian Affairs, Application of the Human Security Concept and the United Nations Trust Fund for Human Security, 10 September 2009. Available online: https://www.unocha.org/sites/dms/HSU/Publications%20and %20Products/Human%20Security%20Tools/Human%20Security%20in%20Theory %20and%20Practice%20English.pdf (accessed 2 June 2020).

Omanovic, E. (2015), 'New Paper Reveals How to Keep Surveillance Tech from Human Rights Abusers', *Access Now* (blog), 13 March. Available online: https:hwww.accessnow .org/new-paper-recommends-how-to-keep-surveillance-tech-from-human-rights -abuser (accessed 20 April 2019).

Omanovic, E. (n.d.), 'Hacking Team's Global Licence Revoked by Italian Export Authorities', *Privacy International* (blog). Available online: https://www.privacyinte rnational.org/node/826 (accessed 22 April 2020).

Omari, A. H. and P. Macaringue. (2007), 'Southern African Security in Historical Perspective', in G. Cawthra, A. du Pisani and A. Omari (eds), *Security and Democracy in Southern Africa*, 45–60, Johannesburg: School of Public and Development Management, Wits University.

O'Neil, A. (2017), 'Australia and the "Five Eyes" Intelligence Network: The Perils of an Asymmetric Alliance', *Australian Journal of International Affairs*, 71 (5): 529–43.

Organization for Economic Cooperation and Development. (2007), *The OECD Handbook on Security Sector Reform: Supporting Security and Justice*, Paris: OECD. Available online: https://www.eda.admin.ch/dam/deza/en/documents/themen/fragile -kontexte/224402-oecd-handbook-security-system-reform_EN.pdf (accessed 29 May 2020).

Oxford, A. (2013), 'Why is X-Keyscore in Zambia and the Sudan?', *HTXT*, 3 August. Available online: http://www.htxt.co.za/2013/08/03/why-is-xkeyscore-in-zambia-and -the-sudan/ (accessed 11 August 2016).

Panitch, L. (2015), 'BRICS, the G20 and the American Empire', in P. Bond and A. Garcia (eds), *BRICS: An Anti-Capitalist Critique*, 61–9, Johannesburg: Jacana Media.

Paret, M. (2017), 'Southern Resistance in Critical Perspective', in M. Paret, C. Runciman and L. Sinwell (eds), *Southern Resistance in Critical Perspective*, 1–18, London: Routledge.

Parliamentary Monitoring Group. (2012), 'State of Ports of Entry and Refugee Reception Offices', (minutes of meeting of Portfolio Committee on Home Affairs), 22 May. Available online: https://pmg.org.za/committee-meeting/14420/ (accessed 12 January 2021).

Parliamentary Monitoring Group. (2016a), 'Border Management Authority Bill [B9–16]: Home Affairs, SAPS and National Treasury Briefing', Minutes of meeting of Portfolio Committee on Home Affairs, 16 August. Available online: https://pmg.org.za/ committee-meeting/23073/ (accessed 18 January 2021).

Parliamentary Monitoring Group. (2016b), 'Status and Collaboration at Harbours and Participation in Protecting the Ocean Economy', *Department of Home Affairs Briefing*,

30 August. Available online: https://pmg.org.za/committee-meeting/23150/ (accessed 18 January 2021).

Parliamentary Monitoring Group. (2017), 'Minutes of a Meeting of the Portfolio Committee on Basic Education'. Available online: https://pmg.org.za/committee -meeting/24650/ (accessed 7 April 2021).

Parshotam, A. (2018), 'Migration Trends in Southern Africa: Southern Africa's Attitude Towards Migration', *Powerpoint Presentation*. South African Institute of International Affairs, 13 November. Available online: https://saiia.org.za/wp-content/uploads/2018 /10/SADC-migration.pdf (accessed 16 October 2020).

Pateman, R. (1992), 'Intelligence Agencies in Africa: A Preliminary Assessment', *Journal of Modern African Studies*, 30 (4): 569–85.

Pauw, J. (2017), *The President's Keepers: Those Keeping Zuma in Power and Out of Prison*, Cape Town: Tafelberg.

Perlo-Freeman, S., A. Fleurant, P. Wezeman and S. Wezeman. (2016), 'Trends in World Military Expenditure 2015', (report), Stockholm: Stockholm International Peace Research Institute. Available online: https://www.sipri.org/publications/2016/sipri-fact -sheets/trends-world-military-expenditure-2015 (accessed 25 April 2020).

Phakati, B. (2020), 'Denel Tries to Limit Job Losses as it Exits the Aircraft Components Business', *Business Day*, 6 February, Available online: https://www.businesslive.co.za/bd /national/2020-02-06-denel-tries-to-limit-job-losses-as-it-exits-aircraft-components -business/ (accessed 17 April 2020).

Piel, S. and J. Tilouine. (2016), 'British Spying: Tentacles Reach Across Africa's Heads of State and Business Leaders', *Le Monde*, 8 December 2016. Available online: https://www .lemonde.fr/afrique/article/2016/12/08/british-spying-tentacles-reach-across-africa-s -heads-of-states-and-business-leaders_5045668_3212.html (accessed 27 April 2020).

Pijoos, I. and J. Wicks. (2020), '#CrimeStats: Police Must 'Follow Data and Focus on Hotspots', *Times Live*, 31 July. Available online: https://www.timeslive.co.za/news/south -africa/2020-07-31-crimestats-police-must-follow-data-and-focus-on-hotspots-iss/.

Poor, N. and R. Davidson. (2016), 'The Ethics of Using Hacked Data: Patreon's Data Hack and Academic Data Standards', Paper published by the Council for Big Data, Ethics and Society. Available online: https://bdes.datasociety.net/wp-content/uploads/2016/10 /Patreon-Case-Study.pdf (accessed 12 February 2020).

Pozo, G. (2015), 'Russia's Neoliberal Imperialism and the Eurasian Challenge', in P. Bond and A. Garcia (eds), *BRICS: An Anti-Capitalist Critique*, 206–27, Johannesburg: Jacana Media.

President of the Republic of South Africa. (1994), *National Strategic Intelligence Act 39 of 1994*. Pretoria: Government Gazette. Available online: https://static.pmg.org.za/docs /120224nsiact_0.PDF (accessed 16 April 2021).

President of the Republic of South Africa. (2002), *National Conventional Arms Control Committee Act 41 of 2002*, Pretoria: Government Gazette. Available online: https:// www.gov.za/documents/national-conventional-arms-control-act (accessed 16 April 2021).

President of the Republic of South Africa. (2020), *Border Management Authority Act 2 of 2020*, Pretoria: Government Gazette. Available online: https://www.gov.za/sites/default /files/gcis_document/202007/43536gon799.pdf (accessed 4 January 2021).

President of the Republic of Zambia. (1973), 'Zambia Security Intelligence Act No. 43', Chapter 109 of the laws of Zambia. Available online: http://www.parliament.gov.zm /sites/default/files/documents/acts/Zambia%20Security%20Intelligence%20Service %20Act.pdf (accessed 7 May 2020).

President of the Republic of Zambia. (2009), 'Electronic Communications and Transactions Act No. 21'. Available online: https://www.zicta.zm/Downloads/The %20Acts%20and%20SIs/ICT%20Acts/ect_act_2009.pdf (accessed 7 May 2020).

President of the Republic of Zimbabwe. (2007), 'Interception of Communications Act No. 6 of 2007'. Available online: http://www.vertic.org/media/National%20Legislation/ Zimbabwe/ZW_Interception_of_Communications_Act.pdf (accessed 22 April 2020).

President of the Republic of Zimbabwe. (2009), *National Security Council Act No. 2 of 2009*, Harare: Government Gazette.

Prevelakis, V. and D. Spinellis. (2007), 'The Athens Affair', *IEEE Spectrum*, 29 June. Available online: https://spectrum.ieee.org/telecom/security/the-athens-affair (accessed 28 April 2020).

Privacy International. (n.d.), 'Challenging the Drivers of Surveillance', (blog post). Available online: https://www.privacyinternational.org/challenging-drivers -surveillance (accessed 14 May 2020).

Privacy International. (2014), 'South African Government Still Funding Vastech, Knows Previous Financing was for Mass Surveillance' (blog), 30 January. Available online: https://www.privacyinternational.org/node/305 (accessed 24 April 2020).

Privacy International. (2016a), 'Switching Hats: Why South Africa's Surveillance Industry Needs Scrutiny', (blog post), 14 December. Available online: https://privacyinte rnational.org/feature/802/switching-hats-why-south-africas-surveillance-industry -needs-scrutiny (accessed 13 April 2020).

Privacy International. (2016b), 'Bulk Powers Equal Mass Surveillance Equals Unlawful Suspicionless Interference with Privacy', (blog post), 5 March. Available online: https:// privacyinternational.org/blog/1153/bulk-powers-equal-mass-surveillance-equals -unlawful-suspicionless-interference-privacy (accessed 9 May 2020).

Privacy International. (2016c), 'The Right to Privacy in Namibia', Universal Periodic Review stakeholder report, 24th session: Namibia, 26 June. Available online: https:// www.privacyinternational.org/advocacy-briefing/734/right-privacy-namibia ?PageSpeed=noscript&PageSpeed=noscript (accessed 14 May 2020).

Privacy International. (2016d), 'The Global Surveillance Industry: A Report by Privacy International', July 2016. Available online: https://privacyinternational.org/sites/default /files/global_ surveillance.pdf (accessed 15 November 2020).

Privacy International. (2017), 'International Human Rights Implications of Reported Mexican Government Hacking Targeting Journalists and Human Rights Defenders', *Briefing*, 28 June. Available online: https://www.privacyinternational.org/sites/ default/files/2017-12/Briefing%20on%20the%20International%20Human%20Rights %20Implications%20of%20Reported%20Mexican%20Government%20Hacking %20Targeting%20Journalists%20and%20Human%20Rights%20Defenders.pdf (accessed 17 March 2021).

Privacy International. (2018a). 'An Open Source Guide to Researching Surveillance Transfers', (blog post), 23 August. Available online: https://privacyinternational.org/ long-read/2225/open-source-guide-researching-surveillance-transfers (accessed 16 May 2020).

Privacy International. (2018b). 'Right to Privacy at the UN in 2017 – Don't Let your Left Hand Know What Your Right Hand is Doing', (blog post). Available online: https:// www.privacyinternational.org/news-analysis/1079/right-privacy-un-2017-dont-let -your-left-hand-know-what-your-right-hand-doing (accessed 19 January 2021).

Privacy International. (2019), 'Responding to the Global Proliferation of Surveillance Technology', (blog post), 17 September. Available online: https://www.privacyinte

rnational.org/advocacy/3218/responding-global-proliferation-surveillance-technology
-our-strategy (accessed 11 April 2020).

Privy Council Office of Canada. (2004), *Securing an Open Society: Canada's National Security Policy*, Ottawa: Privy Council Office of Canada. Available online: http://aix1 .uottawa.ca/~rparis/natsec.pdf (accessed 21 April 2021).

Rakgoadi, P. (1995), 'The Role of Self-Defence Units in a Changing Political Context', (research report). Johannesburg: Centre for the Study of Violence and Reconciliation. Available online: https://www.csvr.org.za/index.php/publications/1466-the-role-of -the-self-defence-units-sdus-in-a-changing-political-context.html (accessed 15 April 2021).

Raptis, M. (1980), *Socialism, Democracy and Self-Management*, London: Allison and Busby Limited.

Ratcliffe, J. (2010), 'Intelligence-Led Policing: Anticipating Risk and Influencing Action', *International Association of Law Enforcement Intelligence Analysts*. Available online: http://citeseerx.ist.psu.edu/viewdoc/download?doi=10.1.1.364.6795&rep=rep1&type =pdf (accessed 10 August 2020).

Remnick, D. (2019), 'Alexandria Ocasio-Cortez on Breaking up Homeland Security', *The New Yorker*, 12 July. Available online: https://www.newyorker.com/podcast/the-new -yorker-radio-hour/alexandria-ocasio-cortez-on-breaking-up-homeland-security (accessed 20 November 2020).

Reporteurs sans Frontiers. (2012), 'Blue Coat', *Enemies of the Internet* Special Edition. Available online: http://surveillance.rsf.org/en/blue-coat-2/ (accessed 23 April 2020).

Republic of Angola. (2002), *National Security Act of 2002 (Lei Segurança Nacional), Angola*. Available online: https://www.policinglaw.info/assets/downloads/2002_Law _on_National_Security.pdf (accessed 8 March 2021).

Republic of Botswana. (2007), 'Intelligence and Security Service Act'. Available online: https://www.botswanalaws.com/alphabetical-list-of-statutes/intelligence-and-security -service (accessed 24 April 2021).

Republic of Mauritius. (2020), 'Seventh National Assembly Parliamentary Debates. First Session', Tuesday 7 August. Available online: https://mauritiusassembly.govmu.org/ Documents/Hansard/2020/hansard322020.pdf (accessed 1 April 2021).

Republic of Namibia. (1997), 'Namibia Central Intelligence Service Act of 1997'. Available online: https://www.lac.org.na/laws/annoNAM/DEFENCE%20(1997)%20-%20 Namibia%20Central%20Intelligence%20Service%20Act%2010%20of%201997%20 (annotated).pdf (accessed 24 April 2020).

Republic of Namibia. (2009), 'Communications Act'. Available online: https://laws .parliament.na/cms_documents/communications-86425fd24c.pdf (accessed 24 April 2020).

Republic of Mozambique. (1997), Defence and Security Act 17.

Republic of South Africa. (1996), 'Constitution of the Republic of South Africa No. 108 of 1996'. Available online: https://www.gov.za/sites/www.gov.za/files/images/a108-96.pdf (accessed 4 January 2021).

Republic of South Africa. (2002), 'Regulation of Interception of Communications and Provision of Communications-related Information Act No 70'. Available online: https://www.justice.gov.za/legislation/acts/2002-070.pdf (accessed 5 June 2020).

Republic of South Africa. (2020), *Border Management Authority Act No. 2 of 2020*, Pretoria: South African Government Gazette, 21 July. Available online: https:// www.gov.za/sites/default/files/gcis_document/202007/43536gon799.pdf (accessed 12 January 2021).

Republic of Zimbabwe. (2013), 'Constitution of the Republic of Zimbabwe', 2013. Available online: https://web.archive.org/web/20190906054210/https://www.constituteproject.or g/constitution/Zimbabwe_2013.pdf (accessed 28 October 2020).

Reuters. (2017), 'Home Affairs to be Central Part of National Security', *DefenceWeb*, Available online: https://www.defenceweb.co.za/security/border-security/home-affairs -to-be-central-part-of-national-security/ (4 January 2021).

Reuters. (2020), 'Denel to Produce Ventilators in Coronavirus Fight', *eNCA*, 5 April 2020. Available online: https://www.enca.com/news/denel-produce-ventilators-coronavirus -fight (accessed 17 April 2020).

Robinson, C. (2000), *Black Marxism: The Making of the Black Radical Tradition*, Chapel Hill: University of North Carolina Press.

Sadoway, D. and S. Shekhar. (2014), '(Re)Prioritizing Citizens in Smart Cities Governance: Examples of Smart Citizenship from Urban India', *Journal of Community Informatics*, 10. Available online: https://openjournals.uwaterloo.ca/index.php/JoCI/article/view /3447/4541 (accessed 31 March 2021).

Said, E. (1993), *Culture and Imperialism*, London: Chatto and Windus.

SANews. (2016), 'Home Affairs Reclassified Under JCPS Cluster', *South African Government News Agency*, 18 February. Available online: https://www.sanews.gov.za/ south-africa/home-affairs-reclassified-under-jcps-cluster (accessed 4 January 2021).

Saul, J. S. (2005), *The Next Liberation Struggle: Capitalism, Socialism and Democracy in Southern Africa*, London: The Merlin Press.

Schlembach, R. (2018), 'Undercover Policing and the Spectre of "Domestic Extremism": The Covert Surveillance of Environmental Activism in Britain', *Social Movement Studies*, 17 (5): 491–506.

Secretaries General of Governing Former Liberation Movements in Southern Africa. (2016), 'Report of the Workshop of Secretaries General of Governing Former Liberation Movements of Southern Africa on the Common Political, Economic and Security Challenges they Face', Victoria Falls, Zimbabwe, 4–8 May.

Segura, M. S. and S. Waisbord. (2019), 'Between Data Capitalism and Data Citizenship', *Television and New Media*, 20 (4): 412–19.

Seiglie, C. and S. Coissard. (2008), 'Economic Intelligence and National Security', *Academia.edu*. Available online: https://www.academia.edu/28798415/Economic _intelligence_and_national_security (accessed 5 June 2020).

Serrano, M. N. R. (2015), 'How Free is Freedom in Angola?' *OpenDemocracy*, 2 November. Available online: https://www.opendemocracy.net/en/democraciaabierta/ how-free-is-freedom-in-angola/ (accessed 9 March 2021).

Serrano, M. N. R. (2017), 'The President, the General and their Country', *OpenDemocracy*, 17 September. Available online: https://www.opendemocracy.net/en /democraciaabierta/president-general-and-their-country/ (accessed 9 March 2021).

Shaw, J. and M. Graham. (2017), 'An Informational Right to the City? Code, Content, Control and the Urbanization of Information', *Antipode*, 49 (4): 907–27.

Shazi, N. (2017), 'David Mahlobo clarifies Vuwani comments. We're Still Not Sure What It Means for State Security', *Huffington Post*, 5 July. Available online: https://www .huffingtonpost.co.za/2017/07/05/david-mahlobo-clarifies-vuwani-comments-to -huffpost-were-still_a_23016707/ (accessed 20 April 2021).

Sherman, M. (2010), 'New Panopticism: The Materiality of Surveillance in Society', *Social Identities*, 16 (5): 621–33.

Silitski, V. (2010), '"Survival of the Fittest": Domestic and International Dimensions of the Authoritarian Reaction in the Former Soviet Union Following the Coloured Revolutions', *Communist and Post-communist Studies*, 43 (4): 339–50.

Smit, S. (2021), 'Austerity Budget Unpacked', *Mail & Guardian*, 4 March. Available online: https://mg.co.za/business/2021-03-04-austerity-budget-unpacked/ (accessed 13 April 2021).

Smith, A. (2014), 'The Lucas Plan: What Can it Tell Us about Democratising Technology Today?' *The Guardian*, 22 January. Available online: https://www.theguardian.com/science/political-science/2014/jan/22/remembering-the-lucas-plan-what-can-it-tell-us-about-democratising-technology-today (accessed 1 April 2020).

Sole, S. and S. Evans. (2016), 'The Smuggler, the Spook and the Grabber', *amaBhungane Centre for Investigative Journalism*, 27 August. Available online: https://amabhungane.org/stories/the-smuggler-the-spook-and-the-grabber/ (accessed 8 April 2020).

Sonne, P. and M. Coker. (2011), 'Firms Aided Libyan Spies', *Wall Street Journal*, 30 August. Available online: http://www.wsj.com/articles/SB10001424053111904199404576538721260166388 (accessed 23 April 2020).

South African Broadcasting Corporation. (2019), 'Cabinet Approves Re-Establishment of National Security Council', *SABC News*, 18 December. Available online: https://www.sabcnews.com/sabcnews/cabinet-approves-re-establishment-of-national-security-council/ (accessed 4 January 2021).

South African Police Service. (2014), 'South African Police Service Strategic Plan 2010–2014'. Available online: www.saps.gov.za/saps_profile/strategic_framework/strategic_plan/2010_2014/strategic_plan_2010_2014_2.pdf (accessed 5 April 2021).

South African Police Service. (2016), 'Annual Report 2015/16'. Available online: https://www.saps.gov.za/about/stratframework/annual_report/2015_2016/saps_annual_report_2015_2016.pdf (accessed 5 April 2021).

South African Police Service. (2017), 'Annual Report 2016/17'. Available online: https://nationalgovernment.co.za/department_annual/201/2017-south-african-police-service-(saps)-annual-report.pdf (accessed 5 April 2021).

South African Police Service. (2018a), 'Media Statement from the Office of the Minister of Police, 17 January'. Available online: https://www.saps.gov.za/newsroom/msspeechdetail.php?nid=14171 (accessed 5 April 2021).

South African Police Service. (2018b). 'Comments on the Border Management Authority Bill, Select Committee on Social Services, 13 February 2018'. *Powerpoint Presentation*. Available online: https://static.pmg.org.za/180213_BMA.pdf (accessed 12 January 2021).

Southern African Regional Police Chiefs Cooperation Organization. (n.d.), 'Our Story', (blog post). Available online: https://sarpcco.com/about/ (accessed 5 April 2021).

South African Treasury. (2021), '*Vote 28: Police*', *National Budget 2021*, Pretoria: South African Treasury. Available online: http://www.treasury.gov.za/documents/National%20Budget/2021/ene/Vote%2028%20Police.pdf (accessed 13 April 2021).

Statistics South Africa. (2019), 'Focus on Improving Civil Registrations and Vital Statistics', (blog post). Available online: http://www.statssa.gov.za/?p=12405 (accessed 5 January 2021).

Stockholm International Peace Research Institute. (2019a), 'Military Expenditure by Region in Constant US Dollars', 1998–2018. Available online: https://www.sipri.org/sites/default/files/Data%20for%20world%20regions%20from%201988%E2%80%932018%20%28pdf%29.pdf (accessed 6 April 2020).

Stockholm International Peace Research Institute. (2019b), *Yearbook: Armaments, Disarmament and International Security*, Stockholm: SIPRI. Available online: https://www.sipri.org/sites/default/files/2019-06/yb19_summary_eng.pdf (accessed 21 January 2021).

South African Law Commission. (1999), 'Review of Security Legislation: The Interception and Monitoring Prohibition Act', Pretoria: Minister of Justice and Constitutional Affairs. Available online: https://justice.gov.za/salrc/dpapers/dp78_prj105_intercept _1998.pdf (accessed 27 March 2021).

Svendsen, A. (2012), *The Professionalization of Intelligence Co-operation*, London: Palgrave Macmillan.

Swart, H. (2016), 'Missed Call: SIM Card Registration "Useless" for Crime Fighting Purposes', *Daily Maverick*, 10 November. Available online: https://www.dailymaverick .co.za/article/2016-11-10-missed-call-rica-registration-useless-for-crime-prevention -purposes/ (accessed 21 March 2021).

Swart, H. (2021), 'Face-off: South Africa's Population Register is on Course to Becoming a Criminal Database – with your Mugshot', *Daily Maverick*, 3 March. Available online: (accessed 15 April 2021).

Swilling, M., H. Bhorat, M. Buthelezi, I. Chipkin, S. Duma, L. Mondi, C. Peter, M. Qobo and H. Friedenstein (pseudonym). (2017), *Betrayal of the Promise: How South Africa is Being Stolen (research report)*, Johannesburg: State Capacity Research Project.

Tait, S. and M. Marks. (2011), 'You Strike a Gathering, You Strike a Rock: Current Debates in the Policing of Public Order in South Africa', *South African Crime Quarterly*, 38: 15–22. Available online: https://www.ajol.info/index.php/sacq/article/view/101428 (accessed 4 April 2021).

Tandon, Y. (2014), 'On Sub-Imperialism and BRICS Bashing', (blog post), 21 May. Available online: htto://yashtandon.com/on-sub-imperialism-and-BRICS-bashing/ (accessed 23 April 2019).

Taylor, O. (2013), 'Iraq War: The Greatest Intelligence Failure in Living Memory', *The Telegraph*, 18 March. Available online: https://www.telegraph.co.uk/news/worldnews/ middleeast/iraq/9937516/Iraq-war-the-greatest-intelligence-failure-in-living-memory .html (accessed 28 March 2021).

Tendi, B. M. (2016), 'State Intelligence and the Politics of Zimbabwe's Presidential Succession', *African Affairs*, 115 (459): 203–24.

Thamm, M. (2020), 'Jacobs vs Sithole: Crime Intelligence Head Takes Suspension Battle to Court, Reveals Historic Deep Rot in the Key Division', *Daily Maverick*, 23 December. Available online: https://www.dailymaverick.co.za/article/2020-12-23-jacobs-vs-sitole -crime-intelligence-head-takes-suspension-battle-to-court-reveals-historic-deep-rot -in-key-division/ (accessed 8 April 2021).

Thamm, M. (2021), '2017: A Year of (Un)clear and Present Danger', *Daily Maverick*, 23 January. Available online: https://www.dailymaverick.co.za/article/2021-01-23-2017-a -year-of-unclear-and-present-danger/ (accessed 8 April 2021).

Thatcher, J., D. O'Sullivan and D. Mahmoudi. (2016), 'Data Colonialism through Accumulation by Dispossession: New Metaphors for Daily Data', *Environment and Planning D: Society and Space*, 34 (6): 990–1006.

Thomas, M. (2008), *Empires of Intelligence: Security Services and Colonial Disorder after 1914*, Berkeley and Los Angeles: University of California Press.

Timm, T. (2012), 'Spy Tech Companies and their Authoritarian Customers Part II: Trovicor and Area Spa', *Electronic Frontier Foundation*, 12 February. Available online: https://www.eff.org/deeplinks/2012/02/spy-tech-companies-their-authoritarian -customers-part-ii-trovicor-and-area-spa (accessed 25 April 2020).

Tormey, S. (2004), *Anti-Capitalism: A Beginner's Guide*, Oxford: One World Publishers.

Tsholofelo, L. (2014), 'A Critical Evaluation of the Intelligence Oversight Regime in Botswana', Unpublished MA thesis, Brunel University. Available online:

https://www.e-ir.info/2014/03/03/a-critical-evaluation-of-the-intelligence-oversight
-regime-in-botswana/#_ftnref26 (accessed 17 February 2021).

Turner, M., N. Cooper and M. Pugh. (2010), 'Institutionalised and Co-Opted: Why
Human Security has Lost its Way', in D. Chandler and N. Hynek (eds), *Critical
Perspectives on Human Security: Rethinking Emancipation and Power in International
Relations*, 83–96, London: Taylor and Francis Group.

United Nations General Assembly. (2012), 'Resolution 66/290', 25 October. Available
online: https://undocs.org/A/RES/66/290 (accessed 8 June 2020).

United States Courts. (2018), 'Wiretap Report 2018'. Available online: https://www
.uscourts.gov/statistics-reports/wiretap-report-2018 (accessed 13 March 2021).

US Code 18 – Crimes and Criminal Procedure. (1948), Available online: https://www.law
.cornell.edu/uscode/text/18 (accessed 15 March 2021).

US Department of State. (2018), 'Voting Practices in the United Nations 2017'. Available online:
https ://www.state.gov/documents/organization/281458 .pdf (accessed 17 April 2021).

Valentino-DeVries, J. and D. Yadron. (2015), 'Cataloguing the World's Cyberforces',
The Wall Street Journal, October 11. Available online: https://www.wsj.com/articles/
cataloging-the-worlds-cyberforces-1444610710 (accessed 13 May 2021).

Van Dijk, M. (n.d.), 'Smart Thinking', *JSE Magazine Supplement*. Available online: http://
www.jsemagazine.co.za/jse-supplement/smart-thinking-2/ (accessed 31 March 2021).

Van Zyl, A. (2016), 'Mayor Denies Role in Vuwani Unrest', *Limpopo Mirror*, 30 May.
Available online: https://limpopomirror.co.za/articles/news/37103/2016-05-30/mayor
-denies-role-in-vuwani-unrest- (accessed 16 April 2021).

Van der Velden, L. (2015), 'Leaky Apps and Data Shots: Technologies of Leakage and
Insertion in NSA Surveillance', *Surveillance & Society*, 13 (2): 182–96.

Verde, R. (2021), *Words and Actions: A Realistic Enquiry into Digital Surveillance in
Contemporary Angola*, Johannesburg: Media Policy and Democracy Project.

Verint. (n.d.), 'About Verint'. Available online: https://cis.verint.com/about/ (accessed
8 April 2020).

Vitale, A. S. (2007), 'The Command and Control and Miami Models at the
2004 Republican National Convention: New Forms of Policing Protests', *Mobilization*,
12 (4): 403–15.

VOA News. (2009), 'South Africa Unrepentant over UN Security Council Role', *VOA
News*, 2 November. Available online: https://www.voanews.com/a/a-13-2009-02-20
-voa23-68712827/409628.1-ffil (accessed 24 July 2020).

Wæver, O. (1995), 'Securitization and Desecuritization', in R. D. Lipshutz (ed.), *On
Security*, 46–53, Columbia: Columbia University Press.

Walia, H. (2013), *Undoing Border Imperialism*, Chico: AK Press.

Warner, M. (2002), 'Wanted: A Definition of Intelligence', *Studies in Intelligence*, 46 (3):
15–22.

The Wassenaar Arrangement (n.d.), 'About Us', (blog post). Available online: https://www
.wassenaar.org/about-us/ (accessed 19 May 2020).

The Wassenaar Arrangement. (2019), 'Compendium of Best Practice Document',
December. Available online: https://www.wassenaar.org/app/uploads/2019/12/WA
-DOC-19-PUB-005-Public-Docs-Vol-III-Comp.-of-Best-Practice-Documents-Dec.
-2019.pdf (accessed 8 April 2020).

Wasserman, H. (2010), *Tabloid Journalism in South Africa*, Indiana: Indiana University Press.

Weigley, S. (2013), '10 Companies Profiting the Most from War', *24/7 Wall Street.com*,
10 March. Available online: http://www.usatoday.com/story/money/business/2013/03
/10/10-companies-profiting-most-from-war/1970997/ (accessed 27 October 2020).

Wells, D. (2016), 'Investigatory Powers Bill – The Case for Mass Surveillance', *Computer Weekly*, 22 September. Available online: https://www.computerweekly.com/opinion/Investigatory-Powers-Bill-the-case-for-mass-surveillance (accessed 4 June 2020).

Wetzling, T. and K. Vieth. (2018), *Upping the Ante on Bulk Surveillance: An International Compendium of Good Legal Safeguards and Oversight Innovations*, Berlin: Stiftung Neue Verantwortung. Available online: https://www.stiftung-nv.de/sites/default/files/upping_the_ante_on_bulk_surveillance_v2.pdf (accessed 23 March 2021).

The White House. (2014), 'Presidential Policy Directive – Signals Intelligence Activities'. *Policy Directive/PPD-28*, 17 January. Available online: https://obamawhitehouse.archives.gov/the-press-office/2014/01/17/presidential-policy-directive-signals-intelligence-activities (accessed 24 March 2021).

Wickremasinghe, C. (2019), 'The United Kingdom's observations on the Grand Chamber's Questions to the Parties. Big Brother Watch and others v The United Kingdom and Intervening Parties', *European Court of Human Rights Grand Chamber*, 2 May. Available online: https://privacyinternational.org/sites/default/files/2019-07/UK%20Gov%20Obs%20-%20Revised%20Version%20-%20May%202019.PDF (accessed 18 March 2021).

Wikileaks. (2011), 'The Spy Files', (blog post). Available online: https://wikileaks.org/the-spyfiles.html (accessed 24 January 2021).

Wilkinson, K. (2015), 'Do Five Million Immigrants Live in South Africa? *New York Times* Inflates Numbers', *AfricaCheck*, 6 May. Available online: https://africacheck.org/reports/do-5-million-immigrants-live-in-s-africa-the-new-york-times-inflates-number/ (accessed 4 January 2021).

Woods, A. (2002), 'On the Constituent Assembly Slogan: Is it Applicable to Argentina?' (blog post). *In Defence of Marxism*. Available online: https://www.marxist.com/constituent-assembly-slogan-applicable-argentina.htm (accessed 20 January 2021).

Wright, E. O. (2015), 'How to Be an Anti-capitalist Today', *Jacobin*, 12 February. Available online: https://www.jacobinmag.com/2015/12/erik-olin-wright-real-utopias-anticapitalism-democracy/ (accessed 24 June 2020).

Yong Jin, D. (2015), *Digital Platforms, Imperialism and Political Culture*, London: Routledge.

Yongo, E. and Y. Theodorou. (2020), 'Access to Mobile Services and Proof of Identity 2020: The Undisputed Linkages', (report). GSM Association. Available online: https://www.gsma.com/mobilefordevelopment/wp-content/uploads/2020/03/Access_to_mobile_services_2020_Singles.pdf (accessed 21 March 2021).

Zimbabwe Lawyers for Human Rights. (2006), 'The Interception of Communications Bill: submission to the Parliamentary Portfolio Committee on Transport and Communications', 4 September. Available online: http://hrlibrary.umn.edu/research/zlhr_submissions%20ON%20INTERCEPTION%20BILL.pdf (accessed 5 May 2020).

Zinn, R. (2011), 'Inaugural Address', University of South Africa, 19 July 2011. Available online: http://uir.unisa.ac.za/bitstream/handle/10500/7649/R_Zinn_Inaugural%20Speech.pdf?sequence=1 (accessed 4 August 2020).

Zuboff, S. (2019), *Surveillance Capitalism: The Fight for a Human Future at the New Frontier of Power*, London: Profile Books.

Zulu, I. (2018), 'People are Expressing their Discontent with PF through Protests, not Incitement, says Mwanakampwe', *The Mast*, 12 November. Available online: https://www.themastonline.com/2018/11/12/people-are-expressing-their-discontent-with-pf-through-protests-not-incitement-says-mwanakampwe/ (accessed 7 May 2020).

INDEX

Note: Page numbers followed by 'n' refer to notes.